Through the Russian Revolution

AMERICANS IN REVOLUTIONARY RUSSIA

Vol. 1
Albert Rhys Williams, *Through the Russian Revolution*,
edited by William Benton Whisenhunt (2016)

Vol. 2
Princess Julia Cantacuzène, Countess Spéransky, *Russian People: Revolutionary Recollections*, edited by Norman E. Saul (2016)

Vol. 3
Ernest Poole, *The Village: Russian Impressions*, edited by Norman E. Saul (2017)

Vol. 4
John Reed, *Ten Days That Shook the World*,
edited by William Benton Whisenhunt (2017)

Vol. 5
Louise Bryant, *Six Red Months in Russia: An Observer's Account of Russia Before and During the Proletarian Dictatorship*, edited by Lee A. Farrow (2017)

Series General Editors

Norman E. Saul and William Benton Whisenhunt

Through the Russian Revolution

Albert Rhys Williams

Edited and Introduction by
William Benton Whisenhunt

ANTHEM PRESS

Anthem Press
An imprint of Wimbledon Publishing Company
www.anthempress.com

First published by Slavica Publishers, Indiana University, USA, 2018

This edition first published in UK and USA 2026
by ANTHEM PRESS
75–76 Blackfriars Road, London SE1 8HA, UK
or PO Box 9779, London SW19 7ZG, UK
and
244 Madison Ave #116, New York, NY 10016, USA

© 2026 William Benton Whisenhunt editorial matter and selection;
individual chapters © individual contributors

The moral right of the authors has been asserted.

All rights reserved. Without limiting the rights under copyright reserved above,
no part of this publication may be reproduced, stored or introduced into
a retrieval system, or transmitted, in any form or by any means
(electronic, mechanical, photocopying, recording or otherwise),
without the prior written permission of both the copyright
owner and the above publisher of this book.

British Library Cataloguing-in-Publication Data
A catalogue record for this book is available from the British Library.

Library of Congress Control Number: 2025940132

ISBN-13: 978-1-83999-669-6 (Hbk)
ISBN-10: 1-83999-669-2 (Hbk)

ISBN-13: 978-1-83999-670-2 (Pbk)
ISBN-10: 1-83999-670-6 (Pbk)

Cover Design: Tracey Theriault

This title is also available as an eBook.

For Meredith

CONTENTS

Photographs and Posters   xi

Acknowledgments   xv

William Benton Whisenhunt

   Editor's Introduction   xvii

THROUGH THE RUSSIAN REVOLUTION

Introduction   5

PART I
THE MAKERS OF THE REVOLUTION:
WITH THE WORKERS, PEASANT AND FIGHTERS

Chapter 1: The Bolsheviks and the City   13

Chapter 2: Petrograd Demonstrates   21

Chapter 3: A Peasant Interlude   29

Chapter 4: The Man on Horseback   41

Chapter 5: Comrades of the Sea   46

PART II
THE REVOLUTION AND THE DAYS AFTER: AMONG THE WHITES AND THE REDS

Chapter 6: "All Power to the Soviets"	55
Chapter 7: November 7—A New Date in History	60
Chapter 8: Looting the Winter Palace	65
Chapter 9: Red Guards, White Guards and Blackguards	75
Chapter 10: Mercy or Death to the Whites?	84
Chapter 11: The War of the Classes	95
Chapter 12: Building the New Order	109

PART III
THE OUTREACH OF THE REVOLUTION: ACROSS SIBERIA ON THE EXPRESS

Chapter 13: The Steppes Rise Up	121
Chapter 14: The Red Convicts of Cherm	128
Chapter 15: The Vladivostok Soviet	134
Chapter 16: The Local Soviet at Work	139

PART IV
THE TRIUMPH OF THE REVOLUTION: THE SOVIETS AGAINST THE CAPITALIST WORLD

Chapter 17: The Allies Crush the Soviet	149
Chapter 18: The Red Funeral	156

CONTENTS

Chapter 19: Exit   162

Chapter 20: Retrospect   166

Appendix I: The Death of a Red Regiment   173

Appendix II: The Death Train of Siberia   175

Appendix III: The Burial of Yanishev   179

Appendix IV: A Circular for British Soldiers   181

Appendix V: Yesterday and Today, by Gorky   183

Appendix VI: Declaration of the Rights of the Toiling and Exploited Peoples   185

Appendix VII: Posters and Placards   189

Index   201

PHOTOGRAPHS AND POSTERS

Children of Darkness and Light	Frontispiece
One of the Ten Thousand Soviets	Figure 1
Lenin Speaks	Figure 2
A Red Horseman	Figure 3
A Cathedral of Communist Faith	Figure 4
"The River of Red"	Figure 5
The Sailors Enter Petrograd	Figure 6
Lying Down to Escape Death	Figure 7
Peasant Paradoxes	Figure 8
The Woodchoppers—The Harvesters	Figure 9
Forward to the Light	Figure 10
Obliterating the Past	Figure 11
The Bronze Czar Beheaded	Figure 12
The Illiterate is a Blind Man	Figure 13
Cossack, with Whom Are You?	Figure 14
A Crack Fighting Regiment	Figure 15
Red Guards Before the Winter Palace	Figure 16

The Trojan Horse of the Bolsheviks	Figure 17
The Sentinel	Figure 18
Antonov, Head of the Red Guards	Figure 19
Bolsheviks at Study	Figure 20
Bolsheviks Under Arms	Figure 21
Bolsheviks At Work	Figure 22
The Sickle and the Book	Figure 23
Palace Passes to the Children	Figure 24
At Play	Figure 25
Bolshevik Milk Maids	Figure 26
Clay Modeling	Figure 27
The Children's Theater	Figure 28
Trotsky Salutes	Figure 29
The Czar's Surprise Party	Figure 30
A Siberian Mother Mourns Her Dead	Figure 31
Ivan Finds a True Friend	Figure 32
The Steel Ring of Bayonets	Figure 33
A Defender of Land and Liberty	Figure 34
Intervention Begins	Figure 35
The Red Funeral	Figure 36

PHOTOGRAPHS AND POSTERS

Comrades! Fight Typhus	Figure 37
A Communist Pays the Price	Figure 38
On the Death Train	Figure 39
Kalinin	Figure 40
The Kremlin in Moscow	Figure 41

ACKNOWLEDGMENTS

I would like to thank Norman E. Saul for not only suggesting Albert Rhys Williams as a research project for me, but for also coediting this series of republications with me. It has been a great pleasure to work with him on this and other projects. I would also like to thank George Fowler and Vicki Polansky at Slavica Publishers for agreeing to take on this series. As I continue to work on Williams as a subject, it is clear that the material at the Rare Book and Manuscript Library at Columbia University is a rich resource, and I thank its staff for assistance. Thanks also to the Hoover Institution for securing some of the images found in the book. As always, my family has been very supportive of my projects. My parents, Don and Betsy Whisenhunt, have been wonderful models for me in so many aspects of life. I appreciate all of their support, especially my dad's work on the index for this volume. My wife, Michele, and kids, Meredith and Matthew, have always been supportive even if they do not know exactly which project I am working on at a given moment. I love them more than they know. Thank you all.

William Benton Whisenhunt

INTRODUCTION
William Benton Whisenhunt

Russia's revolutionary era (1914–21) was marked by tumultuous events: war, revolution, mutinies, famine, political intrigue. Eyewitness accounts of these turbulent times came from people from many countries. Albert Rhys Williams's *Through the Russian Revolution* offered readers a first-hand account of the revolution's most dramatic times (June 1917 to August 1918) by an American who was not only an eyewitness but also a participant. His account offered distinctive insights into how the revolution was affecting the countryside and Russia's Far East. What began as curiosity about the rising role of socialism and communism in Russia quickly became a lifelong passion, as the revolutionary ideals to which Williams bore witness led him to support the Soviet system to the end of his days.

Born to Welsh immigrant parents in Greenwich, Ohio in 1883, Albert Rhys Williams and his family moved often from Ohio to Pennsylvania to New York during his early life. Williams's father abandoned being a miner to become a Congregationalist minister just before Albert was born. Williams and his brothers would follow in their father's footsteps and become clergy themselves. Williams attended Marietta College in Ohio from 1900 to 1904 before pursuing further studies in theology at Hartford Theological Seminary in Connecticut. When he graduated in 1907, he earned a fellowship for further study in Europe. Williams studied in Germany and England, where he was exposed to labor, poverty, and inequality in a profound way. However, all through his theological education he was perplexed by the religious vocation he had undertaken. More than once during his studies, he doubted his future as a minister.[1]

Williams became a minister at the Maverick Congregationalist Church in Boston in 1908, but during his six years there he spent much more time working on labor issues, including campaigning for Socialist candidate Eugene V. Debs in 1908.

---

[1] Marietta College Alumni Records, Marietta College, 1940; email interview with Albert Resis, January 14, 2014; email interview with Eleanor Williams, June 18, 2014; Albert Rhys Williams, "Seminary Diary, 1904–1907," Albert Rhys Williams Papers 1883–1962, Box 2, Rare Book and Manuscript Library, Columbia University (hereafter RBML). This is an unprocessed collection of Albert Rhys Williams's papers that contained seventeen boxes of material when I used it in January 2014. My footnotes reflect the way it was organized at that time.

He took part in many notable labor demonstrations, such as the Lawrence Textile Strike of 1912, where he met journalist John Reed for the first time. Williams's life as a minister in Boston was extremely busy but unsatisfying. His work in the church seemed to bore him, and he still doubted his calling. He dedicated most of his time to working on labor issues in Boston, attending strikes, and holding labor meetings in the church. When the opportunity to go back to Europe came along with the beginning of World War I, he jumped at the chance and took on the role of journalist. He seemed to relish this role for the rest of his life. With this move to Europe for the war, he determined that he would not return to Maverick Congregationalist Church, but rather work as a journalist and writer. In his later notes about his life, he gave a list of reasons why he decided to leave the formal ministry and join the ranks of journalists and socialists. He wrote that he had had a taste of a wider life and found it boring to return to the routine of his church duties. Williams's second reason was that he was "tired of being good and respectable." His third reason was that he felt overwhelmed with the work of the church, and it did not leave him time to think or read. His fourth reason was that the war had become the focus of the world, where the most important decisions and activities were taking place, and he wanted to be a part of it. Lastly, Williams remained most concerned about poverty, and the belief that patience and suffering would bring a later reward was ringing hollow in his mind and heart. He felt he needed to take much more direct action to alleviate the suffering of the people.[2] Even though he never seemed to mention it specifically, he seemed to have moved closer to the ideal of Christian Socialism of this era.

Williams's experience as a journalist was limited, but he had written for a newspaper while a seminary student in Connecticut. Now, though, he was a real war correspondent for the *New York Evening Post* and *Outlook*. After several months in the war zone, where he had many adventures, he returned to the United States and published his first book, *In the Claws of the German Eagle*, in 1917. Many parts of this book had been previously published in newspapers and magazines.[3] While in the war, he had many adventures with German and Belgian troops. The most famous episode was one in which he helped Belgian photographers and soldiers stage a photograph of a German civilian's execution. In the picture Williams posed as the German in front of a Belgian firing squad. While the photograph was intended as a joke, it was reprinted all across Europe in error, highlighting Belgian atrocities against the Germans. Even though the image is somewhat blurred, it is clearly Williams in the

---

[2] Albert Rhys Williams, "Leaving Church—Maverick," Albert Rhys Williams Papers, 1883–1962, Box 1, RBML.

[3] "Biographical Sketch," Joshua Kunitz Papers, 1896–1980, Box 2, RBML; Albert Rhys Williams, *In the Claws of the German Eagle* (New York: E. P. Dutton, 1917); Williams, "From Liege to Holland," *Outlook*, September 30, 1914, 267–69; Williams, "With the Spy Hunters in Belgium," *Outlook*, July 7, 1915, 553–62; and Williams, "With the War Photographers in Belgium," *Outlook*, January 13, 1915, 79–83.

photograph, because the "German civilian" appears in the distinctive overcoat that Williams wore nearly everywhere he went.[4] Not long after his book was published, he heard of the events in Russia and decided he had to witness them for himself. The February revolution of 1917 in Russia and his growing allegiance to socialist ideas prompted him again to seek journalist credentials for his first adventure to Russia.

By the end of March 1917 he had been hired again by the *New York Evening Post* and *Outlook* to report on Russia. The United States government was also organizing an official mission, known as the Root Mission, to observe the events in Russia. Williams briefly considered being part of this mission but preferred to travel as a journalist because he felt that he would have more independence. He departed for Russia in mid-May, stopped off in Stockholm, where he made a brief visit to the Socialist Peace Conference, and arrived in Petrograd in early June. Williams and fellow sympathetic journalist Bessie Beatty arrived at nearly the same time. However they did not know each other and would not meet for several weeks. John Reed and Louise Bryant would not arrive until September.[5] Not long after Williams arrived in St. Petersburg, he began enthusiastically to learn the Russian language, realizing that in order to interview key leaders and better report his observations, he needed to be able to communicate more effectively. Few other American journalists knew any Russian.

Williams depicted the Petrograd to which he arrived as a great and beautiful city with enticing white nights. His initial goal was to hear and, if possible, meet the leaders of the Provisional Government, who had toppled the Romanov dynasty in the February Revolution. They had characterized their revolution as "socialist," and it was this that attracted Williams to them. To more radical socialists like Vladimir Lenin, however, the events of February were not the true revolution, and he and his Bolsheviks were still working to achieve that goal. Williams heard Alexander Kerensky speak and met several ministers of the Provisional Government but left feeling as though something were lacking. He found them pleasant enough but wrote that he felt "they were not real representatives of the masses, that they were 'caliphs of the passing hour.'"[6] He concluded that the true and future power in Russia rested in the workers' soviets.

He attended the First All-Russian Congress of Soviets, which had begun in mid-June. In his memoirs Williams recalls a conversation in which he revealed to the president of the congress his true purpose for being in Russia, that while he had come

---

[4] Williams, "With the War Photographers," 79–83.

[5] Joshua Kunitz, "Biographical Sketch of Albert Rhys Williams," in Albert Rhys Williams, *Through the Russian Revolution* (New York: Monthly Review Press, 1967), i–ix.

[6] Albert Rhys Williams, *Through the Russian Revolution*, ed. William Benton Whisenhunt (Bloomington: Slavica, 2016), 13.

"ostensibly as a journalist ... the real reason [was] the Revolution. It was irresistible. It drew me hear like a magnet. I am here because I could not stay away."[7]

Addressing the congress, Williams told the delegates that he represented the socialists of America and that one day very soon all workers in the world would look upon Russia as the model for true revolution and liberation. The First Congress was dominated by Socialist Revolutionaries, but Williams would find that he had more in common with the more extreme agenda of the Bolsheviks. The Bolsheviks held just over 100 of the 900 seats, making them a significant, yet still minority, voice. Despite the fact that Williams's bourgeois guide described the Bolsheviks as "mostly fools, fanatics, and German agents," Williams decided to seek more information about them. To do this, he headed to the factories.[8]

In the factories, Williams was greeted warmly. One worker invited the American to his home, where he was well fed and found that his host had an intense admiration for Abraham Lincoln and the Bolsheviks. Playing devil's advocate, Williams challenged the worker's beliefs by stating that since the tsar was gone, the revolution was complete. The worker responded that the removal of the tsar was only the beginning and that the workers did not want "to put [the government] into the hands of another ruling class, the bourgeoisie. No matter what name you give it, slavery is the same."[9] The words of the Bolshevik worker impressed and inspired Williams. It was this view of revolution and socialism that Williams had been seeking on his journey. He arrived in Russia believing that the Provisional Government was the revolution that would shape the future of Russia, but by the end of his first month in the country he had embraced a more radical path.

One of Williams's most notable experiences was the "July Days" of 1917. In reaction to the chaos of World War I and the Provisional Government, the Bolsheviks along with sympathetic soldiers and sailors attempted to overthrow the weakened temporary government. He wrote about the glory and splendor of the "red columns" dressed in fanciful garb and singing as they proceeded past St. Isaac's Cathedral on their way to address the First Congress at the Tauride Palace. Williams depicted this spontaneous demonstration in the most positive terms. He noted that there were thousands of banners with Bolshevik slogans on them, "so many that even the Bolsheviks were surprised."[10] It was here, too, that Williams was particularly harsh toward the Root Mission for its failure to see the country changing right before its eyes. On July 1, as the Root Mission attended a mass at Kazan Cathedral, they were confronted with massive protests along Nevsky Prospekt. Williams wrote, "Blind men! They did not see that faith that day was not in the mass within those musty

---

[7] Ibid., 14.

[8] Ibid., 15.

[9] Ibid., 16.

[10] Ibid., 22.

walls, but in the masses without."¹¹ This uprising would result in 56 people being killed and more than 650 wounded, according to Williams. Williams remarked that "three times that night our feet slipped in blood on the ground."¹²

Fellow American journalist Bessie Beatty viewed these events from a different part of Petrograd. She was on Nevsky Prospekt near the Hotel Europe when she saw armed Red Guards patrolling the streets. Beatty also observed the procession of banners in support of the Bolshevik cause, but it was the real threat of violence that dominated her thoughts. Bursts of gunfire up and down Nevsky Prospekt kept her from being able to reach the Hotel Europe. She was shoved to the street and into a doorway before she could find refuge in the hotel. She noted that many on the street felt that a civil war was beginning and that "the streets will run [with] blood before this thing is over."¹³

Like Williams, Russian observer and Socialist Revolutionary Nikolai Sukhanov also witnessed the events of the July Days mostly from the Tauride Palace. Sukhanov writes, "At that time, in the early morning of July 8th, lying on my sofa, I listened to [Anatoly] Lunacharsky's account in utter dejection. The devilish grimacing mask of the July Days, looming over me like a nightmare, passed before my eyes. So then, there had been not only a spontaneous course of events but a malevolent political blunder."¹⁴ For Sukhanov, the radicals in the First Congress had missed a grand opportunity to seize power. Worse yet, in the weeks to come Kerensky's Provisional Government, which Sukhanov had described as having once been a true defender of democracy, was now engaged in conservative reaction in order to preserve the Provisional Government itself.

After his very hectic first few weeks in Russia and the conclusion of the events of July, Williams left Petrograd to spend about a month in the countryside to see how the revolution and, in particular, the Bolsheviks were viewed outside of the capital. Williams spent a month with Mikhail Petrovich Yanishev in Spasskoye, where he seemed to fall in love with the Russian countryside. Yanishev, having once been in America, was a good guide to the culture, food, religion, and daily life of ordinary Russia. While most viewed provincial Russia as traditional, Yanishev, a Bolshevik, proclaimed that the peasantry shared Lenin's vision.¹⁵ When Williams returned to Petrograd in September, the country was on the verge of another revolution. Williams was warmly greeted by his Russian comrades, as they looked for support from foreign

---

[11] Ibid., 22.

[12] Ibid., 23–24; Alexander Rabinowitch, *Prelude to Revolution: The Petrograd Bolsheviks and the July 1917 Uprising* (Bloomington: Indiana University Press, 1968), 4–9.

[13] Bessie Beatty, *The Red Heart of Russia* (New York: Century, 1918), 127.

[14] N. N. Sukhanov, *The Russian Revolution, 1917: A Personal Record*, ed. Joel Carmichael (Princeton, NJ: Princeton University Press, 1984), 481.

[15] Williams, *Through the Russian Revolution*, 24–27.

radicals. It was during this tumultuous summer that Williams seems to have solidified his views on Russia, the Provisional Government, and the Bolsheviks.

Williams's account takes him through the October Revolution itself. He describes how he moved from building to building, close by such main players as Lenin and Leon Trotsky. On November 7 he found himself at the Smolny Institute, where there was a hustle and bustle of soldiers, cars, and officials as power changed hands. While many observers tried to deny that a revolution was coming, Williams asserted that they "may as well refuse to recognize a tidal wave, or an erupting volcano as to refuse to recognize this Revolution."[16] He wrote with great excitement about the movement of the revolution across the city from Smolny to the streets leading to the Winter Palace. Williams seemed excited by the chaos and the new society the revolution promised to bring. With profound respect he records how, as the Bolshevik throngs reached the Winter Palace, some were tempted to loot its treasures but were stopped by revolutionary commanders, who declared, "Take nothing. The Revolution forbids it. No looting. This is the property of the people."[17]

As the revolution continued to unfold, Williams and other sympathetic journalists found themselves in trucks roaming through Petrograd helping to distribute pamphlets to tell the people of the city that the Provisional Government had fallen and the Bolsheviks were in power. As the Bolsheviks took control, Williams observed their interactions, their exhaustion and confusion, and their debates about what to do next, for example, how to confront the White opposition that was forming or whether Russia should continue fighting in the war. The latter discussion was particularly heated, as a central element of Lenin's mission was to withdraw Russia from the First World War, which he viewed as a war of imperialism. This debate would go on for weeks in December 1917 and January 1918, eventually resulting in the signing of the Treaty of Brest-Litovsk in March 1918.[18]

In early 1918, Williams worked with several other people, including Reed, on Bolshevik propaganda that was intended for distribution in Germany. As Russia left the war, the Bolsheviks hoped for the rise in Germany of radical parties, worker discontent, and unrest on the streets. Williams helped draft the pamphlets that would be sent to Germany to help incite a revolution like the one in Russia.

As the Civil War broke out in Russia, Williams tried to volunteer for the Red Army, which had recently been placed under the control of Trotsky. However, Lenin and Trotsky believed he should help form an international brigade of foreign soldiers who would fight on behalf of the Bolsheviks. Williams took up this assignment with enthusiasm. By the spring of 1918, many of the Americans in Russia were leaving.

---

[16] Ibid., 40.

[17] Ibid., 69.

[18] Ibid., 78–108; Orlando Figes, *A People's Tragedy: The Russian Revolution, 1891–1924* (Oxford: Oxford University Press, 1996), 589–630.

Williams stayed a bit longer, but as the civil war intensified in early summer 1918, he set off for the United States via Siberia.[19]

Williams secured two letters from Lenin to guarantee his safety as he crossed Siberia on his way to Vladivostok. Siberia was not fully under Bolshevik control, with White forces holding key territory and often disrupting train service. His journey was long and turbulent, but he arrived safely in Vladivostok, only to find his path home blocked once again, this time by American soldiers who had arrived in the Far East preparing to intervene in the Civil War. Williams was delayed in Vladivostok for weeks. His account of his time in Vladivostok illuminates widespread popular support for the Bolsheviks as well as the role of newly freed prisoners in the first phases of the Civil War. Williams spent a lot of time talking to young Bolshevik soldiers, listening to them sing, and photographing them. The young soldiers were intrigued by Williams, an American so far from home who supported their cause, in contrast to the American soldiers interventionists flooding into the port. By the time Williams was finally able to leave, he had run out of money. He had to borrow money from Bolshevik soldiers to travel to China in an attempt to secure passage to Hawaii and eventually to San Francisco. However, his passage from China was also delayed. He spent nearly another month waiting in Shanghai. He had to send a telegram to his friend and fellow writer Upton Sinclair in order to get more money to pay for the ship's passage to Hawaii. Once he secured the money, he departed for the United States.[20]

Williams carried a large trunk full of papers, notes, placards, and more as he traveled across Siberia and boarded the ship in Shanghai. When he arrived in Hawaii, representatives from the US Naval Intelligence Division were there to greet him. Based on articles Williams had published in the *New York Evening Post*, *Outlook*, and other periodicals, as well as reports by Americans who had encountered him in Russia, Williams had been identified as a communist sympathizer. The Intelligence Division confiscated his materials and sent him on to San Francisco with orders to appear in Washington, DC within a few weeks. By the time he reached San Francisco, it was early September 1918, and he made his way to Washington to be interviewed by various departments of the United States government.

The confiscation of his papers was a great hardship for Williams that significantly altered his plans once back in the United States.[21] He had planned to write an account of his time in the Russian Revolution, but without these notes, manuscripts, and other documents, he did not feel capable of doing this. While he waited for the return of

---

[19] Williams, *Through the Russian Revolution*, 145–85; Figes, *A People's Tragedy*, 595–610.

[20] Albert Rhys Williams, *Journey into Revolution: Petrograd, 1917–1918* (Chicago: Quadrangle Books, 1969), 299–320; Williams, "Diary, 1917–1918," Box 7, RBML.

[21] Williams, *Journey into Revolution*, 302–18; "Biographical Sketch," Joshua Kunitz Papers, 1896–1980, Box 2, RBML.

his papers, he wrote two books. One was a short pamphlet called *The Bolsheviks and the Soviets: The Present Government of Russia, What the Soviets Have Done, Difficulties the Soviets Faced, Six Charges Against the Soviets, the Soviet Leaders and the Bolsheviks, the Russians and America* that was published in 1919 by the Rand School. It consists of a set of questions and answers that Williams thought people who knew nothing of Russia and its revolution would ask. He tried to answer these questions. The other book, which came out later in 1919, was called *Lenin: The Man and His Work*. This work included impressions of Lenin from American Red Cross official Colonel Raymond Robins and British journalist Arthur Ransome. While not a traditional biography, it was perhaps the first biographical treatment of Lenin in English. It was during this time, though, that other observers of the Russian Revolution, like Reed, Bryant, Beatty, and others were publishing their firsthand accounts. Interest in Russia's revolution was high in 1918 and 1919.[22]

In February 1919, Williams was called to testify before the Overman Committee in the US Senate. During this hearing, and in the press, he was depicted as a friend of other known radicals such as John Reed and Louise Bryant (who also testified before the committee) and a Soviet apologist. Nearly all of the questions related to the role of the Industrial Workers of the World (IWW) as an agent of Bolshevik propaganda and whether Williams advocated a Bolshevik system in the United States. Williams gave a favorable account of the Soviet ideal and contested allegations that the Bolsheviks had been engaged in massacres. The exchange between Williams and several senators on the committee was seemingly endless and often humorous. Williams frequently sparred with the senators and was unapologetic for his support of the Bolsheviks despite the political reality of the Red Scare. The senators seemed frustrated by Williams' open acknowledgement of his bias. After the hearings, Williams spent much of 1919 on speaking tours and promoting his book on Lenin.[23]

In 1921, with the return of his confiscated personal papers, Williams was finally able to complete and publish his account of his experiences of 1917–18, *Through the Russian Revolution*. Unfortunately, by that time interest in the revolution had fallen off and the market had been saturated by more famous works, such as Reed's *Ten Days that Shook the World*. Williams's book did not get the attention that he thought it deserved, though a review in the *American Bar Association Journal* noted of his book that "[o]f the books from the pens of friends of the Russian revolution this is among the best."[24] One prominent and sympathetic reviewer, Floyd Dell, wrote of how Williams had made his way through World War I and the Russian Revolution in a dress suit

---

[22] Albert Rhys Williams, "Diary, 1917–1918," Albert Rhys Williams Papers 1883–1962, Box 2, RBML, Columbia University; Williams, *Journey*, 310–20.

[23] Kunitz, "Biographical Sketch," lxxxxvi–c.

[24] Harry A. Bigelow, "Current Legal Literature," *American Bar Association Journal* 8, 5 (May 1922): 302.

despite the trials and tribulations he encountered. Dell concluded that Williams's chapter "Red Funeral" was "one of the most poignant and beautiful chapters of modern prose."[25]

Williams did not linger long in the United States. In 1922, he returned to Russia, where he would spend the next six years investigating the lives of Russian peasants after the revolution. During this time, Williams married Lucita Squier, an American screenwriter who had arrived Russia in 1922 as part of a Quaker mission to make a film about relief efforts in some of the areas hardest hit by the famine. Williams and Squier had met a few years earlier in the United States, but married only in 1923, at an official marriage office of the new Soviet government. Squier worked with the Quakers on their documentary but would often leave Russia for London, where she would work as a screenwriter to earn money that the newlyweds badly needed. During these years, Williams published a handful of articles in American periodicals about his adventures in Russia. Williams and Squier moved often and saw much of the country. Whether because of the rudimentary state of the transportation and communication systems or because, as some speculated, Williams wanted to "get lost" in Russia, he was so out of touch with friends and family that at one point there was even a rumor that he had died in a remote part of Russia. In 1928, the couple returned to the United States and Williams published his new book on Russia, *The Russian Land*, perhaps one of his most insightful works about the life and world of ordinary Russians. The following year the couple's only child, Rhys Williams, was born.[26]

For most of the 1930s, Williams continued to argue strongly for a more moderate approach to the Soviet regime. He had always been an advocate, along with Raymond Robins, for diplomatic recognition of the Soviet Union. In 1930–31, he accompanied a delegation of US senators, including Alben Barkley of Kentucky (later to serve as vice president under Harry Truman), to view the new Soviet Union under Stalin as the United States considered official recognition. In 1937, Williams again returned to the Soviet Union, where he witnessed the show trials of the Purges. Despite this experience, he still held positive views of the Soviet regime. In that same year, he published a book titled *The Soviets*, organized around eighty-eight questions and answers addressing every facet of Soviet life and government in astounding detail.[27]

As World War II began, many Americans wanted to know more about their new ally in the fight against fascism. Even though Williams was often accused of being an apologist for the Soviet government, he was asked to write another account about the USSR for a general audience. In this work, *The Russians: The Land, The People, and Why They Fight*, published in 1943, he gave an overview of some prominent features

---

[25] Floyd Dell, "Through Russia in a Dress Suit," *The Bookman* 55 (March 1922): 68.

[26] "Biographical Sketch," Kunitz Papers, RBML.

[27] Albert Rhys Williams, "The Senators Visit the Soviet Villages" Box 9, RBML.

of Russian and Soviet life. His detailed accounts provided much for the American reader to consider as the war with fascism dominated their lives. Both of these books were generally well reviewed as extremely valuable, if not a bit overly positive.[28]

From 1945 to the end of his life, in 1962, Williams felt forgotten by the Soviet Union and harassed by American officials. The later years of Stalin's reign were marked by increased tensions with the United States. Even though Williams had been a favorite American of the Soviet regime for three decades after the revolution, this friendliness cooled as the Cold War intensified. With the rise of the second Red Scare, Williams was again a target of investigation for his enduring defense of the Soviet regime. While he did face questioning, he did not face the blacklisting that so many other Americans did. This was probably because he was a known quantity, a bit older, and he did not work in any of the key industries like education, government, or entertainment that were the targets of the US government at this time.[29]

In 1957, the Soviets made their successful Sputnik launch. This had repercussions across the world, including the United States. Williams wrote a very positive review of the launch in early 1958 that prompted a re-establishment of positive relations with the Soviet regime, now under the control of Nikita Khrushchev. In 1959, Williams was invited to return to the Soviet Union one last time on a goodwill tour commemorating the success of the Sputnik launch. The trip, which included his wife, Lucita, their son, Rhys, and Rhys's wife, Eleanor, was tremendously successful; it also provided Williams an opportunity to seek special medical care for his recently diagnosed leukemia. Williams's warm reception in the USSR did much to assuage his hurt at having been ignored in later life and reinvigorated his work on a much more extensive account of his revolutionary experience.

In his last years Williams worked with his wife and several research assistants in the United States and Soviet Union to write a more detailed version of *Through the Russian Revolution*, but he died in February 1962 before completing the book. Williams's wife and assistants finished the work in 1969 and published it under the title *Journey into Revolution: Petrograd, 1917–1918*. Lucita Williams would maintain her contacts with Soviet academics and officials until her death in 1980. In 1977, she sent many of her husband's papers to the Lenin Library in Moscow as part of the sixtieth-anniversary celebration of the Russian Revolution.

Williams' dedication to the Soviet regime lasted his entire life and was reflected in his publications and private writings. The book that brought him the most prominence in the minds of those interested in the Russian Revolution, however, was *Through the Russian Revolution*. It is one of a small number of books by Americans who were on the ground, observing and even taking part in the revolution.

---

[28] Albert Rhys Williams, *The Russians: The Land, The People and Why They Fight* (New York: Harcourt, Brace and Co., 1943), 1–10.

[29] "Biographical Sketch," Kunitz Papers, RBML.

SUGGESTED ADDITIONAL READING

Figes, Orlando. *A Peoples Tragedy: The Russian Revolution, 1891–1924*. London: Oxford University Press, 1996.

Francis, David R. *Russia from the American Embassy, April 1916–November 1918*. New York: Charles Scribner's, 1921.

Harrison, Marguerite. *Marooned in Moscow: The Story of an American Woman Imprisoned in Soviet Russia*. Edited and Annotated by William Benton Whisenhunt (Montpelier, VT: Russian Life Books, 2011).

Hoyt, Edwin P. *The Army Without a Country*. New York: Macmillan, 1967.

Ignatieff, Michael. *The Russian Album*. New York: Viking, 1987.

Jackson, George, ed. *Dictionary of the Russian Revolution*. New York: Greenwood Press, 1989.

Lieven, Dominic. *The End of Tsarist Russia: The March to World War I and Revolution*. New York: Viking, 2015.

———. *Russia's Rulers Under the Old Regime*. New Haven: Yale University Press, 1989.

Lincoln, W. Bruce. *Passage Through Armageddon: The Russians in War and Revolution, 1914–1918*. New York: Oxford University Press, 1994.

Luckett, Richard. *The White Generals: An Account of the White Movement and the Russian Civil War*. Edinburgh:

McMeekin, Sean. *History's Greatest Heist: The Looting of Russia by the Bolsheviks*. New Haven: Yale University Press, 2009.

Plokhy, Serhii. *The Gates of Europe: A History of Ukraine*. New York: Basic Books, 2015.

Poole, Ernest. *The Village: Russian Impressions*. Edited by Norman Saul. Bloomington, IN: Slavica Publishers, 2017.

Rabinowitch, Alexander. *How the Bolsheviks Came to Power: the Revolution of 1917 in Petrograd*. New York: W. W. Norton, 1976.

Sanborn, Joshua A. *Imperial Apocalypse: The Great War and the Destruction of the Russian Empire*. Oxford: Oxford University Press, 2014.

Saul, Norman E. *War and Revolution: The United States and Russia, 1914–1921*. Lawrence: University Press of Kansas, 2001.

Smele, Jonathan D. *Civil War in Siberia: The Anti-Bolshevik Government of Admiral Kolchak, 1918–1920*. Cambridge: Cambridge University Press, 1996.

Smith, Douglas. *Former People: The Final Days of the Russian Aristocracy*. New York: Farrar, Straus, and Giroux, 2012.

Thompson, John M. *Russia, Bolshevism, and the Versailles Peace.* Princeton, NJ: Princeton University Press, 1967.

Unterberger, Betty Miller. *America's Siberian Expedition, 1918–1920: A Study of National Policy.* Durham, NC: Duke University Press, 1956.

———. *The United States, Revolutionary Russia, and the Rise of Czechoslovakia.* Chapel Hill: University of North Carolina Press, 1989.

Ward, Colonel John. *With the "Die-Hards" in Siberia.* New York: George H. Doran, 1920.

Weeks, Charles J., Jr. *An American Naval Diplomat in Revolutionary Russia: The Life and Times of Vice Admiral Newton A. McCully.* Annapolis: Naval Institute Press, 1993.

Williams, Albert Rhys. *Journey Into Revolution: Petrograd, 1917–1918.* Chicago: Quadrangle Books, 1969.

———. *The Russian Land.* New York: New Republic, 1928.

THROUGH THE RUSSIAN REVOLUTION
BY
ALBERT RHYS WILLIAMS

Author of
In the Claws of the German Eagle
Lenin, the Man and His Work
76 Questions and Answers

Illustrated with photographs
and Russian posters in color

BONI AND LIVERIGHT
Publishers   New York
1921

Children!

The life of an illiterate is terrible! He lives in a dark forest. Everything frightens him. An owl hoots at night,—the illiterate thinks it is the were-wolf howling; he believes in devils and witches. If lightning strikes his hut, he says God is punishing him for his sins; he does not know how to catch the lightning with a rod! The crop is poor—he will pray to God; but if he knew how better to cultivate Mother Earth, his harvest would be rich. He is cruel to animals—the friends of man. He does not know how to tend them or utilize them. But when the illiterate goes thru school—he, a blind man, immediately has his eyes opened. He begins to understand everything; all things become clear to him. He sees what he did not see before. It is as if he had acquired a hundred eyes; life for him begins to be a joy. All matters begin to take a good turn. And if he is in trouble, he will take advice from his friend, the book—who will not deceive him—and he will learn how to get out of his trouble.

To
THE WORKERS AND PEASANTS OF RUSSIA
WHO FELL IN DEFENSE OF THE REVOLUTION

"Against riches, power and knowledge
for the few you began a war, and with
glory you died in order that riches, power
and knowledge should become universal."

INTRODUCTION

In Moscow I saw two peasant soldiers gazing at a poster being stuck up on a *kiosk*.

"We can't read a word of it," they cried, indignant tears in their eyes. "The Czar only wanted us to plough and fight and pay taxes. He didn't want us to read. He put out our eyes."

"To put out the eyes" of the masses, to put out their minds and consciences, was the deliberate policy of the Russian autocracy. For centuries the people were steeped in ignorance, narcotized by the church, terrorized by the Black Hundreds, dragooned by the Cossacks.[1] The protesters were thrown into dungeons, exiled to hard labor in Siberian mines, and hung up on gibbets.

In 1917 the social and economic fabric of the land was shot to pieces. Ten million peasants dragged from their ploughs were dying in the trenches. Millions more were perishing of cold and hunger in the cities while the corrupt ministers intrigued with the Germans and the court held bacchanalian revels with the notorious monk, Rasputin.[2] Even the Cadet, Milyukov, was forced to say: "History does not know of another government so stupid, so dishonest, so cowardly, so treacherous."[3]

All governments rest upon the patience of the poor. It seems everlasting, but there comes an end to it. It came in Russia in March, 1917.[4]

The masses felt that more vicious even than the Kaiser in Berlin was their own Czar in Petrograd. Their cup of bitterness was full. They marched forth against the palaces to end it all. First, out of the Viborg district, came the working women crying for bread. Then long lines of workingmen. The police turned the bridges to prevent

---

[1] The Black Hundreds were an ultranationalist group who supported the Romanov dynasty and were notorious for their violence. Cossacks are frontier people who live in the Don, Dnieper, Terek, and Ural River area. They have existed for several centuries and are known for their defense of the frontier, cavalry skills, and famous leaders like Stenka Razin and Emelian Pugachev.

[2] Grigory Rasputin (1869–1916) was a Russian faith healer who Russian emperor Nicholas II employed to help heal his hemophiliac son and heir, Aleksei. Many suspected that he had a mystical influence on the royal family, and he was assassinated by members of the Russian elite in late 1916.

[3] Pavel Milyukov (1859–1943) was a Constitutional Democrat (Cadet), historian, and politician who advocated a more moderate path for Russia in its revolutionary period and favored Russia remaining in World War I.

[4] Williams used the New Style or Gregorian calendar, which in the 20th century ran 13 days ahead of the Old Style or Julian calendar. In my notes, I will use the Julian calendar.

them entering the city, but they crossed on the ice. Looking at the red-flagged throngs from his window, Milyukov exclaimed: "There goes the Russian Revolution—and it will be crushed in fifteen minutes!"

But the workingmen came on in spite of Cossack patrols on the Nevsky. They came on in face of wilting fire from machine gun nests. They came on until the streets were littered with their bodies. Still they came on, singing and pleading until soldiers and Cossacks came over to the people's side, and on March 12 the Romanov dynasty, which had misruled Russia for 300 years, went crashing to its doom. Russia went mad with joy while the whole world rose up to applaud the downfall of the Czar.

It was mainly the workers and soldiers who made the Revolution. They had shed their blood for it. Now it was assumed that they would retire in the orthodox manner leaving affairs in the hands of their superiors. The people had taken the power away from the Czarists. Now appeared on the scene the bankers and lawyers, the professors and politicians, to take the power away from the people. They said:

"People, you have won a glorious victory. The next duty is the formation of a new state. It is a most difficult task, but fortunately, we, the educated, understand this business of governing. We shall set up a Provisional Government.[5] Our responsibility is heavy, but as true patriots we will shoulder it. Noble soldiers, go back to the trenches. Brave workingmen, go back to the machines. And peasants, you go back to the land."

Now the Russian masses were tractable and reasonable. So they let these bourgeois gentlemen form their "Provisional Government." But the Russian masses were intelligent, even if they were not literate. Most of them could not read or write. But they could think. So, before they went back to the trenches, the shops and the land, they set up little organizations of their own. In each munitions factory the workers selected one of their number whom they trusted. In the shoe and cotton factories the men did likewise. So in the brickyards, the glass-works and other industries. These representatives elected directly from their jobs were called a *Soviet*[6] *(Council) of Workmen Deputies.*

In like manner the armies formed *Soviets of Soldiers' Deputies*, the villages *Soviets of Peasant Deputies.*

These deputies were elected by trades and occupations, not by districts. The Soviets consequently were filled, not with glibly talking politicians, but with men who knew their business; miners who understood mining, machinists who understood machinery, peasants who understood land, soldiers who understood war, teachers who understood children.

The Soviets sprang up in every city, town, hamlet and regiment throughout Russia. Within a few weeks after the old state-apparatus of Czardom went to pieces, one-sixth the surface of the earth was dotted over with these new social organizations—no more striking phenomenon in all history.

---

[5] The Provisional Government was the temporary government that replaced the government of Nicholas II from February 1917 to October 1917.

[6] Soviets were workers' and later soldiers' councils that were set up as far back at the revolution of 1905 and were very significant political organizations in the Bolshevik Revolution of 1917.

INTRODUCTION

The commander of the Russian battleship *Peresvet*[7] told me his story: "My ship was off the coast of Italy when the news arrived. As I announced the Czar's fall some sailors shouted, 'Long live the Soviet.' That very day on board ship a Soviet was formed, in all aspects like the one in Petrograd. I regard the Soviet as the natural organization of the Russian people, finding its root in the *mir* (commune) of the village and the *artel* (co-operative syndicate) of the city."

Others find the Soviet idea in the old New England town-meetings or the city assemblies of ancient Greece. But the Russian workingman's contact with the Soviet was much more direct than that. He had tried out the Soviet in the abortive Revolution of 1905. He had found it a good instrument then. He was using it now.

After the Czar's overthrow there was a short season of good will amongst all classes known as the "honeymoon of the Revolution." Then the big fight began—a battle royal between the bourgeoisie and the proletariat for the mastery of state power in Russia. On the one side the capitalists, landlords and finally the *intelligentsia* lining up behind the Provisional Government. On the other side the workmen, soldiers and peasants rallying to the Soviets.

I was set down in the midst of this colossal conflict. For fourteen months I lived in the villages with the peasants, in the trenches with the soldiers, and in the factories with the workers. I saw the Revolution through their eyes and took part in most of the dramatic episodes.

I have used the names *Communist* and *Bolshevik* interchangeably, though the party did not officially change its name to *Communist* until 1918.

In the French Revolution the great word was "Citizen." In the Russian Revolution the great word is "Comrade!"—*tovarishtch*. I have written it more simply *tovarish*.

For the right to use here some of my articles I am indebted to the editors of *Asia*, the *Yale Review*, the *Dial*, the *Nation*, the *New Republic*, and the *New York Evening Post*.

The visitor to Soviet Russia is struck by the multitudes of posters—in factories and barracks, on walls and railway-cars, on telephone-poles—everywhere. Whatever the Soviet does, it strives to make the people understand the reason for it. If there is a new call to arms, if rations must be cut down, if new schools or courses of instruction are opened, a poster promptly appears telling *why*, and how the people can co-operate. Some of these posters are crude and hurried, others are works of art. Ten of them are reproduced in this book in almost the exact colors of the originals. The cost has been borne by friends of Russia, and the reader is particularly indebted to Mrs. Jessie Y. Kimball and Mr. Aaron Berkman.

On the next page is reproduced the first issue of the first revolutionary newspaper—the official *Soviet News* (*Izvestia*). It was published on the day of the Czar's fall and every day since then.

---

[7] *Peresvet* was a Russian battleship that was put in service in 1901. It was used in the Russo-Japanese War, captured and used by the Japanese, returned to Russian service, and sank in early 1917 off the coast of Egypt, the victim of a mine.

ИЗВѢСТІЯ ПЕТРОГРАДСКАГО СОВѢТА Рабочихъ депутатовъ.

№ 1—28 февраля 1917 года.   № 1.

Къ населенію Петрограда и Россіи.
Отъ Совѣта Рабочихъ Депутатовъ.

Старая власть довела страну до полнаго развала, а народъ до голоданія. Терпѣть дальше стало невозможно. Населеніе Петрограда вышло на улицу, чтобы заявить о своемъ недовольствѣ. Его встрѣтили залпами. Вмѣсто хлѣба царское правительство дало народу свинецъ.

Но солдаты не захотѣли итти противъ народа и возстали противъ правительства. Вмѣстѣ съ народомъ они захватили оружіе, военные склады и рядъ важныхъ правительственныхъ учрежденій.

Борьба еще продолжается; она должна быть доведена до конца. Старая власть должна быть окончательно низвергнута и уступить мѣсто народному правленію. Въ этомъ спасеніе Россіи.

Для успѣшнаго завершенія борьбы въ интересахъ демократіи народъ долженъ создать свою собственную властную организацію.

Вчера 27 февраля въ столицѣ образовался Совѣтъ Рабочихъ Депутатовъ—изъ выборныхъ представителей заводовъ и фабрикъ, возставшихъ воинскихъ частей, а также демократическихъ и соціалистическихъ партій и группъ.

Совѣтъ Рабочихъ Депутатовъ засѣдающій въ Государственной Думѣ ставитъ своей основной задачей организацію народныхъ силъ и борьбу за окончательное упроченіе политической свободы и народнаго правленія въ Россіи.

Совѣтъ назначилъ районныхъ комиссаровъ для установленія народной власти въ районахъ Петрограда.

Приглашаемъ все населеніе столицы немедленно сплотиться вокругъ Совѣта, образовать мѣстные комитеты въ районахъ и взять въ свои руки управленіе всѣми мѣстными дѣлами.

Всѣ вмѣстѣ, общими силами будемъ бороться за полное устраненіе стараго правительства и созывъ учредительнаго собранія, избраннаго на основѣ всеобщаго равнаго, прямого и тайнаго избирательнаго права.

Совѣтъ Рабочихъ Депутатовъ.

NEWS OF THE PETROGRAD SOVIET
of Workmen Deputies.

№ 1 — March 13, 1917　　　　　　　　　　　　　　№ 1

To the population of Petrograd and Russia
From the Soviet of Workmen's Deputies.

The old authorities brought the country to ruin and the people to starvation. It became impossible to endure it longer. The population of Petrograd came out in the streets to express its discontent. It was met with guns. Instead of bread, the government of the Czar gave the people bullets.

But the soldiers have refused to go against the people and have revolted against the government. Together with the civilians they have seized the armories the military stores and many important government institutions.

The struggle is still going on; it must be brought to an end. The old power must be deposed and replaced by a people's government. This is the salvation of Russia.

To secure a victorious end of this struggle in the interests of democracy, the people must create an organization of its own power.

Yesterday, March the 12th, a Soviet of Workmen Deputies was formed in the Capital. It consists of representatives elected from the shops and factories, the revolting military detachments and also from democratic and socialistic parties and groups.

The Soviet of Workmen Deputies now in session at the Imperial Duma faces as its basic problem, the organization of the people's forces in the battle for permanent political freedom and self-government in Russia.

The Soviet has appointed district commissars to execute the people's authority in the districts of Petrograd.

We call upon the inhabitants of the capital to rally around the Soviet, to form district committees and to take the administration of local affairs in their own hands.

All together, we unite our forces to fight for the complete destruction of the old government, and for the calling of a Constituent Assembly, elected on the basis of a universal, equal, direct and secret ballot.

The Soviet of Workers' Deputies.

[*This is a reproduction in English of the Russian text on the opposite page.*]

PART I

THE MAKERS OF THE REVOLUTION WITH THE PEASANTS, WORKERS, AND FIGHTERS

Chapter 1
THE BOLSHEVIKS AND THE CITY

On a white night of early June, 1917, I first entered Petrograd, the city that lies almost within the Arctic Circle. Though it was midnight, the wide squares and *prospekts* bathed in the soft spectral light of this northern night were all alluring.[1]

Past blue-domed barbaric churches and the silver rippling Catherine Canal we drove along the Neva, while across the river the slender spire of Peter and Paul rose like a golden needle. Then by the Winter Palace, the burnished dome of Saint Isaac's and countless shafts and statues to the memory of Czars who had gone.

But all these were monuments to rulers of the past. They had no hold on me for I was interested in the rulers of the present. I wanted to hear the great Kerensky[2] then at the zenith of his spell-binding powers. I wanted to meet the ministers of the Provisional Government. I met many of them, heard them and talked with them. They were able, amiable and eloquent. But I felt they were not real representatives of the masses, that they were "Caliphs of the passing hour."

Instinctively I sought out the rulers of the future, the men in the Soviets elected directly out of the trenches, factories and farms. These Soviets had sprung up in almost every army city and village of Russia, over one-sixth of the surface of the earth. These local Soviets were now sending their delegates to the First All-Russian Congress of Soviets in Petrograd.

The First All-Russian Congress of Soviets

I found the Soviet in session in the Military Academy. A tablet recording the fact that "His Imperial Majesty, Nicholas II, made this place happy by his presence January 28, 1916," still hung on its walls, the one relic of the glittering past.

The gold-braided officers, the smiling courtiers, and lackeys had been swept from the halls. His Imperial Majesty, the Czar, was gone. His Republican Majesty,

---

[1] Because Petrograd (St. Petersburg) is so far north it experiences what are known as White Nights, where the sun never quite sets at the peak of the summer. Prospekts are wide boulevards that stream across the city, Nevsky being the most famous.

[2] Alexander Kerensky (1881–1970) was the leader of the Provisional Government in the summer and fall of 1917. He lost power to the Bolsheviks and later spent most of the rest of his life in the United States.

the Revolution, ruled here now, acclaimed by hundreds of black-bloused, khaki-clad delegates.

Here were men coming up from the ends of the earth. From the frozen Arctic and burning Turkestan they hailed, slant-eyed Tartars and fair-haired Cossacks, Russians, Big and Little, Poles, Letts and Lithuanians—all tribes and tongues and costumes.[3] Here were toil-scarred delegates from the mines, the forge and the farm, battle-scarred soldiers from the trenches and sea-bronzed sailors from the five fleets of Russia. Here were the "March" revolutionists, colorless, and quiet before the March storm blew the Czar from his throne, but now daubed with red revolutionary paint and calling themselves Socialists. Here were veterans of the Revolution, loyal to the cause through long years of hunger, exile and Siberia, tried and tested by suffering.

Chkheidze,[4] the President of the Soviet Congress, asked me why I came to Russia. "Ostensibly as a journalist," I told him. "But the real reason is the Revolution. It was irresistible. It drew me here like a magnet. I am here because I could not stay away."

He asked me to address the Congress. The "Soviet News" (*Izvestia*) of July 8, reports my words thus:

> *Comrades:* I bring you greetings from the Socialists of America. We do not venture to tell you here how to run a Revolution. Rather we come here to learn its lesson and to express our appreciation for your great achievements.
>
> A dark cloud of despair and violence was hanging over mankind threatening to extinguish the torch of civilization in streams of blood. But you arose, comrades, and the torch flamed up anew. You have resurrected in all hearts everywhere a new faith in freedom.
>
> *Equality, Brotherhood, Democracy,* are great and beautiful words. But to the unemployed millions they are merely words. To the 160,000 hungry children of New York they are hollow words. To the exploited classes of France and England they are mocking words. Your duty is to change these words into reality.
>
> You have made the Political Revolution. Freed from the threat of German militarism your next task is the Social Revolution. Then the workers of the world will no longer look to the West, but to the East—toward great Russia,

---

[3] Turkestan was a broad area of Central Asia under Russian and Soviet control. After 1991, it was divided into several independent countries, including Turkmenistan. Tatars are a Turkic people living in Russia as a result of the Mongol occupation (1220s–1480s). Big and Little Russians is an antiquated way to refer to Russians (from Russia itself) and then Ukrainians as Little Russians and Belorussians as White Russians. Letts is an older term for Latvians.

[4] Nikolai Chkheidze (1864–1926) was a Georgian Social Democrat who was president of the Executive Committee of the Petrograd Soviet for most of 1917. Williams refers to it as the First All-Russian Congress of Soviets.

to the Field of Mars[5] here, in Petrograd, where lie the first martyrs of your Revolution.

"Long live free Russia!" "Long live the Revolution!" "Long live Peace to the World!"

In his reply Chkheidze made a plea for the workers of all nations to bring pressure to bear on their governments to stop "the horrible butchery which is disgracing humanity and beclouding the great days of the birth of Russian freedom."

A storm of cheers, and the Congress took up the order of the day—the Ukraine, Education, War-Widows and Orphans, Provisioning the Front, Repairing the Railways, etc. This should have been the business of the Provisional Government. But that Government was flimsy and incompetent. Its ministers were orating, wrangling, scheming against one another and entertaining diplomats. But somebody must do the hard work. By default it was already passing into the hands of these Soviets of the people.

Enter the Bolsheviks

This First Congress of Soviets was dominated by the *intelligentsia*—doctors, engineers, journalists. They belonged to political parties known as Menshevik and Socialist-Revolutionary.[6] At the extreme left sat 107 delegates of a decided proletarian cast—plain soldiers and workingmen. They were aggressive, united and spoke with great earnestness. They were often laughed and hooted down—always voted down.

"Those are the Bolsheviks," my bourgeois guide informed me, venomously. "Mostly fools, fanatics and German agents." That was all. And no more than that could one learn in hotel lobbies, salons, or diplomatic circles.

Happily, I went elsewhere for information. I went into the factory districts. In Nijni[7] I met Sartov, a mechanic who invited me to his home. A long rifle stood in the corner of the main room.

"Every workingman has a gun now," Sartov explained. "Once we used it to fight for the Czar—now we fight for ourselves."

In another corner hung an *ikon* of Saint Nicholas, a tiny flame burning before it.

"My wife is still religious," Sartov apologized. "She believes in the Saint—thinks he will fetch me safely through the Revolution. As though a saint would help a Bolshe-

---

[5] The Field of Mars is a large park in the center of St. Petersburg named for the Roman god of war.

[6] The Mensheviks were a part of the Russian Social Democratic Labor Party when the party split in 1903. They were the larger group that advocated a more gradual path to revolutionary change. The Socialist Revolutionaries were a large left-wing group that had significant political power in Russia and right and left factions.

[7] Williams probably meant Nizhnii-Novogorod, which was established in the thirteenth century about 250 miles east of Moscow. It was a vibrant trade center for many centuries.

vik!" he laughed. *"Yeh! Bogu!* There's no harm in it. Saints are queer devils. No telling what one of them may do."

The family slept on the floor, insisting that I take the bed, because I was an American. In this room I found another American. In the soft gleam of the ikon-light his face looked down at me from the wall, the great, homely, rugged face of Abraham Lincoln. From that pioneer's hut in the woods of Illinois he had made his way to this workingman's hut here upon the Volga. Across half a century, and half a world, the fire in Lincoln's heart had leaped to touch the heart of a Russian workman groping for the light.

As his wife paid her devotion to Saint Nicholas, the great Wonder-Worker, so he paid his devotion to Lincoln, the great Emancipator. He had given Lincoln's picture the place of honor in his home. And then he had done a startling thing. On the lapel of Lincoln's coat he had fixed a button, a large red button bearing on it the word, B-o-l-s-h-e-v-i-k.

Of Lincoln's life Sartov knew little. He knew only that he strove against injustice, freed the slaves, that he was reviled and persecuted. To Sartov, that was the earnest of his kinship with the Bolsheviks. As an act of highest tribute he had decorated Lincoln with this emblem of red.

I found that factories and boulevards were different worlds. A world of difference, too, in the way they said the word "Bolshevik." Spoken on the boulevards with a sneer and a curse, on the lips of the workers it was becoming a term of praise and honor.

The Bolsheviks did not mind the bourgeoisie. They were busy expounding their program to the workers. This program I got first hand from delegates coming up to the Soviet Congress from the Russian army in France.

"Our demand is, not to continue the war, but to continue the Revolution," these Bolsheviks blurted out.

"Why are you talking about Revolution?" I asked, taking the rôle of Devil's Advocate. "You have had your Revolution, haven't you? The Czar and his crowd are gone. That was what you were aiming at for the last hundred years, wasn't it?"

"Yes," they replied. "The Czar is gone, but the Revolution is just begun. The overthrow of the Czar is only an incident. The workers didn't take the government out of the hands of one ruling class, the monarchists, in order to put it into the hands of another ruling class, the bourgeoisie. No matter what name you give it, slavery is the same."

I said the world at large held that Russia's task now was to create a republic, like France or America; to establish in Russia the institutions of the West.

"But that is precisely what we don't want to do," they responded. "We don't cherish much admiration for your institutions or governments. We know that you have poverty, unemployment and oppression. Slums on one hand, palaces on the other. On the one side, capitalists fighting workmen with lockouts, blacklists, lying press, and thugs. Workmen on the other side, fighting back with strikes, boycotts, bombs. We want to put an end to this war of the classes. We want to put an end to poverty. Only the workers can do this, only a communistic system. That is what we are going to have in Russia."

"In other words," I said, "you want to escape the laws of evolution. By some magic you expect suddenly to transfer Russia from a backward agricultural state into a highly organized co-operative commonwealth. You are going to jump out of the eighteenth century into the twenty-second."

"We are going to have a new social order," they replied, "but we don't depend on jumping or magic. We depend upon the massed power of the workmen and peasants."

"But where are the brains to do this?" I interrupted. "Think of the colossal ignorance of the masses."

"Brains!" they exclaimed hotly. "Do you think we bow down before the brains of our 'betters'? What could be more brainless and stupid and criminal than this war? And who are guilty of it? Not the working classes, but the governing classes in every country. Surely the ignorance and inexperience of workmen and peasants could not make a worse mess than generals and statesmen with all their brains and culture. We believe in the masses. We believe in their creative force. And we must make the Social Revolution anyhow."

"And why?" I asked.

"Because it is the next step in the evolution of the race. Once we had slavery. It gave way to feudalism. That in turn gave way to capitalism. Now capitalism must leave the stage. It has served its purpose. It has made possible large-scale production, world-wide industrialism. But now it must make its exit. It is the breeder of imperialism and war, the strangler of labor, the destroyer of civilization. It must in its turn give place to the next phase—the system of Communism. It is the historic mission of the working-class to usher in this new social order. Though Russia is a primitive backward land it is for us to begin the Social Revolution. It is for the working-class of other countries to carry it on."

A daring program—to build the world anew.

No wonder the ideas of James Duncan of the Root Mission[8] seemed trivial as he came with tedious talk of craft unions, the union label, and the eight-hour day. His hearers were amused or bored. Next day a newspaper reported the two-hour speech thus: "Last night the Vice-President of the American Federation of Labor addressed the Soviets. Coming over the Pacific he evidently prepared two speeches, one for the Russian people and the other for the ignorant Eskimos—obviously last night he thought he was addressing the Eskimos."

For the Bolsheviks to put forward a big revolutionary program was one thing; to get it accepted by a nation of 160,000,000 was quite another—especially as the Bolshevik Party counted then not more than 150,000.

---

[8] The Root Mission was sent to Russia in the spring of 1917 by Woodrow Wilson to assess Russia's future role in World War I. It also tried hard to keep Russia in the war. Secretary of State Elihu Root headed the mission and greatly underestimated the power of Vladimir Lenin and the Bolshevik Party.

Bolsheviks Trained in America

Many factors, however, were conspiring to give Bolshevik ideas prestige with the people. In the first place the Bolsheviks understood the people. They were strong among the more literate strata, like the sailors, and comprised largely the artisans and laborers of the cities. Sprung directly from the people's loins they spoke the people's language, shared their sorrows and thought their thoughts.

It is not quite correct to say that the Bolsheviks understood the people. They *were* the people. So they were trusted. The Russian workingman, betrayed so long by the classes above him, puts faith only in his own.

This was brought home to a friend of mine in a grotesque manner. Krasnoschekov[9] is his name, now President of the Far East Republic. Coming from the Workers' Institute in Chicago, he entered the lists as a champion of the workers. An able, eloquent man, he was elected President of the City Council of Nikolaievsk. The bourgeois paper promptly appeared with an assault upon him as an "immigrant roustabout."

"Citizens of great Russia," it asked, "do you not feel the shame of being ruled by a porter, a window cleaner from Chicago?"

Krasnoschekov wrote out a hot reply, pointing out his distinction in America as lawyer and educator. On the way to the newspaper with his article he turned in at the Soviet, wondering how much this assault had hurt him in the eyes of the workers.

"Tovarish Krasnoschekov!" someone shouted as he opened the door. With a cheer the men rose to their feet. *"Nash! Nash!"* (Ours! Ours!) they cried, grasping his hand. "We just read the paper, comrade. It made us all glad. We always liked you, though we thought you were a bourgeois. Now we find out you are one of us, a real workingman, and we love you. We'll do anything for you."

Ninety-six per cent of the Bolshevik Party were workingmen. Of course the Party had its intelligentsia, not sprung directly from the soil. But Lenin and Trotsky[10] lived close enough to the hunger line to know the thoughts of the poor.

The Bolsheviks were mostly young men not afraid of responsibility, not afraid to die[11] and, in sharp contrast to the upper-classes, not afraid to work. Many of them

---

[9] Alexander Krasnoschekov (1880–1937) was born in Chernobyl in Ukraine. He immigrated to Chicago and earned a degree in law from the University of Chicago. In 1917, he returned to Russia before the Bolshevik Revolution through Siberia, where he worked in the Far East during the Civil War, Allied intervention, and beyond. He was arrested several times, suffered from health problems for more than ten years, and was eventually executed at Stalin's order.

[10] Vladimir I. Lenin (1870–1924), whose real name was Vladimir I. Ulianov, was the primary leader of the Bolshevik Party, led the October Revolution, and was the first leader of the Soviet Union (1917–24). Leon Trotsky (1879–1940), whose real name was Lev D. Bronstein, was a Marxist revolutionary who was part of the Menshevik and Bolshevik parties. He led the Red Army in the Russian Civil War. He was exiled by Joseph Stalin in the late 1920s and later killed in Mexico.

[11] [William's note]: Appendix I, "The Death of a Red Regiment."

became my friends, particularly the exiles returning on the immigrant tide now flowing back from America.

There was Yanishev, who was literally a workman of the world. Ten years earlier he had been driven out of Russia for inciting his fellow peasants against the Czar. He had lived like a water rat on the docks of Hamburg; he had dug coal in the pits of Austria and had poured steel in the foundries of France. In America he had been tanned in leather vats, bleached in textile mills and clubbed in strike lines. His travels had given him a knowledge of four languages and an ardent faith in Bolshevism. The peasant had become now an industrial proletarian.

Some satirist has defined a proletarian as a "talking workingman." Yanishev was not a talker by nature. But now he had to talk. The cry of millions of his fellow-workers for the light drew the words to his lips, and in mills and mines he spoke as no intellectual could speak. Night and day he toiled until midsummer came and he took me on a memorable trip to the villages.

Another comrade was Woskov,[12] formerly agent of New York Carpenters' Union No. 1008, now in the Workers' Committee that ran the rifle factory at Sestroretsk. Another was Volodarsky,[13] virtually a galley-slave of the Soviet and deliriously happy in it. Once he exclaimed to me: "I have had more real joy in these few weeks than any fifty men ought to have in all their lives!" There was Neibut,[14] with his pack of books and with eyes glowing over the English in Brailsford's *The War of Steel and Gold!* To Bolshevik propaganda these immigrants brought Western speed and method. In Russian there is no word "efficient." These young zealots were prodigies of efficiency and energy.

The center of Bolshevik action was Petrograd. In this there is the fine irony of history. This city was the pride and glory of the great Czar Peter. He found a swamp here and left a brilliant capital. To make a foundation he sunk into these marshes forests of trees and quarries of stone. It is a colossal monument to Peter's iron will. At the same time it is a monument of colossal cruelty, for it is built not only on millions of wooden piles, but on millions of human bones.

Like cattle the workmen were herded in these swamps to perish of cold and hunger and scurvy. As fast as they were swallowed up more serfs were driven in. They dug the soil with bare hands and sticks, carrying it off in caps and aprons. With thudding hammers, cracking whips, and groans of the dying, Petrograd rose like the Pyramids, in the tears and anguish of slaves.

Now the descendants of these slaves were in revolt. Petrograd had become the Head of the Revolution. Every day it started out missionaries on long crusading tours.

---

[12] Woskov, also known as Samuel Voskov, was a carpenter who organized a union in Boston and Russia.

[13] V. Volodarsky (1891–1918), whose real name was Moisei M. Goldstein, was a Marxist revolutionary who briefly lived in the United States. He advocated the overthrow of the Provisional Government and was a member of the All-Russian Central Executive Committee.

[14] Arnold Neibut, was a prominent artisan and lover of great books who had been a leader of the Chicago section of the American Socialist Party.

Every day it poured out bales and carloads of Bolshevik gospel in print. In June, Petrograd was publishing *Pravda (Truth)*,[15] *The Soldier, The Village Poor* in millions of copies. "All done on German money," said the Allied observers, as ostrich-like, they sat with heads buried in the boulevard cafés, believing what they preferred to believe. Had they turned the corner they would have seen a long line of men filing past a desk, each laying on it a contribution, ten copecks, ten rubles, maybe a hundred. These were workers, soldiers, even peasants doing their bit for the Bolshevik press.

The greater the success of the Bolsheviks, the louder the hue and cry against them. While the bourgeois press praised the sense and moderation of the other parties, it called for an iron fist for the Bolsheviks. While "Babushka" and Kerensky[16] were given regal quarters in the Winter Palace, the Bolsheviks were thrown into jail.

In the past all parties suffered for their principles. Now it was chiefly the Bolsheviks who suffered. They were the martyrs of today. This gave them prestige. Persecution lifted them into prominence. The masses, now giving heed to Bolshevik doctrine, found it strangely akin to their own desires.

But it was not the sacrifice and enthusiasm of the Bolsheviks that was finally to bring the masses under their banner. More powerful allies were working with them. Hunger was their chief ally—a threefold hunger: a mass hunger for bread, and peace, and land.

In the rural Soviets rose again the ancient cry of the peasants, "The land belongs to God and the people." The city-workers left out God and cried, "The factories belong to the workers." At the front the soldiers proclaimed, "The war belongs to the devil. We want nothing to do with it. We want peace."

A great ferment was working in the masses. It set them organizing Land Committees, Factory Committees, Committees of the Front. It set them talking, so that Russia became a nation of a hundred million orators. It sent them into the streets in tremendous mass demonstrations.

---

[15] [Williams's note]: Reproduction of this newspaper on pages 194–95.

[16] Babushka was the nickname for Russian socialist leader Ekaterina K. Breshko-Breshkovskaya (1844–1934), who was originally an anarchist but who supported the Provisional Government after the February Revolution of 1917.

Chapter 2
PETROGRAD DEMONSTRATES

The spring and summer of 1917 was a series of demonstrations. In this Russia always excelled. Now the processions were longer, led not by priests but by the people, with red banners instead of *ikons,* and instead of church hymns, songs of revolution.

Who can forget Petrograd of July first! Soldiers in drab and olive, horsemen in blue and gold, white-bloused sailors from the fleet, black-bloused workmen from the mills, girls in vari-colored waists, surging through the main arteries of the city. On each marcher a streamer, a flower, a riband of red; scarlet kerchiefs around the women's heads, red *rubashkas*[1] on the men. Above, like crimson foam, sparkled and tossed a thousand banners of red.

As this human river flowed it sang.

Three years before I had seen the German war machine rolling down the valley of the Meuse on its drive towards Paris. The cliffs resounded then to ten thousand lusty German voices singing *"Deutschland über Alles,"* while ten thousand boots struck the pavement in unison. It was powerful but mechanical, and, like every act of those grey columns, ordered from above.

But the singing of these red columns was the spontaneous outpouring of a people's soul. Some one would strike up a revolutionary hymn; the deep resonant voices of the soldiers would lift the refrain, joined by the plaintive voices of the working-women; the hymn would rise, and fall, and die away; then, down the line, it would burst forth again—the whole street singing in harmony.

Past the golden dome of Saint Isaac's, past the minarets of the Mohammedan Mosque, marched forty creeds and races, welded into one by the fire of the Revolution. The mines, the mills, the slums and trenches were blotted from their minds. This was the day the people had made. They would rejoice and be glad in it.

But in their joy they did not forget those who, to bring this day, had marched bound and bleeding to exile and death on the plains of Siberia. Close at hand, too, were the martyrs of the March Revolution; a thousand of them lying in their red coffins on the Field of Mars. Here the militant strains of the *Marseillaise* gave way to the solemn measures of Chopin's *Funeral March.* With muffled drums and lowered banners, with bowed heads, they passed the long grave, weeping or in silence.

---

[1] A *rubashka* is a shirt with shoulderboards that became common during Soviet times.

One incident, trivial in itself, but significant, marred the peace of the day. It was on Sadovaya where I was standing with Alex Gumberg,[2] the little Russian-American, friend and pilot to so many Americans in the days of the Revolution. The wrath of the sailors and workingmen was roused by a red banner with the inscription *"Long live the Provisional Government."* They started to tear it down and in the mêlée some one shouted "The Cossacks are coming."

The very name of these ancient enemies of the people struck terror into the crowds. White-faced, they stampeded like a herd, trampling the fallen and yelling like madmen. Happily it was a false alarm. The ranks re-formed and with songs and cheers took up the march again.

But this procession was more than an outburst of emotion. It was sternly prophetic, its banners proclaiming: *"Factories to the Workers! Land to the Peasants! Peace to All the World! Down with the War! Down with the Secret Treaties! Down with the Capitalist Ministers!"*

This was the Bolshevik program crystallized into slogans for the masses. There were thousands of banners, so many that even the Bolsheviks were surprised. Those banners were signals indicating a big storm brewing. Everybody could see that, and everybody did see it, except those sent to Russia specifically commissioned to see it— the Root Mission, for example. While these gentlemen were in revolutionary Russia they were absolutely isolated from the Revolution. As the Russian proverb goes: "they went to the circus, but they did not see the elephant."

On this July 1 the Americans were invited to a special service in the Cathedral of Kazan. In the church they knelt to receive the kisses and blessings of the priests, while the streets outside rang with songs and cheers from the vast procession of exalted people. Blind men! They did not see that faith that day was not in the mass within those musty walls, but in the masses without.

Yet they were no blinder than the rest of the diplomats cheering the first glowing reports of Kerensky's drive on the Eastern Front. The drive, like its leader, a dazzling success at first, turned into a tragic fiasco. It slaughtered 30,000 Russians, shattered the morale of the army, enraged the people, forced a cabinet crisis, and brought the disastrous repercussion in Petrograd, the armed upheaval of July 16.

The Armed Demonstration

July 1 gave warning of the coming storm. July 16 saw it break in fury. First long files of older peasant soldiers with placards: *"Let the 40-year-old men go home and harvest the crops."* Then barrack, slum and factory belching out torrents of men in arms who

---

[2] Alexander Gumberg (1877–1939) was born in Russia and immigrated to the United States in 1903. He returned to Russia in 1917 sympathetic to the Bolshevik Revolution. He worked with the American Red Cross and the Committee on Public Information. He worked with American journalists like Williams, John Reed, Louise Bryant, and Bessie Beatty. He also lobbied for the establishment of diplomatic relations between the new Soviet Union and the United States.

converged on the Tauride Palace,[3] and, for two nights and a day, roared through its gates. Armored cars, with sirens screaming and red flags flying from the turrets, raced up and down the streets. Motor trucks, crammed with soldiers, bayonets jutting out on every side, dashed by like giant porcupines on a rampage. Stretched full length on the car fenders lay sharpshooters, rifles projecting beyond the lamps, eyes on the watch for provocators.

This outpouring was much bigger than the river that ran through these streets on July 1, and more sinister, for it glittered with steel and hissed with curses—a long grey line of wrath. It was the spontaneous outburst of men against their rulers—ugly, reckless, furious.

Under a black banner marched a band of Anarchists, with Yarchuk[4] the tailor at the head. On him was the stamp of the sweat-shop. Long bending over the needle had left him undersized. Now, in place of a needle, he was wielding a gun—the symbol of his deliverance from slavery to the needle.

Gumberg asked him, "What are your political demands?"

"Our political demands?" hesitated Yarchuk.

"To hell with the capitalists!" interjected a big sailor. "And our other political demands," he added, "are—to hell with the war and to hell with the whole damn Cabinet."

Backed up in an alley was a taxi-cab, the nozzles of two machine-guns poking through the windows. In answer to our query, the driver pointed to a banner reading, *"Down with the Capitalist Ministers."*

"We are tired of begging them not to starve and kill the people," he explained. "When we talk they won't listen; but wait till these two pups *(sobachki)* speak!" He patted the guns affectionately. "They will listen then all right."

A mob with nerves at trigger-tension, with such weapons in its hands, and such temper in its soul, did not need much provocation. And provocators were everywhere. Agents of the Black Hundred[5] plied their trade of dissension among the crowds, inciting to riot and pogroms. They turned loose two hundred criminals from Kresty[6] to pillage and loot. In the ensuing ruin they hoped to see the Revolution killed and the Czar restored. In some places they did bring on frightful slaughter.

---

[3] The Tauride Palace was built in St. Petersburg by Prince Grigory Potemkin between 1783 and 1790. He died in 1791.

[4] Efim Yarchuk (1882/1886?–1937) was an anarchist who had agitated during the 1905 Revolution, was exiled to Siberia, and immigrated to the United States in 1913. He returned to Russia after the February Revolution and was a key anarchist figure at the Kronstadt Naval Base just outside of Petrograd. He later fled to Paris, returned to the Soviet Union in 1925, and was arrested and executed by Stalin in 1937.

[5] The Black Hundreds were an ultranationalist group that supported the Romanov dynasty, Russocentric ideas, anti-Semitism, and xenophobia.

[6] Kresty is an old wine warehouse from the 1730s that was converted to a prison in the later nineteenth century.

At a tense moment, in the tight-packed concourse of the Tauride, a provocatory shot was fired. From that shot sprang a hundred. From every quarter rifles blazed, comrades firing point blank into comrades. The crowd screamed, crashed up against the pillars, surged back again, and then fell flat upon the ground. When the firing ceased, sixteen could not rise. During this massacre a military band two blocks away was playing the *Marseillaise*.

Fighting in the streets is panicky business. At night, with bullets spitting from hidden loopholes, from roofs above and cellar-ways below, with the enemy invisible and friends pouring volleys into friends, the crowds stampeded, back and forth, fleeing from a hail of bullets in one street only to plunge into leaden gusts sweeping through the next.

Three times that night our feet slipped in blood on the pavement. Down the Nevsky was blazed a trail of shattered windows and looted shops. The fighting ranged from little skirmishes, with nests of provocators, to the battle on Liteiny, which left twelve horses of the Cossacks stretched upon the cobbles. [Over these horses stood a big *izvoschik* (cabman), tears in his eyes. In time of Revolution the killing of 56 and wounding of 650 men might be endured, but the loss of 12 good horses was too much for an *izvoschik's* heart to bear.]

The Bolsheviks Control the Rising

Only Petrograd's long experience in barricade and street fighting, and the native good sense of the people, prevented the shambles from being more bloody than they were. Upon the chaotic insurgent masses was brought to bear a stabilizing force in tens of thousands of workingmen, backed by the directing mind of the Bolshevik Party. The Bolsheviks saw clearly that this uprising was a spontaneous elemental thing. They saw these masses striking out powerfully but rather blindly. They determined that they should strike to some purpose. They determined to let the full force of this demonstration reach the Soviet Central Executive Committee. This was a committee of 200 selected by the First All-Russian Congress of Soviets before it adjourned. It was in permanent session in the Tauride Palace, and upon it the masses were converging.

The Bolsheviks alone had influence over these masses. All parties implored them to use it. Placing their speakers upon the central portico, they met each regiment and delegation with a short address.

From our vantage point we could view the whole concourse crammed with people, with here and there a man lifted upon his artillery horse, while many banners marked out a red current through the solid mass.

Below us was a sea of upturned faces, the fears, and hopes, and angers written on them but half legible in the twilight of the Russian night. From down the street could be heard the roar of marching hosts, cheering the armored cars. The automobile searchlights focusing on the speaker silhouetted him against the walls of the Palace, a gigantic figure in black. Every gesture, ten times magnified, cut a sweeping shadow across the white façade.

"Comrades," said this giant Bolshevik, "you want revolutionary action. The only way to get it is through a revolutionary government. The Kerensky Government is revolutionary in name only. They promise land, but the landlords still have it. They promise bread, but the speculators still hold it. They promise to get from the Allies a declaration of the objects of the war, but the Allies simply tell us to go on fighting.

"In the cabinet a fundamental conflict rages between the Socialist and the bourgeois ministers. The result is a deadlock and nothing at all is done.

"You men of Petrograd come here to the Soviet Executive Committee saying, 'Take the Government. Here are the bayonets to back you!' You want the Soviets to be the government. So do we Bolsheviks. But we remember that Petrograd is not all of Russia. So we are demanding that the Central Executive Committee call delegates from all over Russia. It is for this new congress to declare the Soviets the government of Russia."

Each crowd met this declaration with cheers and loud cries, *"Down with Kerensky"*; *"Down with the Bourgeois Government"*; *"All Power to the Soviets."*

"Avoid all violence and bloodshed," was the parting admonition to each contingent. "Do not listen to provocators. Do not delight your enemies by killing each other. You have amply shown your power. Now go home quietly. When the occasion for force arises we will call you."

In the swirling flood were cross currents made by the Anarchists, the Black Hundreds, German agents, hoodlums, and those volatile elements which always join the side with the most machine-guns. One thing was now clear to the Bolsheviks: the revolutionary workmen and soldiers around Petrograd were overwhelmingly *against* the Provisional Government and *for* the Soviet. They wanted the Soviet to be the government. But the Bolsheviks were afraid this would be a premature step. As they said, "Petrograd is not Russia. The other cities and the army at the front may not be ripe for such drastic action. Only delegates from the Soviets of all Russia can decide that."

Inside the Tauride, the Bolsheviks were using every argument to persuade the members of the Soviet Executive Committee to call another All-Russian Congress. Outside the Tauride, they were using every exhortation to quiet and appease the clamoring masses. This was a task that taxed all their wits and resources.

The Sailors Demand "All Power to the Soviets"

Some contingents came to the Tauride very belligerent. The Kronstadt sailors arrived in a particularly ugly temper. In barges they came up the river, eight thousand strong. Two of their number had been killed along the way. It had been no holiday excursion, and they had no intention of gazing at the walls of the palace, filling the courtyard with futile clamor, then turning around and going home. They sent in a demand that the Soviet produce a Socialist Minister, and produce him at once.

Chernov,[7] Minister of Agriculture, came out. He took for his rostrum the top of a cab.

"I come to tell you that three bourgeois ministers have resigned. We now look to the future with great hope. Here are the laws which give the land to the peasant."

"Good," cried the hearers. "Will these laws be put into operation at once?"

"As soon as possible," Chernov answered.

"Soon as possible!" they mocked him. "No, no! We want it *now, now*. All the land for the peasant *now!* What have you been doing all these weeks anyhow?"

"I am not answerable to you for my deeds," Chernov replied, white with rage. "It is not you that put me in my office. It was the Peasants' Soviet. To them alone I make my reckoning."

At this rebuff a howl of derision went up from the sailors. With it went the cry: "Arrest Chernov! Arrest him!" A dozen hands stretched out to clutch the minister and drag him off. Others sought to drag him back. In a vortex of fighting friends and foes, his clothes torn, the Minister was being borne away. But Trotsky, coming up, secured his release.

Meanwhile, Saakian[8] scrambled up on the cab. He struck an attitude of stern command.

"Listen!" he cried. "Do you know who is now addressing you?"

"No," a voice called out. "And we don't give a damn."

"The man who is now addressing you," resumed Saakian, "is the Vice-President of the Central Executive Committee of the First All-Russian Congress of Soviets of Soldiers' and Workmen's Deputies."

This prodigious title, instead of serving to impress and quiet the crowd, was greeted by laughter and cries of *"Down with him!" (doloi, doloi)*. But he had come out to tame this mob, and with great vim he fired into it a fusillade of short abrupt sentences.

"My name—Saakian!" (The mob: "Down with him!")

"My party—Socialist Revolutionary!" ("Down with him!")

"My official religion—according to the passport—Armenian-Gregorian!" ("Down with him!")

"My real religion—Socialism!" ("Down with him!")

"My relation to the war—two brothers killed." A voice: "There should have been a third."

"My advice to you—trust us, your leaders and best friends. Stop this foolish demonstration. You are disgracing yourself, disgracing the Revolution, bringing disaster to Russia."

These sailors were already enraged. To slap them in the face thus was an idiotic act. Pandemonium broke loose. Again Trotsky to the rescue.

---

[7] Victor M. Chernov (1873–1952) was a founding member of the Socialist Revolutionary Party and served in the Provisional Government. After the Bolsheviks seized power, he fled Russia and eventually died in the United States.

[8] Sargis (Sako) Saakian was an Armenian Socialist Revolutionary who served in the Provisional Government.

He steps upon the platform, the hero and idol of the Kronstadt sailors. He knows the temper of his hearers. He knows, today, they have no ears for censure.

"Revolutionary sailors, pride and flower of the revolutionary forces of Russia!" he began. "In this battle for the Social Revolution we fight together. Together, comrades, our fists beat upon the doors of this Palace until the ideals for which our blood has flowed shall at last be incarnated in the constitution of this country. Hard and long has been the heroic struggle! But out of it will come a free life for free men in a great free land. Am I not right?"

"Right you are, Trotsky," yells the crowd.

Trotsky moves away.

"But you haven't told us anything," they cry. "What are you going to do about the Cabinet?" They may be a mob, with an appetite for flattery, but they are not so unthinking as to be pacified by phrases, even from Trotsky.

"I am too hoarse to talk more," he pleads. "Riazanov[9] will tell you."

"No, you tell us!" Trotsky again mounts the cab.

"Only the All-Russian Congress can assume full power of government. The Labor Section has agreed to call this congress. The Military Section will without doubt follow. In two weeks the delegates can be here."

"Two weeks!" they cry in astonishment. "Two weeks is too long. We want it now!"

But Trotsky prevails. The sailors acquiesce, cheering the Soviets and the coming Revolution.

They move peacefully away, convinced that the Second All-Russian Congress will be called.

Downing the Demonstration, then the Bolsheviks

This is precisely what the leaders in the Soviet Executive Committee do not want. They are dead set against the Soviet becoming the government. They have many reasons to give. But the real reason is fear of these very masses by whom they have been lifted to their exalted stations. The intelligentsia distrust the masses below them. At the same time they exaggerate the abilities and good intentions of the grand bourgeoisie above them.

They do not want the Soviets to take the power. They have no intention of calling a Second All-Russian Congress in two weeks, two months, or at all. But they are frightened by these turbulent crowds crashing into the courtyard, hammering at the doors. Their tactics are to placate the mob, and they seek help from the Bolsheviks. At the same time these intelligentsia play another game. They join the Provisional Government in calling regiments from the front "to quell the mutiny and restore order in the city."

On the third day the troops arrive. Bicycle battalions, the reserve regiments, and then long grim lines of horsemen, the sun glancing on the tips of their lances. They

---

[9] David B. Riazanov (1870–1938) was a leading Marxist revolutionary. He founded the Marx-Engels Institute. He was executed in the purges of the 1930s.

are the Cossacks, ancient foes of the revolutionists, bringing dread to the workers and joy to the bourgeoisie. The avenues are filled now with well-dressed throngs cheering the Cossacks, crying *"Shoot the rabble." "String up the Bolsheviks."*

A wave of reaction runs through the city. Insurgent regiments are disarmed. The death penalty is restored. The Bolshevik papers are suppressed. Forged documents attesting the Bolsheviks as German agents are handed to the press. Alexandrov, the Czar's prosecutor, hales them before the bar, indicted for high treason under section 108 of the Penal Code. Leaders like Trotsky and Kollontai are thrown into prison. Lenin and Zinoviev are driven into hiding. In all quarters sudden seizures, assaults, and murder of workingmen.[10]

In the early morning of July 18, I am suddenly wakened by piercing cries from the Nevsky. With the clattering of horses' hoofs are mingled shouts, desperate pleas for mercy, curses—one terrible blood-curdling scream. Then, the thud of a falling body, the groans of a man dying, and silence. An officer coming in explains that some workingmen had been caught pasting up Bolshevik posters along the Nevsky. A squad of Cossacks had ridden them down, lashing out with whips and sabres, cleaving one man open and leaving him dead on the pavement.

At this new turn of events the bourgeoisie are elated. Ill-based elation! They do not know that the screams of this murdered workman will penetrate the furthermost corners of Russia, rousing his comrades to wrath and arms. This July day they cheer the Volynsk regiment, as with band playing it enters the city to suppress this uprising, whose purpose is to offer all power to the Soviets. Ill-starred cheers! They do not know that on a coming November night they will see this regiment in the forefront of the rising that triumphantly delivers all power to the Soviets.

The troops are called in to conquer Petrograd; but in the end Petrograd conquers them. The infection of this Bolshevik stronghold is irresistible. It is a huge blast furnace of the Revolution, burning away all dross and indifference. No matter how cold and sluggish they may enter the city, out of it they go fired by the spirit of the Revolution.

The city rose in tears and blood, in hunger and cold, in the forced labor of myriads of the starved and beaten. Their bones lie buried deep in the mud below. But their outraged spirits seem to live again in the Petrograd workingmen of today—spirits powerful and avenging. The serfs of Peter built the city; presently their descendants will be coming into their own. It does not appear thus in midsummer 1917. The black shadow of reaction hovers over them. But the Bolsheviks bide their time. History, they feel, is on their side. Their ideas are working out in the villages, in the fleet and at the front.

To these places I now make my way.

---

[10] Alexandra M. Kollontai (1872–1952) was originally a Menshevik, then a Bolshevik, and later the Soviet ambassador to Norway. She was a key Bolshevik theorist. Grigory Zinoviev (1883–1936), born Ovsei-Gershon A. Radomyslsky, was a long-time Bolshevik and head of the Communist International.

Chapter 3
A PEASANT INTERLUDE

"Go out among the forests and the people," said Bakunin.

In the capitals the orators thunder and rage.
But in the village is the silence of centuries.

We craved a taste of this silence. Three months we had heard the roar of Revolution. I was saturated with it: Yanishev was exhausted by it. His voice had failed through incessant speaking and he had been ordered by the Bolshevik Party to take a ten days' respite. So we started out for the Volga basin bound for the little village of Spasskoye (Salvation), from which Yanishev had been driven out in 1907.

It was high noon one August day when we left the Moscow train and set out on the road leading across the fields. Sun-drenched in these last weeks of summer, the fields had turned into wide rolling seas of yellow grain, dotted here and there with islands of green. These were the tree-shaded peasant villages of the province of Vladimir. From a rise in the road we could count sixteen of them, each with its great white church capped with glistening domes. It was a holiday and the distant belfries were flooding the fields with music as the sun had flooded them with color.

After the cities this was to me a land of peace and quiet. But to Yanishev it was a land of poignant memories. After ten years of wandering the exile was returning home.

"In that village over there," he said, pointing to the west, "my father was a teacher. The people liked his teaching, but one day the gendarmes came, closed the school, and led him off. In that next village Vera lived. She was very pretty and very kind and she was my sweetheart. I was too bashful to tell her then, and now it is too late. She is in Siberia. In the woods yonder a few of us used to meet to talk about the revolution. One night the Cossacks came riding down on us. That bridge is where they killed Yegor, the bravest of our comrades."

It was not a happy home-coming for the exile. Every turn in the road started up some recollection. Handkerchief in hand Yanishev walked along, pretending that it was only perspiration he was wiping from his face.

As we came across the village green of Spasskoye we saw an old peasant in a bright blue smock, sitting on a bench before his hut. He shaded his eyes, puzzled by the appearance of these two dust-stained foreigners. Then in joyful recognition he cried "Mikhail Petrovich!" and throwing his arms around Yanishev, kissed him on both cheeks. Then he turned to me. I told him that my name was Albert.

"And your father's name?" he inquired gravely.

"David," I replied.

"Albert Davidovich (Albert, son of David), welcome to the home of Ivan Ivanov. We are poor, but may God give you his richest blessing."

Ivan Ivanov stood straight as an arrow, long-bearded, clear-eyed, hard-muscled. But it was not his strength of body, nor his warmth of feeling, nor his quaint formality of speech that struck me. It was his quiet dignity. It was the dignity of a natural object, a tree whose roots run deep into the soil. And it was indeed out of the soil of this *mir* that Ivan Ivanov for sixty years had drawn his sustenance, as had his fathers for generations. His little *izba* was made of logs, its deep thatched roof now green with weeds, its garden gay with flowers.

Ivan's wife, Tatyana, and daughter, Avdotia, having saluted us, brought a table from the house. On it they set a samovar, and lifting its top, placed eggs along the steaming sides. Ivan and his household made the sign of the cross and we sat down at the table.

"Of what we are rich in, we gladly give you," said Ivan *(Chem bogaty, ty ee rady)*.

The women brought in a big bowl of cabbage-soup *(shtchee)*, and for each person a wooden spoon.

Every one was supposed to dip his soup from the common bowl. Seeing this, I stood not upon the order of the dipping, but dipped at once. When the first bowl was empty, they brought a second, full of porridge *(kasha)*. It was followed by a bowl of boiled raisins. Ivan presided at the samovar, dispensing tea, black bread, and cucumbers. It was a special feast, for this was a special holiday in Spasskoye.

Even the crows seemed to be aware of it. Great flocks wheeling overhead threw swift cloud-shadows across the ground, or alighted on the church roof and covered it completely. The domes, all green or glistening gold, would in a minute be blackest jet.

I told Ivan that in America farmers killed crows because they ate the grain.

"Yes," said Ivan, "our crows eat the grain. But they eat the field-mice, too. And even if they are crows, they are like us and want to live."

Tatyana held a like attitude toward the flies that swarmed around the table. Descending on a piece of sugar they would turn it as black as the crow-covered church.

"Never mind the flies," said Tatyana. "Poor things, in a month or two they'll be dead, anyhow."

The Village Takes a Holiday

It was the Feast of Transfiguration, and from all the countryside around came the poor, the crippled and the aged. Again and again we heard the tapping of a cane and a plaintive voice asking alms *radi Christa*, for the Christ's sake. Yanishev and I dropped a few copecks into the bags they thrust before them. The women followed with large pieces cut from the big black loaves, while Ivan solemnly deposited in each sack a great green cucumber. Cucumbers were scarce this year, so it was truly a gift of love. But whether we gave cucumbers or bread or copecks, back to each of us came the plaintive sing-song blessing of the beggar.

Even the roughest, poorest Russian peasant is moved to profound pity by the spectacle of human misery. His own life teaches him the meaning of pain and privation. But this does not dull his sympathy; it makes him the more sensitive to the sufferings of others.

To Ivan the city workingmen cooped up in their hot dusty streets were "poor fellows" *(bedniakee);* the criminals locked up in jails were "unfortunates" *(neschastnenkie);* while a group of war-prisoners in Austrian uniforms cut him deepest of all. They seemed jolly enough as they came rollicking by, and I said so.

"But they are so far away from home," said Ivan. "How can they be happy?"

"Well," I said, "here am I, farther from home than they are, and I am happy."

"Yes," assented the others, "that is right."

"No," said Ivan Ivanov, "that is wrong. Albert Davidovich is here because he wanted to come. The prisoners are here because we made them come."

Naturally two foreigners sitting at the table of Ivan Ivanov made a sensation among the natives of Spasskoye. But the elders did not let their curiosity overcome their sense of the proprieties. Only a few children came down, and fixed their gaze upon us. I smiled at the children and they looked thunderstruck. Again I smiled, and three of them almost fell backwards. This seemed a peculiar reaction to my friendly overtures. At the third smile they cried, *"Zolotiyeh zooby!"* and clasping hands they ran away. Before I could grasp the meaning of this behavior they came rushing back with a score of recruits. In semi-circle they stood around the table with all their wistful eyes converged on me. There was nothing for me to do but smile again. "Yes, yes!" they cried. *"Zolotiyeh zooby!* He is the man with golden teeth!" This was why my smile had startled them. And what could be more marvelous than the arrival of a foreigner whose mouth grew golden teeth? Had I arrived in Spasskoye with a golden crown upon my head I could not have more deeply stirred the community than by wearing a golden crown upon my tooth. But this I learned on the morrow.

Now from the farther end of the village came the strains of music. There was a chorus of young voices accompanied by the thrumming of the *balalaika,*[1] the clanging of cymbals, and the throbbing of a kind of tambourine *(bouben).* Clearer and nearer came the music, until suddenly around the corner of the church emerged the procession of players and singers. The girls were in the gay rich costumes of the peasants; the boys wore smocks of green and orange and brightest hue, belted by cords with tasseled ends. The boys played the instruments, while the girls sang in response to the precentor, a clean-looking, tousle-haired lad of seventeen, one of the last to be drafted to the front. In clear lusty voice, with abandon of emotion he sang an old folk song, adding new verses of his own as he strode along. Later he wrote them down for me.

> At the window a birch tree stands
>   The golden days are gone
> Pity us, fair maidens all,
>   We are now recruits!

---

[1] A balalaika is a three-stringed instrument that is a traditional instrument in Russia.

> Why have they taken me as a soldier?
>> I, my father's only son?
> The reason probably is this,
>> I've courted the maidens all too long.
>
> From the trenches a lad steps out
>> Crying, "Oh, my fathers!
> All my comrades have been killed!
>> Soon my turn will come."
>
> Why, my darling, don't you meet me
>> In the midst of fields?
> Don't you feel some pain or sorrow
>> That a soldier boy am I?
>
> Father, mother, dig a grave,
>> Bury me deep below.
> For my courting, for my freedom,
>> Bury my naughty head.

Three times they circled the village green. Then gathering on the grass before the church, they sang and danced till morning. The rush and joyous fling of the dancers, the colors of their costumes lit by the pine-torches, the laughter and snatches of song rising out of the dark, the young lovers with their caresses frank and unashamed, the church bell at intervals crashing like a great temple gong, and the startled birds wheeling overhead, all combined to create an impression of primitive energy and beauty. It carried me back across the centuries to the days when the race was young, and men drew life and inspiration directly from the soil.

Yanishev Tells of America

It was a dream world, an idyllic commune, bound together in a fellowship of toil and play and feasting. With its spell upon me I made my way to the *izba*, opened the door, and came suddenly face to face with the twentieth century again. It was in the person and words of Yanishev, Yanishev the artisan, the Socialist, and the Internationalist. To the peasants ringed around him he was describing the America of today. It was not the usual story of the bitter experiences of the Russian in America, the story of slums and strikes and poverty that thousands of returning exiles have spread over Russia. Yanishev, with husky voice but face aglow, was telling the wonders of America. To peasants with houses one story high he pictured the houses of New York, forty, fifty and sixty stories high. To men who had never seen a shop larger than the blacksmith's, he told of great plants where a hundred trip hammers pounded night and day. From their serene Muscovite plain he took them to great cities with subway trains tearing up the night, Great White Ways flooded with pleasure-seekers, and clanging factories where millions surged in and out.

The villagers listened attentively. They were not overawed or wonderstruck. Yet we could not complain of any lack of appreciation.

"The Americans do wonderful things," said one old mujik,[2] shaking our hands.

"Yes," agreed his companion, "they do things more wonderful than even the *leshey* (the wood spirit)."

But in their kindly comments we felt a certain reserve, as if they were trying to be polite to strangers. Next morning a conversation overheard by chance gave us their real opinion.

Ivan was speaking. "No wonder Albert and Mikhail are white-faced and tired. Think of being brought up in a country like that." And Tatyana said, "It's a hard life we live, but God knows it looks harder over there."

I glimpsed for the first time a truth that grew clearer as the months went by. The peasant has a mind of his own, which he uses to make judgments of his own. This is startling to the foreigner, to whom the Russian peasant is a shambling creature of the earth, immersed in the night of mediaevalism, chained by superstition, steeped in poverty. It is startling to discover that this peasant, unable to read or write, is able to think.

His thought is primal, elemental, with the stamp of the soil on it. It reflects the centuries of living on the far-stretching plains and steppes under the wide Russian sky and through the long winter. He brings a fresh untutored mind to bear upon all questions in a manner penetrating and often disconcerting. He challenges our long-held convictions. He revises our estimate of western civilization. It is not at all obvious to him that it is worth the price we pay for it. He is not mesmerized by machinery, efficiency, production. He asks, "What is it for? Does it make men happier? Does it make them more friendly?"

His conclusions are not always profound. Sometimes they are only naïve and curious. When the *mir* assembled on Monday morning the village Elder (*starosta*) politely extended to me the greetings of the village. He said apologetically that the children had brought home a report about my golden teeth, but that it did not seem reasonable, and they didn't know whether to believe it or not. There was nothing to do but demonstrate. I opened my mouth while the Elder peered long and intently into it and then gravely confirmed the report. Thereupon the seventy bearded patriarchs formed in line while I stood with mouth agape. Each gazed his fill and then moved along to give place to the next man until all the members of the *mir* had filed past my open mouth.

I had to explain that it is the custom of Americans to put cement and gold and silver in their crumbling teeth. One old man of eighty, whose fine clean teeth showed not the slightest need of dentistry, gave his opinion that Americans must eat food very strange and strong to work such havoc. Several said it might be all right for Americans to have golden teeth, but that it would never do for Russians, who were always drinking so much tea and such very hot tea that it would surely melt the gold. At this point Ivan Ivanov, who had been enjoying the prestige of harboring the unusual vis-

---

[2] *Mujik* or *muzhik* is a reference to a Russian peasant.

itors, spoke up. He insisted that his tea was as hot as any in the village, and testified that he had drawn at least ten glasses for me, yet there had been no melting.

Abroad the term "American" is almost synonymous with "man of wealth." Gold on my eye-glasses and on my fountain pen convinced them that I must be a man of super-wealth. Yet I came to marvel at their lavish display of gold quite as much as they at mine. For this peasant village had gold in abundance, only it was not on the persons of the villagers. It was in their church. As one stepped through the church doors there loomed up a beautiful reredos twenty or thirty feet high, covered with a glistening sheen of gold. At one time the villagers had raised ten thousand rubles to decorate this temple.

While this little village was far removed from the currents of Europe and America, still there were marks of culture and civilization advancing from the West. There were cigarettes and Singer sewing-machines, men whose limbs had been shot off by machine-guns, and two boys from the factory-towns with store-clothes and celluloid collars—ugly contrasts to the smocks and kaftans of the village.

One night standing before a neighbor's hut we were startled to hear through the curtains a soft and modulated voice asking *"Parlez-vous Français?"* It was a pretty peasant girl raised in the village but with all the airs and graces which belong to a girl raised in a court. She had served in a French household in Petrograd and had come home to give birth to her child.

Thus, in varied ways the outside world was filtering into the village, stirring it from the slumber of centuries. Stories of big cities and of lands across the seas came by way of prisoners and soldiers, traders and *zemstvo*[3] men. It resulted in a strange miscellany of ideas about foreign lands—a curious compound of facts and fancies. One time a grotesque half-fact about America was brought home to me pointedly and in an embarrassing manner.

We were at the supper table and I was explaining that in my notebook I was writing down all the customs and habits of the Russians that struck me as strange and peculiar.

"For example," I said, "instead of having individual dishes you eat out of one great common bowl. That is a curious custom." "Yes," said Ivan. "I suppose we are a curious people."

"And that big stove! It takes up a third of the room. You bake bread in it. You sleep on top of it. You get inside and take a steam bath in it. You do everything with it and in a most peculiar manner." "Yes," nodded Ivan again, "I suppose we are a peculiar people."

I felt something step on my foot. I thought it was a dog but it proved to be a pig. "There!" I exclaimed. "That is the most peculiar custom of all. You let pigs and chickens walk right into your dining-room."

At this moment the baby in Avdotia's arms began kicking its feet up and down upon the table in baby fashion. Addressing the child, she said, "Here, baby! Take

---

[3] A zemstvo was a form of local government that was instituted during the Great Reforms of Alexander II in the 1860s.

your feet off the table. Remember you are not in America." And turning to me she added courteously, "What peculiar customs you have there in America."

We Harvest the Crops

It was the day after the holiday, and the visitors from neighboring towns still tarried. There were games and dancing on the village green; and a band of children, having come into possession of an accordion, paraded solemnly about, singing the songs of yesterday, quaint little understudies of their elder brothers and sisters. An after-the-holiday lethargy lingered over most of the village. But not over the household of Ivan Ivanov. Everybody was busy there. Avdotia was twisting straw into bands to bind the sheaves. Tatyana was plaiting strips of bark and shaping them into sandals. Olga, Avdotia's elder child, was forcibly teaching the cat to drink tea. Ivan sharpened the scythes, and we all set out for the fields.

At this move the young people came out of the *izbas*. "Please don't go to the fields. Stay at home," they teased. As we proceeded they became quite serious. I asked why we should not go.

"If one family starts for the fields all the others follow," they said. "Then our holiday fun will be over. Please don't go!"

But the ripened harvest was calling. The sun was shining, and there was no telling how soon the rains would fall. So Ivan marched along, and when, fifteen minutes later, we reached a rise of ground, we looked back to see the paths dotted with black figures making for the fields. Like a beehive the village was sending out its workers to garner its food-stores for the oncoming winter. As we reached the rye field Yanishev quoted from Nekrasov's[4] national epic, *Who Can Be Happy and Free in Russia?*

> You full yellow cornfields!
>   To look at you now
> One would never imagine
>   How sorely God's people
> Had toiled to array you.
>   'Tis not by warm dewdrops
> That you have been moistened;
>   The sweat of the peasant
> Has fallen on you.
>
> The peasants are gladdened
>   At sight of the oats,
> And the rye and the barley,
>   But not by the wheat,
> For it feeds but the chosen.
>   "We love you not, Wheat!

---

[4] Nikolai A. Nekrasov (1821–77) was a Russian writer and poet who served as an inspiration to Russian revolutionaries of the time and later.

But the rye and the barley
>   We love—they are kind,
> They feed all men alike."

As each one turned to his task I joined in the work, fetching water, tying sheaves, swinging a scythe, watching the light-brown stalks come tumbling down. The scythe demands skill and practice. So the figure I cut and the swathe I cut were not heroic, nor did I add to the prestige of American reapers. Ivan was too polite to criticize my technique but I could see that it was inciting him to suppressed merriment. In his comment to Avdotia I picked up the Russian word for camel. I was indeed hunched over like a camel while Ivan Ivanov stood erect, handling his scythe like a master-craftsman. I turned upon Ivan and accused him of likening me to a camel. He was embarrassed. But when he saw that I was amused, and admitted my likeness to that humped creature, he laughed and laughed.

"Tatyana! Mikhail!" he roared. "Albert Davidovich says that when he cuts the grain he looks like a camel. Ho! ho! ho!" Two or three times after that he broke into sudden laughter. The camel must have helped him through many weary wastes in the long winter.

Writers dwell upon the laziness of the Russian peasant. Watching the *mujik* lounging around market places and vodka shops gives one that impression. But trying to keep up with the *mujik* in the fields very quickly takes it away. With the sun beating down on their heads and the dust rising from under their feet they mowed and raked and bound and stacked until the last straw had been gleaned from the field. Then they tramped back into the village.

The Peasants Wary of Bolshevism

Since our arrival the villagers had been asking Yanishev to make a speech. In the early evening there arrived a delegation beseeching him.

"Think of it," said Yanishev. "Ten years ago if these peasants had suspected that I was a Socialist they would have come to kill me. Now, knowing that I am a Bolshevik, they come begging me to talk. Things have gone a long, long way since then."

Yanishev was not a gifted man unless it be a gift to be deeply sensitive to the sorrows of the world. Tormented by the sufferings of others, he had chosen privation for himself. As an artisan in America he earned six dollars a day. Out of this he took enough for a cheap room and meals. With the rest he bought "literature" and carried it from door to door. In the poor quarters of Boston, Detroit, Moscow, and Marseilles, they still speak of Yanishev as the comrade who gave everything to the cause.

In Tokyo a fellow-exile once found an excited coolie trying to drag Yanishev, protesting, into a rickshaw. "I just got in his rickshaw," Yanishev explained, "and he began pulling and sweating like a horse. I may be a fool, but I can't let a man work like a beast for me. So I paid him and got out. I'll never get into a rickshaw again."

Since his return to Russia he had travelled night and day addressing enormous crowds until his voice failed him and he could only whisper and gesture. He had come to his home village to recuperate. But even here the revolution would not let him rest.

"Will Mikhail Petrovich give us a little speech?" the peasants pleaded. "Only a little speech."

Yanishev could not deny them. The committee drew a wagon out upon the village green and when the throng was thick around it, Yanishev mounted this rostrum and began telling the Bolshevik story of the Revolution, the War, and the Land.

They stood listening while evening darkened into night. Then they brought torches, and Yanishev talked on. His voice grew husky. They brought him water, tea, and *kvass*.[5] His voice failed, and they waited patiently till it came back again. These peasants who had labored all day in the fields stood there late into the night, more eager to gather stores for their mind than they had been to gather food for their bodies. It was a symbolic sight, this torch of knowledge flaming in the darkness of the village—one of tens of thousands scattered over the Ukrainian steppes, the plains of Muscovy and the far stretches of Siberia. In hundreds of them that night torches were flaming and other Yanishevs were telling the story of the Revolution.

So much reverence and age-old longings in those eager faces pressing around the speaker. So much hunger in these questions rising out of the dark. Yanishev toiled on until he was utterly exhausted. Only when he could go no further did they reluctantly disperse. I listened to their comments. Were these "ignorant illiterate *mujiks*" ready to swallow this new doctrine, to be swayed by the passion of a propagandist?

"Mikhail Petrovich is a good man," they were saying. "We know that he has gone far and seen many things. What he believes may be good for some people, but we do not know whether it is good for us." Yanishev had poured out his soul, explaining, expounding the creed of Bolshevism—and not a single convert. Yanishev himself said so, as he dragged himself up into the hayloft where we had gone to escape from the stuffy cabin. One young, peasant, Fedossiev, seemed to divine the loneliness and spiritual emptiness of a preacher who gives his best and seemingly is rejected.

"It is all so new, Mikhail Petrovich," he said. "We are a slow people. We must have time to think it over and talk it over. Only today we reaped the grain in the fields; it was months and months ago that we sowed it in the ground."

I tried to add a reassuring word. "Never mind," whispered Yanishev, with the zealot's confidence in the ultimate triumph of his faith. "Of course, they will believe." He lay in collapse on the hay, his body trembling and coughing, but with serenity in his face.

I doubted. But Yanishev was right. Eight months later he made another speech on the village green. It was on invitation of the Communist Party of the village of Spasskoye. Fedossiev was chairman of the meeting.

---

[5] Kvass is a Slavic fermented drink made from rye bread.

Yanishev Talks of the Land

Morning brought many peasants to the door with questions. Above all was the problem of the land. The Bolshevik solution at that time was, "Leave it to the local land committees. Let them take over the great estates and put them into the hands of the people." The peasants pointed out that this did not solve the land problem of Spasskoye, for here there were no crown or church or private domains.

"All the land around here already belongs to us," said the Elder. "It is too little, for God gives us many children. The Bolsheviks may be as good as Mikhail Petrovich says, they are, but if they take the government, can they make more land? No. Only God can do that. We want a government with money enough to send us to Siberia or to any place where there is land in plenty. Will the Bolsheviks do that?"

Yanishev explained the colonizing scheme, and then turned to the agricultural commune which the Bolsheviks were projecting for Russia. It was ultimately to change the *mir* into a cooperative large-scale farming enterprise. He pointed out the wastage of the present system in Spasskoye. Here, as usual, the land was divided into four sections. One was held for common pasturage. To make sure of a fair division of the good, the bad and the medium ground, each peasant was allotted a field in each of these respective sections. Yanishev pointed out the time lost in going from field to field. He showed the gain that would come if the fields, instead of being cut into checkerboards, were worked as a unit on a grand scale. He pictured the gang-plow and the harvester at work. Two of the peasants had seen their magic performances in another province and testified that for working they were regular "devils" *(cherti)*.

"And will America send them to us?" the peasants asked.

"For a while," Yanishev replied. "Then we shall build great shops and make them right here in Russia."

Again he took his hearers out of their quiet rural haunts into the roar and clamor of a great modern plant. And again there was that same uneasy reaction to his tale. They were more afraid than enamored of modern industrialism. They wanted our wonderful machinery. But they thought it would be a dubious blessing if they must pay the price of seeing chimneys belching black smoke-clouds over their land of green and white. The peasants dread the idea of "being cooked in a factory boiler." Necessity goaded some of them into mines and mills, but since the Revolution they have gone flocking back to the land.

Besides their social questions, there were, many personal problems that confronted Yanishev. Should he recommend his political creed by compromising his personal convictions? For example, should he who had left the Greek Church, make the sign of the cross before and after meals. Yanishev decided against it and prepared himself for questions from Ivan Ivanov. But though the old peasant looked perplexed and his wife grieved when Yanishev omitted the ceremony, they never asked for explanations.

In Russia the customary salutation to the toiler in the fields is "God's help to you" (*Bog v Pomoshch*). Yanishev decided to use that greeting instead of the formal "Good morning." He also stood through the long service for Fedossiev's baby. In Russian villages bells toll often for the death of a child.

"Many children God gives us," said the Elder. "And to keep bread in the mouths of those that live we must not neglect the fields." So the others went to their work while the priest and the parents, Yanishev and I, went to the church. Beside the mother stood her nine children. Each year she had borne a child and, ranged according to age, they formed a flight of steps with here and there a gap. That year the child had died. And now this year's child was dead. It was a tiny thing, no larger than the lily beside it, so small and fragile in its little blue coffin, with the massive walls and pillars of the church rising around it.

This village of Spasskoye was fortunate in its priest. He was a kind and sympathetic man, liked and trusted by the people. Though called so often to say the children's mass, he was trying not to make it a thing of routine. Gently he lit the candles on the coffin, laid the cross on the baby's breast, and began the mass, filling the church with his resonant voice. Priest and deacon chanted the service, while father, mother and children crossed themselves and knelt and touched their foreheads to the floor. Opposite the priest Yanishev stood stolidly with half-bowed head.

They faced each other with the mystery of life and death between them; the one a priest of the Holy Orthodox church, the other a prophet of the Social Revolution; the one consecrating himself to making children happy and secure in the paradise beyond, the other devoting his life to making the earth secure and happy for living children.

I went with Yanishev upon many of his missionary journeys through the Russian towns and cities. From the skilled artisans in the textile center of Ivanovo, we ranged through all ranks of the proletarians down to the slum of the thieves in Moscow, immortalized in Maxim Gorky's[6] *The Night Asylum*. But always the thoughts of Yanishev were going back to the villages.

Six months later I said good-bye to him at the Fourth Soviet Congress in Moscow. Clinging to his arm was a woman of seventy, very withered and bent. Yanishev introduced her reverently as his "teacher." Beyond the confines of Russia or outside the working-classes her name was quite unknown. But to the young rebels among the workers and peasants her name was everything. With them she had shared hardship, pain and prison. The long years of toil and hunger had left her white and feeble, an object inspiring pity until one saw her eyes. In them were still the fires which had kindled the spirits of scores of young men like Yanishev and sent them out as flaming apostles of the Social Revolution. For the Revolution she had given her life, but had hardly dared dream that she would see it.

Now it had come and she was sitting among her own, with hands clasped in the hand of her young disciple. True, industry was in ruin, the Germans were at the gates, and hunger and cold walked through the city, yet as she sat in the ancient Hall

---

[6] Maxim Gorky (1868–1936), born Aleksei Maksimovich Peshkov, was a Russian/Soviet writer who founded the socialist realist form. He supported the Bolshevik regime under Lenin but ran afoul of Stalin and spent much of the 1920s and 1930s abroad. He returned to the Soviet Union in 1932 and died there in 1936.

of Nobles, listening to Lenin, she was seeing the new day coming, bringing peace to all people and to her a chance to live on the land. "We both came from the land and we both love it," she whispered to me. "And when the Revolution is complete Mikhail and I are going back to live in the villages."*

* Appendix III. The Burial of Yanishev.

Chapter 4

THE MAN ON HORSEBACK

In the summer of 1917, I travelled far and wide through Russia. From all sides rose the lamentation of a stricken people. I heard it in the textile mills of Ivanovo, the Fair grounds of Nijni [Nizhnii-Novgorod] and the market-squares of Kiev. It came to me from the holds of steamers on the Volga and at night from rafts and barges drifting down the Dnieper. The burden of the people's sorrow was the war, "The cursed war!"

Everywhere I saw the blight and wreckage of war. In the Ukraine I drove out over those rolling lands which made Gogol[1] exclaim: "You steppes! O God! How lovely you are!" We stopped at a little village folded in the hills and about three hundred women, forty old men and boys and a score of crippled soldiers gathered round our *zemstvo* wagon. When I stood up to address them I asked: "How many ever heard of Washington?" One lad raised his hand. "How many have heard of Lincoln?" Three hands. "Kerensky?" About ninety. "Lenin?" Ninety again. "Tolstoy?" One hundred and fifty hands.

They enjoyed this, laughing together at the foreigner and his funny accent. Then a foolish blunder. I asked, "Who of you have lost someone in the war?" Nearly every hand went up, and a wail swept through that laughing throng, like a winter wind moaning in the trees. Two old peasants fell against the wagon wheels sobbing, and shaking my platform. A lad ran out of the crowd, crying: "My brother—they killed my brother!" And the women, drawing their *platoks*[2] to their eyes, or clasped in each other's arms, wept and wept, until I wondered where all the tears could come from. Who would have dreamed that behind those placid faces lay so much grief?

This was but one of the thousands of Russian villages which the war had stripped of every able-bodied man. It was one of countless villages to which the wounded came crawling back, crippled, eyeless, or armless. Millions never returned at all. They lay in that great grave, 1,500 miles long, stretching from the Black Sea to the Baltic—the Russian front against the Germans. There peasants with only clubs in their hands, driven up against the machine guns of the Germans, were mowed down *en masse*.

---

[1] Nikolai Gogol (1809–52) was a Russian-Ukrainian novelist who was best known for his novel *Dead Souls*.

[2] A *platok* is a Russian traditional scarf.

There were plenty of guns in Archangel. They had even been loaded on cars, and started for the front. But merchants who wanted those cars for their wares, slipped a few thousand rubles to the officials; so, ten miles out of Archangel, the munitions were dumped and the cars shunted back to be reloaded with champagnes, automobiles, and Parisian dresses.

Life was gay and dazzling in Petrograd and the big cities—big profits in this war business—but it was cold and bloody business for 12,000,000 soldiers driven into the trenches by order of the Czar.

And now under Kerensky there were still 12,000,000 under arms. They were conscripts, dragged from ploughs and workshops to have guns thrust in their hands. The ruling-class used every device to keep those weapons in the soldiers' hands. It waved the flag and screamed "Victory and glory." It organized Women's Battalions of Death[3] crying "Shame on you men to let girls do your fighting." It placed machine-guns in the rear of rebelling regiments declaring certain death to those who retreated. But all to no avail.

The Soldiers in Revolt

In thousands the soldiers were throwing down their guns and streaming from the front. Like plagues of locusts they came, clogging railways, highways and waterways. They swarmed down on trains, packing roofs and platforms, clinging to car-steps like clusters of grapes, sometimes evicting passengers from their berths. A Y.M.C.A. man swears he saw this sign: *"Tovarish Soldiers:* Please do not throw passengers out of the window after the train is in motion." Perhaps an exaggeration. But they did throw our suitcases out of the window.

It happened on a trip I made to Moscow with Alex Gumberg. Our compartment was crowded, and the Russians, having almost hermetically sealed door and window against the night air, went blissfully to sleep. The place, soon steaming like a Turkish bath, became unbearable. To let in a breath of air, I slid the door open, then joined the sleepers. In the morning I woke to a harsh surprise. Our suitcases were gone.

"Some *tovarish* robbers in uniform threw them out of the window and then jumped off the train," explained the old conductor. His consolation for our grief was that they had likewise stolen the baggage of an officer in the next compartment. We grieved not so much for the loss of our clothes as for the invaluable passports, notebooks and letters of introduction our bags contained.

Two weeks later we got another surprise—a summons from the station-master in Moscow. There was one of our suitcases forwarded to us by the robbers. It contained none of our clothes but all our documents and the officers' papers—not a single one was missing. After all, considering the plight of the hordes of deserting soldiers that

---

[3] The Women's Battalion was formed after the February Revolution to inspire weary soldiers to continue to fight in the summer of 1917.

swept across the land, one wonders not at the number of thefts and excesses they committed but at the fewness of them. And if the tales of awful conditions in the trenches were true, the wonder is not that so many soldiers deserted but that so many still remained at the front.

I wanted to see conditions for myself. Many times I tried to get a pass to the front. At last in September I succeeded. With John Reed and Boris Reinstein,[4] I started for the Riga Sector.

With us was a Russian priest, a big bearded fellow, gentle and amiable, but with a terrible thirst for tea and conversation. On the door of our compartment the guard slapped up a sign that said: *"American Mission."* Under this aegis we slept and ate as the train crept through the autumn drizzle and the priest talked endlessly on about his soldiers.

"In the old text of the church prayers," he said, "God is called *Czar of Heaven* and the Virgin, *Czarina*. We've had to leave that out. The people won't have God insulted, they say. The priest prays for peace to all nations. Whereupon the soldiers cry out, 'Add "without annexations and indemnities."' Then we pray for travellers, for the sick and the suffering. And the soldiers cry 'Pray also for the deserters.' The Revolution has made havoc with the Faith, yet the masses of soldiers are religious. Much can still be done in the name of the cross.

"But the Imperialists tried to do too much with it. 'On with the war!' they cried. 'On with the war, until we plant the cross glittering over the dome of Saint Sophia's in Constantinople.' And the soldiers replied: 'Yes! But before we plant the cross on Saint Sophia's, thousands of crosses will be planted on our graves. We don't want Constantinople. We want to go home. We don't want other people to take our land away from us. Neither will we fight to take other people's land away from them.'"

But even if they had the will to fight, what could they fight with? At Wenden, the old city of the Teutonic Knights, we were set down in the midst of an army in ruins. Out of a gray sky the rain poured down, turning roads into rivers, and the soldiers' hearts into lead. Out of the trenches gaunt skeletons rose up to stare at us. We saw famine-stricken men falling on fields of turnips to devour them raw. We saw men walking barefoot in the stubbled fields, summer uniforms arriving at the beginning of winter, horses dropping dead in mud up to their bellies. Above the lines brazenly hovered the armored planes of the enemy watching every move. There were no aircraft guns, no food, no clothes. And to crown all, no faith in their superiors.

Because their officers and government would or could do nothing for them the soldiers were doing things for themselves. On all sides, even in trenches and gun-

---

[4] John Reed (1887-1920) was a sympathetic American journalist with whom Williams associated. He wrote *Ten Days That Shook the World* in 1919 and died in the Soviet Union in 1920. Boris Reinstein (1866-1947), born in Russia but active in the American Socialist Worker's Party until he returned to Russia in 1917 before the Bolshevik Revolution.

positions, new Soviets were springing up. Here in Wenden there were three (*Is-ko-sol, Is-ko-lat, Is-ko-strel*).

We were guests of the last, the Soviet of Lettish [Latvian] Sharp-Shooters, the most literate, the most valiant, the most revolutionary of all. For protection against the German planes, they convened in a tree-screened valley, ten thousand brown uniforms blending with the autumn tinted leaves. Even with the threat above them, every mention of Kerensky's name drew gales of laughter, every mention of peace thunders of applause.

"We are not cowards or traitors," declared the spokesmen. "But we refuse to fight until we know what we are fighting for. We are told this is a war for democracy. We do not believe it. We believe the Allies are land-grabbers like the Germans. Let them show that they are not. Let them declare their peace terms. Let them publish the secret-treaties. Let the Provisional Government show it is not hand in glove with the Imperialists. Then we will lay down our lives in battle to the last man."

This was the root of the debacle of the great Russian armies. Not primarily that they had nothing to fight *with* but that they felt they had nothing to fight *for*.

Backed by the workingmen the soldiers were determined that the war should stop.

Fate of the Man on Horseback

The bourgeoisie backed by the Allies and the General Staff were equally determined that the war should go on. Continuing the war would give three things to the bourgeoisie: (1) It would continue to give them enormous profits out of army contracts. (2) In case of victory it would give them, as their share in the loot, the Straits and Constantinople. (3) It would give them a chance of staving off the ever more insistent demands of the masses for land and factories.

They were following the wisdom of Catherine the Great who said: "The way to save our empire from the encroachment of the people is to engage in war and thus substitute national passions for social aspirations." Now the social aspirations of the Russian masses were endangering the bourgeois empires of land and capital. But if the war could go on, the day of reckoning with the masses would be postponed. The energies absorbed in carrying on the war could not be used in carrying on the Revolution. "On with the war to a victorious end!" became the rallying cry of the bourgeoisie.

But the Kerensky government no longer could control the soldiers. They no longer responded to the eloquence of this romantic man of words. The bourgeoisie set out to find a Man of the Sword.... "Russia must have a strong man who will tolerate no revolutionary nonsense, but who will rule with an iron hand," they said. "Let us have a Dictator."

For their Man on Horseback they picked the Cossack General, Kornilov.[5] At the conference in Moscow he had won the hearts of the bourgeoisie by calling for a policy of blood and iron. On his own initiative he had introduced capital punishment in the army. With machine-guns he had destroyed battalions of refractory soldiers and placed their stiffened corpses in rows along the fences. He declared that only drastic medicine of this kind could cure the ills of Russia.

On September 9, Kornilov issued a proclamation declaring: "Our great country is dying. Under pressure of the Bolshevik majority in the Soviet, the Kerensky government is acting in complete accord with the plans of the German General Staff. Let all who believe in God and the temples pray to the Lord to manifest the miracle of saving our native land."

He drew 70,000 picked troops from the front. Many of them were Mohammedans [Muslims]—his Turkoman bodyguard, his Tartar horsemen and Circassian mountaineers. On the hilts of their swords the officers swore that when Petrograd was taken, the atheist Socialists would be forced to finish building the great mosque or be shot. With aeroplanes, British armored cars and the blood-thirsty Savage Division, he advanced on Petrograd in the name of God and Allah.

But he did not take it.

In the name of the Soviets and the Revolution the masses rose as one man to the defense of the capital. Kornilov was declared a traitor and an outlaw. Arsenals were opened and guns put in the hands of the workingmen. Red Guards patrolled the streets, trenches were dug, barricades hastily erected. Moslem Socialists rode into the Savage Division and in the name of Marx and Mohammed exhorted the mountaineers not to advance against the Revolution. Their pleas and arguments prevailed. The forces of Kornilov melted away and the "Dictator" was captured without firing a single shot. The bourgeoisie were depressed as the White Hope of the Counter-Revolution went down so easily before the blows of the Revolution. The proletarians were correspondingly elated. They saw the strength and unity of their forces. They felt anew the solidarity binding together all sections of the toiling masses. Trench and factory acclaimed one another. Soldiers and workingmen paid special tribute to the sailors for the big part they played in this affair.

---

[5] Lavr G. Kornilov (1870–1918) was a general who tried to assert power in the late summer of 1917, which led to his arrest by Kerensky.

Chapter 5

COMRADES OF THE SEA

When the news of Kornilov's advance on Petrograd was flashed to Kronstadt and the Baltic fleet, it aroused the sailors like a thunderbolt. From their ships and island citadel they came pouring out in tens of thousands and bivouacked on the Field of Mars. They stood guard at all the nerve centers of the city, the railways and the Winter Palace. With the big sailor Dybenko[1] leading, they drove headlong into the midst of Kornilov's soldiers exhorting them not to advance. They put the fear of the Revolution into the hearts of the Whites and the fire and zest of the Revolution into the blood of their fellow Reds.

In July, Trotsky had hailed them as "Pride and Flower of the Revolutionary Forces!" When they had been damned on all sides for some brash deeds at Kronstadt he had said: "Yes, but when a counter-revolutionary general tries to throw a noose around the neck of the Revolution, the Cadets will grease the rope with soap, while the sailors will come to fight and die with us together!"

So it proved in this adventure of Kornilov. And it was always so. All over Russia I had met these blue-bloused men with the roll of the sea in their carriage and the tang of the salt winds in their blood. Everywhere they went expounding the doctrines of Socialism. I had heard them in forum and marketplaces stirring the sluggish to action. I had seen them in remote villages starting the flow of food to the cities. Later when the Yunkers[2] rose against the Soviets I was to see these sailors heading the storming party that rushed the telephone-station and dug the Yunkers from their nests. Always they were first to sense danger to the Revolution, always first to hurry to its rescue.

The Revolution was precious to the Russian sailor because it meant deliverance from the past. That past was a nightmare. The old Russian naval officers came exclusively from the privileged caste. The count against them was that they imposed, not a rigid discipline, but one that was arbitrary and personal. The weal of a sailor was at the mercy of the whims, jealousies and insane rage of petty officers whom he

---

[1] Pavel E. Dybenko (1889–1948) was a sailor and leading revolutionary who was married to Alexandra Kollontai.

[2] *Yunker* is a reference to a counterrevolutionary movement against the Bolsheviks in 1917.

despised. He was treated like a dog and humiliated by signs that read: "For Dogs and Sailors."

Like the soldier's, the sailor's replies to his superior were limited to the three phrases "Quite so" (*tak tochno*) "No indeed" (*nekak niet*), [and] "Glad to try my best" (*rad staratsa*), with the salutation, "Your nobility." Any added remark might bring him a blow in the face. The most trivial offense met with the most severe penalty. In four years 2,527 men were executed, sent to the penitentiary or to hard labor. All done in the name of the Czar.

Now the Czars were gone; their very names were being blotted out. The ships were being re-christened with names fitting the new republican order.

By this ceremony the *Emperor Paul the First* became *The Republic*. The *Emperor Alexander II* emerged from its baptism of paint as the *Dawn of Liberty*. Here was revolution enough to make these ancient autocrats turn in their graves. But it was even harder on the living Czar and his son. The *Czarevich* was renamed the *Citizen*, while Nicholas II came forth as the good ship *Comrade*. Comrade! This ex-Czar, now living in exile in Tobolsk, knew that the meanest coal-heaver was now a "comrade."

The new names appeared in gold on the jaunty-ribboned caps of the sailors. And the sailors appeared everywhere as missionaries of Liberty, Comradeship and the Republic.

To make these changes in the names of the ships was very easy. Yet they were not mere surface changes, but symbolized a change in reality. They were the outward and visible signs of an inward and spiritual fact—the democratization of a great fleet.

The Sailors Rule the Navy

In September I had my first contact with the sailor at home. It was at Helsingfors,[3] where the Baltic fleet stood as a barricade on the water-road to Petrograd. Tied up to the dock was the *Polar Star*, the yacht of the former Czar. Our guide, an old ex-officer, pointed out a strip of yellow wood that ran around the ship.

"That molding is of best mahogany," he whispered to us. "It cost twenty-five thousand rubles, but these damned Bolsheviks are too lazy now to keep it polished, so they painted it yellow. In my day a sailor was a sailor; he knew that his job was to scrub and polish, and he tended to his job. If he didn't we knocked him down. But the devil is loose among them now. Think of it! On this very yacht belonging to the Czar himself, ordinary seamen sit about making laws for managing the ships, the fleet and the country. And they don't stop there. They talk about managing the world. Internationalism and democracy they call it, but I call it downright treason and insanity."

---

[3] Helsinki, Finland.

There in brief was the issue between the old régime and the new. In the old order, discipline and control were superimposed from above; in the new, they proceeded from the men themselves. The old was a fleet of officers, the new a fleet of sailors. In the change a new set of values had been created. Now the polishing of the sailor's wits upon democracy and internationalism had higher rating than polishing the brass and mahogany.

The second index of the temper of the new fleet came to us as we climbed the gangway of the *Polar Star*, where Rasputin and his associates once had their fling. Here Bessie Beatty,[4] the American correspondent, was gravely informed that the presence of her sex upon the ships was taboo—it was one of the new rules of the Soviet of Sailors. The captain was polite, much adorned with gold braid, but very helpless.

"I can do nothing at all," he explained dolefully. "Everything is in the hands of the 'Committee.'"

"But she has come ten thousand versts[5] to see the fleet."

"Well, we can see what the Committee says," he answered.

The messenger came back with a special dispensation from the Committee and we were on our way again. Everywhere members of the crew would challenge the presence of a woman in our party, politely capitulating, however, as the captain explained, "By special permit of the Committee."

This Central Committee of the Baltic Sea, or, as it was familiarly known, the *Centrobalt*, sat in the great cabin *de luxe*. It was simply a Soviet of the ships. Each contingent of 1,000 sailors had a representative in the committee, which consisted of 65 members, 45 of whom were Bolsheviks. There were four general departments: Administrative, Political, War, and Marine, transacting all the affairs of the fleet. The captain had one of the former princes' suites, but from the great cabin he was debarred. Happily my credentials were an open sesame to the committee and the cabin.

The irony of history! Here in these chairs a few months ago lolled a medieval autocrat with his ladies and his lackeys. Now big-bronzed seamen sat in them, hammering out problems of the most advanced Socialism. The cabin had been cleared for action. The piano and many decorations had been placed in a museum. The tables and lounges were covered with brown canvas burlap. The grand salon was now a workshop. Here hard at work were ordinary seamen suddenly turned legislators, directors and clerks. They were a bit awkward in their new role, but they clung to it with desperate earnestness, sixteen hours a day. For they were dreamers gripped by an idea, the drive and scope of which appear in the following address:

---

[4] Elizabeth "Bessie" Beatty (1886–1947) was a sympathetic American journalist from California who wrote *The Red Heart of Russia* in 1918.

[5] A *verst* is a Russian unit of measure equaling about 3,500 feet.

*To the Representative of the American Social Democracy,
Albert Williams, in Reply to his Greetings.*

The Russian democracy in the person of the representatives of the Baltic Fleet sends warm greetings to the proletariat of all countries and hearty thanks for the greetings from our brothers in America.

Comrade Williams is the first swallow come flying across to us on the cold waves of the Baltic Sea, which now for over three years has been dyed by the blood of the sons of one family, the International.

The Russian proletariat will strive, up to its last breath, to unite everybody under the red banner of the International. When starting the Revolution, we did not have in view a Political Revolution alone. The task of all true fighters for freedom is the making of a Social Revolution. For this the advance guard of the Revolution, in the person of the sailors of the Russian Fleet, and the workmen, will fight to the end.

The flame of the Russian Revolution, we are sure, will spread over the world and light a fire in the hearts of the workers of all lands, and we shall obtain support in our struggle for a speedy general peace.

The free Baltic Fleet impatiently awaits the moment when it can go to America and relate there all that Russia suffered under the yoke of Czarism, and what it is feeling now when the banner of the struggle for the freedom of peoples is unfurled.

LONG LIFE TO THE AMERICAN SOCIAL-DEMOCRACY.
LONG LIVE THE PROLETARIAT OF ALL LANDS.
LONG LIVE THE INTERNATIONAL.
LONG LIVE GENERAL PEACE.

The Central Committee of the Baltic Fleet, Fourth Convention

On this table where in good will and amity they had written this address to me, these sailors dipped their pens in vitriol and wrote another. It was addressed to their Commander-in-Chief, Kerensky. He was unable to explain his part in the Kornilov mix-up and had just made an offensive reference to the sailors. They returned the compliment in this wise:

We demand the immediate removal from the government of the "Socialist" political adventurer, Kerensky, who is ruining the great Revolution by his shameless political blackmail in behalf of the bourgeoisie.

To you, Kerensky, traitor to the Revolution, we send our curses. When our comrades are drowning in the Gulf of Riga, and when all of us, as one man, stand ready to lay down our lives for freedom, ready to die in open fight on the sea or on the barricades, you strive to destroy the forces of the fleet. To you we send our maledictions....

This day, however, the men were in festive mood. They were happy over a big fund just raised for their soldier comrades on the Riga front, and now were playing host to their first foreign comrade. The Secretary of the Committee escorted me on the pilot-boat to his battleship, the *Republic*. The entire crew was on deck cheering our approach across the waters. After an official welcome there were loud demands for a speech. My knowledge of Russian was very meager then, and my interpreter knew but little English. I had to fall back on the current revolutionary phrases. But the mere reiteration of the new battle cries had power to charm these new disciples of Socialism. The sounding of these slogans in my foreign accent drew an outburst of applause that echoed like a salvo from all the ship's batteries.

It was in these waters that the historic meeting between the Kaiser and the Czar had been staged. The applause could not have been more thunderous (certainly not so spontaneous) than when, as an American Internationalist, I shook hands with Averishkin, the Russian Internationalist, on the bridge of this battleship off the coast of Finland.

A Ship's Menu, a Club, and a College

After our love-feast on deck we retired to the quarters of the ship's committee. I was plied with innumerable questions about the American navy, ranging from "Do American navy officers reflect solely the viewpoint of the upper classes?" to "Are American battleships kept as clean as this one of ours?" As we talked, eggs and steak were brought to me, while each member of the committee was served with a large plate of potatoes. I commented on the difference in the dishes.

"Yours is officer's fare, ours is sailor's," they explained.

"Then why did you make a revolution?" I asked banteringly.

They laughed and said, "The Revolution has given us what we wanted most—freedom. We are masters of our ships. We are masters of our own lives. We have our own courts. We can have shore leave when not on duty. Off duty we have the right to wear civilian clothes. We do not demand everything of the Revolution."

The world-wide rise of the workers, however, is based on their desire, not solely for the first necessities of life, but for a larger part in its amenities. Driving through Helsingfors one night we missed the usual bands of sailors rolling down the streets. Suddenly we were brought sharply up before a building with façade and dimensions of a great modern hotel. We entered and were guided by the music to the dining hall. There, in a room set with palms and glistening with mirrors and silver, sat the diners, listening to Chopin and Tchaikovsky, interspersed with occasional ragtime from the American conductor. It was a hotel of the first class, but instead of the usual clientele of a big hotel—bankers, speculators, politicians, adventurers and ornate ladies—it was crowded with bronzed seamen of the war fleet of the Russian Republic, who had commandeered the entire building. Through its curtained halls now streamed a procession of laughing, jesting, arguing sailors in their suits of blue.

Outside in big letters was the sign *"Sailors' Club"* with its motto, "A welcome to all the sailors of the world." It opened with ten thousand dues-paying members, ninety per cent of whom were literate. The club boasted a much-used magazine room, the nucleus of a library, and an excellent illustrated weekly, *The Seaman* (*Moryak*).

They had founded, too, a "University," with courses ranging from the most elementary to the most advanced. In the committee on curriculum I blunderingly asked the chairman from what university he came.

"No university, no school," he replied regretfully. "I come from the dark people, but I am a revolutionist. We did away with the Czar, but a worse enemy is ignorance. We shall do away with that. That is the only way to get a democratic fleet. Now we have a democratic machine, but most of our officers have not the democratic spirit. We must train our officers out of the ranks." In his courses he had enlisted professors from the university, men from the scientific societies, and some officers.

How did all this new discipline and comfort affect the fleet? Opinions differed. Many officers said that in destroying the old discipline the technical efficiency was lowered. Others said that considering its ordeal by war and revolution the fleet was in good trim. As the test of its moral efficiency, they pointed to the battle of the Monsund Isles. Out-numbered by the Germans, and out-distanced in speed and gun-range, these revolutionary sailors had fought a brilliant engagement with the enemy. All admitted that their fighting morale was superb.

There was no doubt of the enthusiasm of the sailors for their fleet. They had a feeling of communal ownership in it. When the pilot boat carried me away from the *Republic*, Averishkin with a gesture that took in all the gray ships riding in the bay, exclaimed, "Our fleet! Our fleet! We shall make it the best fleet in the world. May it always fight for justice!" Then, as if looking through the gray mists which hung above the water and beyond the red mists of the world war, he added, "Until we make the Social Revolution and the end of all wars."

In Russia this Social Revolution was coming on apace and these men of the fleet were shortly to be in the vortex of it.

PART II

THE REVOLUTION AND THE DAYS AFTER AMONG THE WHITES AND THE REDS

Chapter 6

"ALL POWER TO THE SOVIET"

Another winter is bearing down upon hungry, heartsick Russia. The last October leaves are falling from the trees, and the last bit of confidence in the government is falling with them.

Everywhere recklessness—and orgies of speculation. Food trains are looted. Floods of paper money pour from the presses. In the newspapers endless columns of hold-ups, murders and suicides. Night life and gambling-halls run full blast with enormous stakes won and lost.

Reaction is open and arrogant. Kornilov, instead of being tried for high treason, is lauded as the great patriot by the bourgeoisie. But with them patriotism is tawdry talk and a sham. They pray for the Germans to come and cut off Petrograd, the Head of the Revolution. Rodzianko,[1] ex-President of the Duma, brazenly writes: "Let the Germans take the city. Tho they destroy the fleet they will throttle the Soviets." The big insurance companies announce one-third off in rates after the German occupation. "Winter always was Russia's best friend," say the bourgeoisie. "It may rid us of this cursed Revolution."

Despair Foments Rebellion

Winter, sweeping down out of the North, hailed by the privileged, brings terror to the suffering masses. As the mercury drops toward zero, the prices of food and fuel go soaring up. The bread ration grows shorter. The queues of shivering women standing all night in the icy streets grow longer. Lockouts and strikes add to the millions of workless. The rancor in the hearts of the masses flares out in bitter speeches like this from a Viborg workingman:

"Patience, patience, they are always counseling us. But what have they done to make us patient? Has Kerensky given us more to eat than the Czar? More words and promises—yes! But not more food. All night long we wait in the lines for shoes and

---

[1] Mikhail V. Rodzianko (1859–1924) was the chair of the fourth Duma in Russia in 1917. He was instrumental in Nicholas II's abdication. He supported the Whites in the Russian Civil War.

bread and meat, while, like fools, we write *'Liberty'* on our banners. The only liberty we have is the same old liberty to slave and starve."

It is a sorry showing after eight months of pleading and parading through the streets. All they have got are lame feet, aching arms, and the privilege of starving and freezing in the presence of mocking red banners: *"Land to the Peasants!" "Factories to the Workers!" "Peace to all the World!"*

But no longer do they carry their red banners through the streets. They are done with appealing and beseeching. In a mood born of despair and disillusion they are acting now—reckless, violent, iconoclastic, but—acting.

In the cities revolting employees are driving mill-owners out of their offices. Managers try to stop it, and are thrown into wheel-barrows and ridden out of the plant. Machinery is put out of gear, materials spoiled, industry brought to a standstill.

In the army soldiers are throwing down their guns and deserting the front in hundreds of thousands. Emissaries try to stop them with frantic appeals. They may as well appeal to a landslide. "If no decisive steps for peace are taken by November first," the soldiers say, "all the trenches will be emptied. The entire army will rush to the rear." In the fleet is open insubordination.

In the country, peasants are overrunning the estates. I ask Baron Nolde,[2] "What is it that the peasants want on your estate?"

"My estate," he answers.

"How are they going to get it?"

"They've got it."

In some places these seizures are accompanied by wanton spoliation. The skies around Tambov are reddened with flames from the burning hay-ricks and manor-houses. Landlords flee for their lives. The infuriated peasants laugh at the orators trying to quiet them. Troops sent down to suppress the outbursts go over to the side of the peasants.

Russia is plunging headlong towards the abyss.

Over this spectacle of misery and ruin presides a handful of talkers called the Provisional Government. It is almost a corpse, treated to hypodermic injections of threats and promises from the Allies. Before tasks calling for the strength of a giant it is weak as a baby. To all demands of the people it has just one reply, "Wait." First, it was "Wait till the end of the war." Now, "Wait till the Constituent Assembly."

But the people will wait no longer. Their last shred of faith in the government is gone. They have faith in themselves; faith that they alone can save Russia from going over the precipice to ruin and night; faith alone in the institutions of their own making. They look now to the new authority created out of their own midst. They look to the Soviets.

---

[2] Baron Boris E. Nolde (1876–1948) was a Constitutional Democrat (Cadet) who worked in the Provisional Government in 1917.

"Let the Soviets Be the Government"

Summer and fall have seen the steady growth of the Soviets. They have drawn to themselves the vital forces in each community. They have been schools for the training of the people, giving them confidence. The net-work of local Soviets has been wrought into a wide firmly built organization, a new structure which has risen within the shell of the old. As the old apparatus was going to pieces, the new one was taking over its functions. The Soviets in many ways were already acting as a government. It was necessary only to proclaim them the government. Then the Soviets would be in name what they were already in reality.

From the depths now lifted up a mighty cry: *"All Power to the Soviets."* The demand of the capital in July became the demand of the country. Like wildfire it swept through the land. Sailors on the Baltic Fleet flung it out to their comrades on the Black and White and Yellow Seas, and from them it came echoing back. Farm and factory, barracks and battlefront joined in the cry, swelling louder, more insistent every hour.

Petrograd came thundering into the chorus on Sunday, November 4th, in sixty enormous mass meetings. Trotsky, having read the Reply of the Baltic Fleet to my greetings, asked me to speak at the People's House.

Here great waves of human beings dashed against the doors, swirled inside, and sluiced along the corridors. They poured into the halls, filling them full, splashing hundreds up on the girders where they hung like garlands of foam. Out of the eddying throngs, a mighty voice rose and fell and broke like surf, thundering on the shore—hundreds of thousands of throats roaring *"Down with the Provisional Government." "All Power to the Soviets."* Hundreds of thousands of hands were raised in a pledge to fight and die for the Soviets.

The patience of the poor at an end; the pawns and cannon-fodder in revolt! The dark masses, long inert, but roused at last, refusing longer to be brow-beaten or hypnotized by the word-juggling of statesmen, scorning their threats, laughing at their promises, take the initiative into their own hands, demanding of their "leaders" to move forward into revolution or resign. For the first time the slaves and the exploited, consciously choosing the time of their deliverance, vote for insurrection, investing themselves with the government of one-sixth of the world. A big venture for men unschooled in state affairs. Are they equal to these tasks? Can they control the currents now being loosed in the city? At any rate these masses show complete control of themselves. From these blood-stirring revolutionary. meetings they pour forth in orderly fashion.

The poor frightened bourgeoisie are reassured. They see no houses looted, no shops wrecked, no white-collared gentry shot down in the streets. To their minds, therefore, all is well; there will be no insurrection. The true import of this restraint quite escapes them. The people indulge in no sporadic outbursts because they have better use for their energies. They have a Revolution to make, not a riot. And a Revolution requires order, plan, labor—much hard intensive labor.

The Masses Conducting Their Revolution

These insurgent masses go home to organize committees, draw up lists, form Red Cross units, collect rifles. Hands lifted in a vote for Revolution now are holding guns. They get ready for the forces of the Counter-Revolution now mobilizing against them. In Smolny[3] sits the Military Revolutionary Committee from which these masses take orders. There is another committee, the Committee of a Hundred Thousand; that is, the masses themselves. There are no bystreets, no barracks, no buildings where this committee does not penetrate. It reaches into the councils of the Black Hundred, the Kerensky Government, the intelligentsia. With porters, waiters, cabmen, conductors, soldiers, and sailors, it covers the city like a net. They see everything, hear everything, report everything to headquarters. Thus, forewarned, they can checkmate every move of the enemy. Every attempt to strangle or sidetrack the Revolution they paralyze at once.

Attempt is made to break the faith of the masses in their leaders by furious assault upon them. Kerensky cries from the tribunal "Lenin, the state criminal, inciting to pillage ... and the most terrible massacres which will cover with eternal shame the name of free Russia." Immediately the masses reply by bringing Lenin out of hiding with a tremendous ovation and turning Smolny into an arsenal to guard him.

Attempt is made to drown the Revolution in blood and disorder. The Dark Forces keep calling the people to rise up and slaughter Jews and Socialist leaders. Forthwith the workmen placard the city with posters saying "Citizens! We call upon you to maintain complete quiet and self-possession. The cause of order is in strong hands. At the first instance of robbery and shooting, the criminals will be wiped off the face of the earth."

Attempts are made to isolate the different sections of the revolutionists. Telephones are cut off between Soviets and barracks; immediately communications are established by setting up telephonograph apparatus. The Yunkers turn the bridges, cutting off the working-class districts; the Kronstadt sailors close them again. The offices of the Communist papers are locked and sealed, cutting off the flow of news; the Red Guards break the seals and set the presses running again.

Attempt is made to suppress the Revolution by force of arms. Kerensky begins calling "dependable" troops into the city; that is, troops that may be depended upon to shoot down the rising workers. Among these are the Zenith Battery and the Cycle

---

[3] Smolny is the Smolny Convent, a school for noble girls, that was established in the mid-eighteenth century.

Corps.[4] Along the highroads, on which these units are advancing into the city the Revolution posts its forces. They attack the enemy, not with guns but with ideas. They subject these troops to a withering fire of arguments and pleas. Result: these troops that are being rushed to the city to crush the Revolution enter instead to aid and abet it.

To these zealots of the Communist faith, all soldiers succumb, even the Cossacks. "Brother Cossacks!" reads the appeal to them, "You are being incited against us by grafters, parasites, landlords, and by our own Cossack generals who wish to crush our Revolution. Comrade Cossacks! Do not fall in with this plan of Cain." And the Cossacks likewise line up under the banner of the Revolution.

---

[4] The Zenith Battery was a British horse-drawn machine gun unit. The Cycle Corps were infantry units that were loyal to the Kerensky government but decided to support the Soviets in the summer of 1917.

Chapter 7
NOVEMBER 7TH—A NEW DATE IN HISTORY

While Petrograd is in a tumult of clashing patrols and contending voices, men from all over Russia come pouring into the city. They are delegates to the Second All-Russian Congress of Soviets convening at Smolny. All eyes are turned towards Smolny.

Formerly a school for the daughters of the nobility, Smolny is now the center of the Soviets. It stands on the Neva, a huge stately structure, cold and grey by day. But by night, glowing with a hundred lamp-lit windows, it looms up like a great temple—a temple of Revolution. The two watch fires before its porticos, tended by long-coated soldiers, flame like altar fires. Here are centered the hopes and prayers of untold millions of the poor and disinherited. Here they look for release from age-long suffering and tyranny. Here are wrought out for them issues of life and death.

That night I saw a laborer, gaunt, shabbily-clad, plodding down a dark street. Lifting his head suddenly he saw the massive façade of Smolny, glowing golden through the falling snow. Pulling off his cap, he stood a moment with bared head and outstretched arms. Then, crying out *"The Commune! The People! The Revolution!"* he ran forward and merged with the throng streaming through the gates.

Out of war, exile, dungeons, Siberia, come these delegates to Smolny. For years no news of old comrades. Suddenly, cries of recognition, a rush into one another's arms, a few words, a moment's embrace, then a hastening on to conferences, caucuses, endless meetings.

Smolny is now one big forum, roaring like a gigantic smithy with orators calling to arms, audiences whistling or stamping, the gavel pounding for order, the sentries grounding arms, machine-guns rumbling across the cement floors, crashing choruses of revolutionary hymns, thundering ovations for Lenin and Zinoviev as they emerge from underground.

Everything at high speed, tense and growing tenser every minute. The leading workers are dynamos of energy; sleepless, tireless, nerveless miracles of men, facing momentous questions of Revolution.

At ten-forty on this night of November 7th, opens the historic meeting so big with consequences for the future of Russia and the whole world. From their party caucuses the delegates file into the great assembly-hall. Dan,[1] the anti-Bolshevik chairman, is on the platform ringing the bell for order and declares, "The first session of the Second Congress of Soviets is now open."

First comes the election of the governing body of the congress (the presidium). The Bolsheviks get 14 members. All other parties get 11. The old governing body steps down and the Bolshevik leaders, recently the outcasts and outlaws of Russia, take their places. The Right parties, composed largely of intelligentsia, open with an attack on credentials and orders of the day. Discussion is their forte. They delight in academic issues. They raise fine points of principle and procedure.

Then, suddenly out of the night, a rumbling shock brings the delegates to their feet, wondering. It is the boom of cannon, the cruiser *Aurora*[2] firing over the Winter Palace. Dull and muffled out of the distance it comes with steady, regular rhythm, a requiem tolling the death of the old order, a salutation to the new. It is the voice of the masses thundering to the delegates the demand for *"All Power to the Soviets."* So the question is acutely put to the Congress: "Will you now declare the Soviets the government of Russia, and give legal basis to the new authority?"

The Intelligentsia Desert

Now comes one of the startling paradoxes of history, and one of its colossal tragedies—the refusal of the intelligentsia. Among the delegates were scores of these intellectuals. They had made the "dark people" the object of their devotion. "Going to the people" was a religion.[3] For them they had suffered poverty, prison and exile. They had stirred the quiescent masses with revolutionary ideas, inciting them to revolt. The character and nobility of the masses had been ceaselessly extolled. In short, the intelligentsia had made a god of the people. Now the people were rising with the wrath and thunder of a god, imperious—and arbitrary. They were acting like a god.

But the intelligentsia rejects a god who will not listen to them and over whom they have lost control. Straightway the intelligentsia became atheists. They disavow all faith in their former god, the people. They deny their right to rebellion.

Like Frankenstein before this monster of their own creation, the intelligentsia quails, trembling with fear, trembling with rage. It is a bastard thing, a devil, a terrible calamity, plunging Russia into chaos, "a criminal rebellion against authority."

---

[1] Fyodor I. Dan (1871–1947) was a leading Menshevik in the Petrograd Soviet in 1917. After the Bolsheviks seized power, he went into exile.

[2] The cruiser *Aurora* was constructed in 1900 and signaled the beginning of the Bolshevik Revolution with a blank shot in the Neva River in October 1917.

[3] The "To the People" movement was created by the Narodniks of the 1860s and 1870s, middle-class students in Russia who took their populist message of empowering the ordinary people to the countryside. This movement ended in failure mainly because rural Russians did not trust them.

They hurl themselves against it, storming, cursing, beseeching, raving. As delegates they refuse to recognize this Revolution. They refuse to allow this congress to declare the Soviets the government of Russia.

So futile! So impotent! They may as well refuse to recognize a tidal wave, or an erupting volcano as to refuse to recognize this Revolution. This Revolution is elemental, inexorable. It is everywhere, in the barracks, in the trenches, in the factories, in the streets. It is here in this congress, officially, in hundreds of workmen, soldier and peasant delegates. It is here unofficially in the masses crowding every inch of space, climbing up on pillars and windowsills, making the assembly hall white with fog from their close-packed steaming bodies, electric with the intensity of their feelings.

The people are here to see that their revolutionary will is done; that the congress declares the Soviets the government of Russia. On this point they are inflexible. Every attempt to becloud the issue, every effort to paralyze or evade their will evokes blasts of angry protest. The parties of the Right have long resolutions to offer. The crowd is impatient. "No more resolutions! No more words! We want deeds! We want the Soviet!"

The intelligentsia, as usual, wish to compromise the issue by a coalition of all parties. "Only one coalition possible," is the retort. "The coalition of workers, soldiers and peasants."

Martov[4] calls out for "a peaceful solution of the impending civil war." "Victory! Victory!—the only possible solution," is the answering cry.

The officer Kutchin tries to terrify them with the idea that the Soviets are isolated, and that the whole army is against them. "Liar! Staff!" yell the soldiers. "You speak for the staff—not the men in the trenches. We soldiers demand 'All Power to the Soviets!'"

Their will is steel. No entreaties or threats avail to break or bend it. Nothing can deflect them from their goal.

Finally stung to fury, Abramovich[5] cries out, "We cannot remain here and be responsible for these crimes. We invite all delegates to leave this congress." With a dramatic gesture he steps from the platform and stalks towards the door. About eighty delegates rise from their seats and push their way after him.

"Let them go," cries Trotsky, "let them go! They are just so much refuse that will be swept into the garbage-heap of history."

In a storm of hoots, jeers and taunts of "Renegades! Traitors!" from the proletarians, the intelligentsia pass out of the hall and out of the Revolution. A supreme trag-

---

[4] Julius Martov (1873–1923), whose real name was Yuly O. Tsederbaum was a leading Menshevik. He was a member of the Constituent Assembly and a supporter of the Red Army in the Russian Civil War, but a critic of the Red Terror of the early Bolshevik regime. He left Russia in the early 1920s and died in Germany in 1923 due to illness.

[5] Raphael Rein Abramovich (1880–1963) was a Menshevik who was arrested in 1918, but escaped to Europe and lived a long life advocating socialist causes.

edy! The intelligentsia rejecting the Revolution they had helped to create, deserting the masses in the crisis of their struggle. Supreme folly, too. They do not isolate the Soviets, they only isolate themselves. Behind the Soviets are rolling up solid battalions of support.

The Soviets Proclaimed the Government

Every minute brings news of fresh conquests of the Revolution—the arrest of ministers, the seizure of the State Bank, telegraph station, telephone station, the staff headquarters. One by one the centers of power are passing into the hands of the people. The spectral authority of the old government is crumbling before the hammer strokes of the insurgents.

A commissar, breathless and mud-spattered from riding, climbs the platform to announce: "The garrison of Tsarskoye Selo for the Soviets. It stands guard at the gates of Petrograd." From another: "The Cyclists' Battalion for the Soviets. Not a single man found willing to shed the blood of his brothers." Then Krylenko,[6] staggering up, telegram in hand: "Greetings to the Soviet from the Twelfth Army! The Soldiers' Committee is taking over the command of the Northern Front."

And finally at the end of this tumultuous night, out of this strife of tongues and clash of wills, the simple declaration: *"The Provisional Government is deposed. Based upon the will of the great majority of workers, soldiers and peasants, the Congress of Soviets assumes the power. The Soviet authority will at once propose an immediate democratic peace to all nations, an immediate truce on all fronts. It will assure the free transfer of lands ... etc."*

Pandemonium! Men weeping in one another's arms. Couriers jumping up and racing away. Telegraph and telephone buzzing and humming. Autos starting off to the battle-front; aeroplanes speeding away across rivers and plains. Wireless flashing across the seas. All messengers of the great news!

The will of the revolutionary masses has triumphed. The Soviets are the government.

This historic session ends at six o'clock in the morning. The delegates, reeling from the toxin of fatigue, hollow-eyed from sleeplessness, but exultant, stumble down the stone stairs and through the gates of Smolny. Outside it is still dark and chill, but a red dawn is breaking in the east.

---

[6] Nikolai V. Krylenko (1885–1938) was a Bolshevik politician who held the position of Commissar of Justice. He was later executed during the Purges of the 1930s.

Chapter VIII
LOOTING THE WINTER PALACE

THE Russian poet Tyutchev[1] writes:

> Blessed is he who visited this world
> In moments of its fateful deeds:
> The highest Gods invited him to come,
> A guest, with them to sit at feast
> And be a witness of their mighty spectacle.

Twice blessed were five Americans: Louise Bryant,[2] John Reed, Bessie Beatty, Gumberg, and myself. We were spectators of the great drama enacted in the halls of Smolny: we also saw the other big event of the night of November 7th—the taking of the Winter Palace.

We had been sitting in Smolny, gripped by the pleas of the speakers, when out of the night that other voice crashed into the lighted hall—the cannon of the cruiser *Aurora*, firing at the Winter Palace. Steady, insistent, came the ominous beat of the cannon, breaking the spell of the speakers upon us. We could not resist its call and hurried away.

Outside, a big motor-truck with engines throbbing was starting for the city. We climbed aboard and tore through the night, a plunging comet, flying a tail of white posters in our wake. From alleys and doorways dim figures darted out to snatch them up and read:

---

[1] Fyodor I. Tyutchev (1803–73) was a Romantic era Russian poet with strong Pan-Slavic views.

[2] Louise Bryant (1885–1936) was an American journalist reporting on the Russian situation. She was married to John Reed in 1916 and sympathetic to the Bolshevik cause as well. She would write her own account of her time in Russia entitled *Six Red Months in Russia*.

Отъ Военно-Революціоннаго Комитета при Петроградскомъ Совѣтѣ Рабочихъ и Солдатскихъ Депутатовъ.

Къ Гражданамъ Россіи.

Временное Правительство низложено. Государственная власть перешла въ руки органа Петроградскаго Совѣта Рабочихъ и Солдатскихъ Депутатовъ Военно-Революціоннаго Комитета, стоящаго во главѣ Петроградскаго пролетаріата и гарнизона.

Дѣло, за которое боролся народъ: немедленное предложеніе демократическаго мира, отмѣна помѣщичьей собственности на землю, рабочій контроль надъ производствомъ, созданіе Совѣтскаго Правительства — это дѣло обезпечено.

ДА ЗДРАВСТВУЕТЪ РЕВОЛЮЦІЯ РАБОЧИХЪ, СОЛДАТЪ И КРЕСТЬЯНЪ!

Военно-Революціонный Комитетъ
при Петроградскомъ Совѣтѣ
Рабочихъ и Солдатскихъ Депутатовъ.

25 октября 1917 г. 10 ч. утра.

From the War-Revolutionary Committee of the Petrograd Soviet of Workmen and Soldiers Deputies.

To the Citizens of Russia:

The Provisional Government is deposed. The State power has passed into the hands of the organ of the Petrograd Soviet of Workers' and Soldiers' Deputies, the Military Revolutionary Committee, which stands at the head of the Petrograd proletariat and garrison.

The aims for which the people were fighting – immediate proposal of a democratic peace, abolition of landlord property-rights in the land, labor control over production, creation of a Soviet Government, – these aims have been achieved.

LONG LIVE THE REVOLUTION OF WORKMEN, SOLDIERS AND PEASANTS!

Military-Revolutionary Committee of the Petrograd Soviet of Workers and Soldier's Deputies.

NOVEMBER 7, 1917

[*Reproduction in English of the Russian text on opposite page.*]

This announcement is a trifle previous. The ministers of the Provisional Government, minus Kerensky, still sit at council in the Winter Palace. That is why the guns of the *Aurora* are in action. They are thundering into the ears of the ministers the summons to surrender. True, only blank shells are firing now, but they set the air shivering, shaking the building and the nerves of the ministers within.

As we come into the Palace Square the booming of the guns dies away. The rifles no longer crackle through the dark. The Red Guards are crawling out to carry off their dead and dying. Out of the night a voice cries, "The Yunkers surrender." But mindful of their losses, the besieging sailors and soldiers cling to cover.

The Mob Enters the Palace

New throngs gather on the Nevsky. Forming a column, they pour through the Red Arch and creep forward, silent. Near the barricade they emerge into the light blazing from within the Palace. They scale the rampart of logs, and storm through the iron gateway into the open doors of the east wing—the mob swarming in behind them.

From cold and darkness, these proletarians come suddenly into warmth and light. From huts and barracks they pass into glittering salons and gilded chambers. This is indeed Revolution—the builders entering into the Palace they built.

And such a building! Ornate with statues of gold and bronze, and carpeted with Oriental rugs, its rooms hung with tapestries and paintings, and flooded with a million lights from the twinkling crystal chandeliers, its cellars crammed with rare wines and liquors of ancient vintage. Riches beyond their dreams are within their grasp. Why not grasp them?

A terrible lust lays hold of the mob—the lust that ravishing beauty incites in the long starved and long denied—the lust of loot. Even we, as spectators, are not immune to it. It burns up the last vestige of restraint and leaves one passion flaming in the veins—the passion to sack and pillage. Their eyes fall upon this treasure-trove, and their hands follow.

Along the walls of the vaulted chamber we enter there runs a row of huge packing cases. With the butts of their rifles, the soldiers batter open the boxes, spilling out streams of curtains, linen, clocks, vases and plates.

Scorning such petty booty, the throngs swirl past to richer hunting-grounds. The vanguard presses forward through gorgeous chambers opening into ever more gorgeous ones, lined with cabinets and wardrobes. They fall upon them with shouts of expectant joy. Then cries of anger and chagrin. They find mirrors shattered, panels kicked in, drawers rifled—everywhere the trail of vandals who have gone before. The Yunkers have taken the cream of the plunder.

So much is gone! So much intenser, then, the struggle for what remains. Who shall gainsay them the right to this Palace and its contents? All of it came out of their sweat and the sweat of their fathers. It is theirs by right of creation. It is theirs, too, by right of conquest. By the smoking guns in their hands and the courage in their hearts they have taken it. But how long can they keep it? For a century it was the Czar's. Yesterday it was Kerensky's. Today it is theirs. Tomorrow it shall be—whose? No one can tell. This day the Revolution gives. Next day the Counter-Revolution may snatch away. Now while the prize is theirs shall they not make the most of it? Here where courtiers wantoned for a century shall they not revel for a night? Their outraged past, the feverish present, the uncertain future—everything urges them to grasp what they can now.

Pandemonium breaks loose in the Palace. It rolls and echoes with myriad sounds. Tearing of cloth and wood, clatter of glass from splintered windows, clumping of heavy boots upon the parquet floor, the crashing of a thousand voices against the ceiling. Voices jubilant, then jangling over division of the spoils. Voices hoarse, high-pitched, muttering, cursing.

Then another voice breaks into this babel—the clear, compelling voice of the Revolution. It speaks through the tongues of its ardent votaries, the Petrograd workingmen. There is just a handful of them, weazened and undersized, but into the ranks of these big peasant soldiers they plunge, crying out—"Take nothing. The Revolution forbids it. No looting. This is the property of the people."

Children piping against a cyclone, dwarfs attacking an army of giants. So seem these protesters, trying to stem with words the onslaught of soldiers flushed with conquest, pillage-bent. The mob goes on pillaging. Why should it heed the protest of a handful of workmen?

The Restraining Hand of Revolution

But these workmen will be heeded. Back of their words they feel the will of the Revolution. It makes them fearless and aggressive. They turn upon the big soldiers with fury, hurl epithets into their faces, wrest the booty out of their hands. In a short time they have them on the defensive.

A big peasant making off with a heavy woolen blanket is waylaid by a little workingman. He grabs hold of the blanket, tugs away at one end of it, scolding the big fellow like a child.

"Let go the blanket," growls the peasant, his face convulsed with rage. "It's mine."

"No, no," the workingman cries, "it's not yours. It belongs to all the people. Nothing goes out of the Palace tonight."

"Well, this blanket goes out tonight. It's cold in the barracks!"

"I'm sorry you're cold, *tovarish*. Better for you to suffer cold than the Revolution to suffer disgrace by your looting."

"Devil take you," exclaims the peasant. "What did we make the Revolution for, anyhow? Wasn't it to give clothes and food to the people?"

"Yes, *tovarish*, the Revolution will give everything you need in due time, but not tonight. If anything goes out of here we will be called hooligans and robbers—not true Socialists. Our enemies will say that we came here not for revolution, but for loot. So we must take nothing. For this is the property of the people. Let us guard it for the honor of the Revolution."

"Socialism! The Revolution! Property of the People!" With this formula the peasant saw his blanket taken away from him. Always these abstract ideas adorned with capital letters taking things away from him. Once it was done with "Tsardom, the Glory of God." Now it was being done with "Socialism, Revolution, Property of the People."

Still there was something in this last concept that the peasant could grasp. It was in line with his communal training. As it took hold of his brain his hold on the blanket relaxed, and with a last tragic look at his precious treasure he shambled away. Later I saw him expounding to another soldier. He was talking about the "Property of the People."

Relentlessly the workingmen press home their advantage, using every tactic, pleading, explaining, threatening. In an alcove is a Bolshevik workingman, furiously shaking one hand at three soldiers, the other hand on his revolver.

"I hold you responsible, if you touch that desk," he cries.

"Hold us responsible!" jeer the soldiers. "Who are you? You broke into the palace just as we did. We are responsible to no one but ourselves."

"You are responsible to the Revolution," retorts the workingman sternly. So deadly earnest is he that these men feel in him the authority of the Revolution. They hear and obey.

The Revolution loosed the daring and ardor in these masses. It used them to storm the Palace. Now it leashes them in. Out of bedlam it brings forth a controlling power—quieting, imposing order, posting sentries.

"All out! Clear the Palace!" sounds through the corridors, and the throng begins to flow toward the doors. At each exit stands a self-appointed Committee of Search and Inspection. They lay hold of each man as he comes along, exploring his pockets, shirt, and even his boots, gathering in a varied line of souvenirs; statuettes, candles, clothes-hangers, damask, vases. The owners plead like children for their trophies, but the committee is adamant, repeating constantly, "Nothing goes out of the Palace tonight."

And nothing does go out that night on the persons of the Red Guards, though prowlers and vandals later on make off with many valuables.

The commissars now turn to the Provisional Government and their defenders. They are rounded up and escorted to the exit. First, come the ministers, seized in session around the green baize table in the Hall of State. They file down in silence. From the crowd inside not a word or a jeer. But from the mob outside rises a blast of denunciation when a sailor calls for an automobile. "Make them walk, they have ridden long enough," the mob yells, making a lunge at the frightened ministers. The Red Sailors, with fixed bayonets, close around their captives and lead them out across the bridges of the Neva. Towering above all the convoy is Tereshchenko,[3] the Ukrainian capitalist, bound now from the Ministry of Foreign Affairs to the Prison of Peter-Paul, reversing the journey of the Bolshevik, Trotsky, from the Prison of Peter-Paul to the office of Foreign Affairs.

The Yunkers were led out to cries of "Provocators! Traitors! Murderers!"—a sorry crestfallen lot. That morning each Yunker had vowed to us that he would fight until just one bullet was left. This last one, he would put through his own brain rather than surrender to the Bolsheviks. Now he was giving up his arms to these Bolsheviks, solemnly promising never to take weapons against them again. (Unhappy fellows! They were to break their promise.)

Last of the captives to leave the Palace were the members of the Women's Battalion. Most of them were of proletarian birth. "Shame! Shame!" cried the Red Guards, "Working-women fighting against workingmen." To drive home the indignation they felt, some grabbed the girls by the arms, shaking and scolding them.

This was about the sum total of the casualties among the soldier girls, though later one of them committed suicide. Next day the hostile press spread tales of gruesome atrocities against the Women's Battalion, alongside stories of sack and pillage of the Palace by the Red Guards.

Yet nothing is more alien to the essential nature of the working-class than destructiveness. Were it not so, history might have a different story to tell of the morning of November 8th. It might have to record that the magnificent edifice of the Czars was left a heap of crumbling stones and smoking embers by the vengeance of a long-suffering people.

For a century it had stood there upon the Neva, a cold and heartless thing. The people had looked to it for light, and it had brought forth darkness. They had cried to it for compassion, and it had answered with the lash, the knout, the burning of villages, exile in Siberia. One winter morning in 1905 thousands of them had come here, defenseless, petitioning the Little Father for redress of wrongs. The Palace had answered with rifle and cannon, reddening the snow with their blood. To the masses the building was a monument of cruelty and oppression. Had they razed it to the ground, it would have been but one more instance of the wrath of an outraged people, removing from their eyes forever the hated symbol of their suffering.

Instead they proceeded to remove the historic landmark from all likelihood of damage.

Kerensky had done the opposite. He had recklessly put the Winter Palace in the arena of conflict by making it the center of his cabinet and his own sleeping quarters.

---

[3] Mikhail I. Tereshchenko (1886–1956) was minister of foreign affairs for the Provisional Government. Arrested in October 1917, he escaped in 1918, and supported anti-Bolshevik causes abroad.

But the representatives of these storming masses who had captured the palace declared that it was not theirs nor the Soviets', but the heritage of all. By Soviet decree it was made the Museum of the People. The custody of it was formally placed in the hands of a committee of artists.

A New Attitude towards Property

So events gave the lie to another dire prophecy. Kerensky, Dan, and other of the intelligentsia had shrieked against the Revolution, predicting a hideous orgy of crime and plunder, the loosing of the basest passions of the mob. Once the hungry and embittered masses got in motion, they said, like a maddened herd they would go trampling down, wrecking, and destroying everything. "Even Gorky was prophesying the end of the world" (Trotsky).

And now the Revolution has come. There are, indeed, isolated acts of vandalism; rich-clad bourgeois still return home minus their great fur coats; mobs work havoc before the Revolution can rein them in.

But there is one outstanding fact. The first fruits of the Revolution are law and order. Never was Petrograd safer than after passing into the hands of the masses. Unprecedented quiet reigns in the streets. Hold-ups and robberies drop almost to zero. Robbers and thugs quail before the iron hand of the proletariat.

It is not merely negative restraint—order rising out of fear. The Revolution begets a singular respect for the rights of property. In the shattered windows of the shops, within hands' reach of passing men in desperate need, are foodstuffs and clothing. They remain untouched. There is something pathetic in the sight of hungry men having food within their grasp and not grasping it, something awesome in the constraint engendered by the Revolution. It exerts its subtle influence everywhere. Into the far-off villages it reaches. No longer are the peasants burning the great estates.

Yet it is the upper classes who assert that in them lies true respect of the sanctity of property. A curious claim at the end of the World War for which the governing classes are responsible. By their fiat, cities were given to the torch, the face of the land covered with ashes, the bottom of the sea strewn with ships, the structure of civilization shot to pieces, and even now still more terrible instruments of destruction are being prepared.

What basis is there for true respect of property in the bourgeoisie? Actually they produce little or nothing. To the privileged, property is something that comes by cleverness, by chance inheritance, by stroke of fortune. With them it is largely a matter of titles, deeds and papers.

But to the working classes, property is a thing of tears and blood. It is an exhausting act of creation. They know its cost in aching muscles and breaking backs.

With shoulders back and breast astrain,
And bathed in sweat that falls like rain,
Through midday heat with gasping song,
He drags the heavy barge along.

… goes the song of the Volga boatmen.

What men have brought forth in pain and labor they cannot wantonly annihilate, any more than a mother can destroy her child. They, out of whose thews and muscles the thing has issued, will best guard and cherish it. Knowing its cost, they feel its sacredness. Even before works of art the rude, untaught masses stand with reverence. Only vaguely do they glimpse their meaning. But they see in them the incarnation of effort. And all labor is holy.

The Social Revolution is in truth the apotheosis of the rights of property. It invests it with a new sanctity. By transferring property into the hands of the producers it gives the keeping of wealth into the hands of its natural and zealous guardians—the makers of it. The creators are the best conservators.

Chapter 9
RED GUARDS, WHITE GUARDS, AND BLACKGUARDS

The Soviets declared themselves the government on November 7. But it was one thing to take power; another thing to keep it. It was one thing to write out decrees; another to back them with bayonets.

The Soviets soon found a big fight on their hands. They found, too, a crippled military-apparatus to fight with. It was all out of gear, sabotaged by officers. The Revolutionary General Staff could not straighten out the tangle from above. It appealed directly to the workers.

They uncovered stores of benzine and motors, whipping the transport into shape. They assembled guns, gun-carriages, and horses, to form artillery units. They requisitioned provisions, forage, and Red Cross supplies, rushing them to the front. They seized 10,000 rifles being shipped to Kaledin[1] and distributed them among the factories.

The stamp of hammers in the factories gives way to the tramp of marching feet. The foreman's orders give way to the commands of sailors drilling awkward squads. Through the streets hurry the motorcars spreading this call to arms:

---

[1] Aleksei M. Kaledin (1861–1918) was a Don Cossack general and leader of the White movement against the Bolsheviks in the Russian Civil War.

РАЙОННЫМЪ
Совѣтамъ Рабочихъ Депутатовъ Фабрично-Заводскимъ Комитетамъ

ПРИКАЗЪ.

Корниловскія банды Керенскаго угрожаютъ подступамъ къ столицѣ. Отданы всѣ необходимыя распоряженія для того, чтобы безпощадно раздавить контръ-революціонное покушеніе противъ народа и его завоеваній.

Армія и Красная Гвардія революціи нуждаются въ немедленной поддержкѣ рабочихъ.

Приказываемъ районнымъ Совѣтамъ и фабр.-зав. Комитетамъ:

1) выдвинуть наибольшее количество рабочихъ для рытья окоповъ, воздвиганія баррикадъ и укрѣпленія проволочныхъ загражденій;

2) гдѣ для этого потребуется прекращеніе работъ на фабрикахъ и заводахъ, немедленно исполнить;

3) собрать всю имѣющуюся въ запасѣ колючую и простую проволоку, а равно всѣ орудія, необходимыя для рытья окоповъ и возведенія баррикадъ;

4) все имѣющееся оружіе имѣть при себѣ;

5) соблюдать строжайшую дисциплину и быть готовыми поддержать армію революціи всѣми средствами.

Предсѣдатель Петроградскаго Совѣта Раб. и Солд. Депутатовъ
Народный Комиссаръ ЛЕВЪ ТРОЦКІЙ.

Предсѣдатель Военно-Революціоннаго Комитета
Главнокомандующій ПОДВОЙСКІЙ.

TO THE DISTRICT SOVIETS OF WORKER'S DEPUTIES AND SHOP-FACTORY COMMITTEES

ORDER

THE KORNILOV BANDS OF KERENSKY ARE THREATENING THE OUTSKIRTS OF OUR CAPITAL. ALL NECESSARY ORDERS HAVE BEEN GIVEN TO CRUSH MERCILESSLY EVERY COUNTER-REVOLUTIONARY ATTEMPT AGAINST THE PEOPLE AND ITS CONQUESTS.

THE ARMY AND THE RED GUARD OF THE REVOLUTION ARE IN NEED OF IMMEDIATE SUPPORT OF THE WORKERS.

THE DISTRICT SOVIETS AND SHOP-FACTORY COMMITTEES ARE ORDERED:

1) To bring forward the largest possible number of workers to dig trenches, erect barricades and set up wire defenses;

2) Wherever necessary for this purpose to **SUSPEND WORK** in shops and factories, it must be done **IMMEDIATELY.**

3) To collect all available plain and barbed wire, as well as all tools **FOR DIGGING TRENCHES AND ERECTING BARRICADES;**

4) **ALL AVAILABLE ARMS TO BE CARRIED ON PERSONS;**

5) Strictest discipline must be preserved and all must be ready to support the Army of the Revolution to the utmost.

President of the Petrograd Soviet of Workers & Soldiers Deputies
People's Commissar **LEV TROTSKY.**

President of the Military-Revolutionary Committee
Chief Commander **PODVOISKY.**

[*Reproduction in English of the Russian text on opposite page.*]

In answer, everywhere appear workmen with cartridge belts outside of overcoats, blankets strapped on their backs, spades, tea kettles, and revolvers tied on with strings. Long, irregular lines of slanting bayonets winding through the dark.

Red Petrograd rises in arms to repel the Counter-Revolutionary forces marching up out of the south. Over the roofs, now hoarse, now shrill, comes the sound of factory-whistles blowing the tocsin to war.

On all roads leading out of the city pours a torrent of men, women and boys, carrying kit-bags, picks, rifles and bombs. A drab and motley throng. No banners, no drums to cheer them on. Plunging trucks splash them with mud, freezing slush oozes through their shoes, winds from the Baltic chill to the bone. But they push on to the front, unresting, as the grey day turns to sullen night. Behind them the city flings its lights into the sky, and still they press forward into the dark. Fields and forests are swarming now with dim shapes, pitching tents, building campfires, cutting trenches, stretching wire. One brief day, and tens of thousands have moved out twenty miles from Petrograd, and stand, a bulwark of living flesh against the forces of the Counter-Revolution.

To military experts it is a rag-tag army, a rabble. But in this "rabble" there is a drive and power not reckoned with in the books of strategy. These dark masses are exalted with visions of a new world. Their veins burn with a crusading fire. They fight with reckless abandon, often with skill. They plunge forward into the black copse against hidden foes. They stand up to the charging Cossacks and tear them from their horses. They lie flat before the machine-gun fire. Bursting shells send them fleeing, but they rally again. They carry back the stricken, binding their wounds. Into the ears of their dying comrades they whisper, *"The revolution! The people!"* They die, gasping out *"Long live the Soviet! Peace is coming!"*

Disorder, confusion, panic, of course, in these raw levies of the shops and slums. But the ardor of these hungry, work-scarred men and women, fighting for their faith, is more effective than the organized battalions of their foes. It destroys these battalions. It shatters their morale. Hardened Cossacks come, see and are conquered by it. "Loyal" divisions, ordered to the front, flatly refuse to shoot down these workmen-soldiers. The whole opposition crumples up or melts away. Kerensky flees from the front in disguise. The commander of the grand armies that were to crush the Bolsheviks cannot find a corporal's guard to fly with him. The proletarians are victors all along the line.

The Whites Take the Telephone Station

While the Soviet masses are battling on the plains outside Petrograd, the Counter-Revolution rises suddenly, in the rear. It sets out to paralyze the Soviet power at its base in the city.

The Yunkers, who were paroled after their capture at the Winter Palace, break their parole to join this White Guard[2] uprising. They are detailed to seize the telephone station.

The telephone station is one of the vital centers of the city; from it run a million wires, which like a million nerves, help make the city a unit. In Petrograd the telephone station is housed in a massive stone citadel on the Morskaya.[3] Here some Soviet sentries are posted. Through the tedium of the day they have one thing to look forward to—the change of sentries at night.

Night comes and with it twenty men marching down the street. The sentries think it is the relief-squad bringing them liberty. But it is not. It is a squad of officers and Yunkers disguised as Reds. Their guns are slung slant-wise in orthodox Red Guard fashion. They give the Red Guard pass-word to the sentries. In good faith the sentries stack guns and turn to go. In a flash twenty revolvers are pointed at their heads.

"*Tovarishe!*" (Comrades!) exclaim the astounded Reds.

"You damned swine!" shout the officers. "Get into that hall there, and keep your mouths shut or we will blow your heads open."

The doors slam behind the bewildered sentries, who find not release and freedom, but imprisonment at the hands of the Whites. The telephone station is in the hands of the Counter-Revolution.

In the morning the new masters finished fortifying the place under the supervision of a French officer. Suddenly the officer turned on me with a stern, "What are you doing here?"

"Correspondent—American," I replied. "Dropped in to see what was up."

"Your passport," he demanded. I produced it. He was impressed and apologized. "Of course, this is none of my business. Like you, I just glanced in to see what was happening." But he went on directing the work.

On both sides of the archway the Yunkers ran out barricades of boxes, automobiles and piles of logs. They levied toll on passing autos, bringing in supplies and weapons, and corralled all passers-by who might possibly serve as soldiers of the Soviet.

A great prize came their way in the person of Antonov,[4] the Soviet Commissar of War. Driving by in his auto, he was suddenly yanked from the seat; and before he could recover from the shock, he was behind barred doors. With the fate of the Revolution hanging in the balance, he found himself a prisoner of the Counter-Revolutionists.

---

[2] White Guards were mainly monarchists who opposed the Bolsheviks in the Russian Civil War (1918–20).

[3] The Morskaya River runs through the center of St. Petersburg.

[4] Vladimir A. Antonov-Ovseyenko (1883–1938) was a Bolshevik who led the attack on the Winter Palace in the October Revolution and later fought in the Red Army in the Russian Civil War. He was executed in the Purges of the 1930s.

His anguish at being jailed was only exceeded by their joy at jailing him. They were jubilant. For among the unorganized masses of revolutionary Petrograd, leaders were as yet desperately few. They knew—according to all the laws of military science—that the masses, leaderless, could not move effectively against their citadel; and the master military brain of the Reds was now in their hands.

The Revolution Rallies Its Forces

Some things these officers did not know. They did not know that the Revolution was not dependent upon any single brain, or set of brains, but upon the collective brains of the Russian masses. They did not know how deeply the Revolution had roused the brain, the initiative, and the resources of these masses, and wrought them into a living unit. They did not know that the Revolution was a living organism, self-sustaining, self-directing, rallying at the danger-call all its latent powers for self-preservation.

When an evil germ enters the blood of the human organism the whole body senses the danger, as if an alarm had been sent out. Along a hundred arteries the special corpuscles or phagocytes come hurrying to attack the poison-center. Fastening on the intruder, they attempt to expel it. This is not the conscious act of the brain. It is the unconscious intelligence inherent in the human organism.

Now into the body of Red Petrograd, threatening its very life, enters the malignant poison of the Counter-Revolution. The reaction is immediate. Spontaneously along a hundred streets and arteries, the corpuscles (in this case red ones) come hurrying to the contagion center—the telephone station.

Ping! Crash! A bullet splintering a log announces the arrival of the first Red corpuscle carrying a gun. Ping! Ping! Crash! Crash! A gust of lead, biting stone chips from the wall, heralds the advent of more attacking units.

Peering through the barricades, the Counter-Revolutionists already see swarms of Red Guards at the ends of the street. The sight of them arouses an old Czarist officer to savagery. "Turn on the guns!" he shouts. "Kill the rabble!" Up and down the streets they let loose a storm of rifle and machine-gun fire. Like a canyon the street is filled with noise and ricocheting bullets. But there are no Red corpses. The revolutionary masses have no appetite for martyrdom. Provokingly they refuse to be killed.

It is different from former days. Then the mobs obligingly put themselves in the way of the guns. In hundreds they were spattered over the Winter Palace Square, blown to pieces by the artillery, trampled under the hoofs of the Cossacks, massacred by machine guns. It was so easy! How easy now, too, to annihilate them, if they would but rush the barricades.

But the Revolution is careful of its material. It has made these masses cautious. It has taught them the first lesson in strategy: find out what your enemy wants you to do, and then don't do it. The barricades, the Reds see, are intended to destroy them; they intend to destroy the barricades.

They inspect them and decide the tactics of assault. They pick out every vantage-point. They hide behind stone pillars. They scale walls. They crawl along the copings. They lie flat upon the roofs. They ambuscade themselves in windows and chimney-pots. From every angle they train their guns upon the barricades. Then suddenly they open fire, raking the barricades with hails of lead. As precipitately as they began, they stop, and steal up into new positions. Another outburst and another silence. The officers begin to feel like trapped animals, around whom invisible hunters are drawing a circle of fire.

New units are constantly arriving, filling the gaps in the circle. The ring draws tighter and tighter and seals up the Counter-Revolution in the center. Then, having isolated its plague-spot the Revolution prepares to eradicate it.

A gale of bullets forces the Whites to abandon the barricade and find refuge under the archway. Behind stone ramparts, now, they pause for counsel. The first plan is to make a sortie, break through the Red cordon, and escape. But this they see is suicide. A scout crawls out on the roof and is driven back, a ball through his shoulder. They play for time, begging a peace parley, but the besiegers reply:

"Three days ago we captured you in the Winter Palace; we paroled you then. You broke your parole. You shot down our comrades. We do not trust you."

They sue for amnesty, offering to give up Antonov.

"Antonov! We'll take him ourselves," the Reds reply. "Harm him and we'll kill you—every one of you."

Red Guards Tricked by the Red Cross Car

Desperate situations induce desperate ventures.

"Oh, for a Red Cross car," sighed an officer. "The Reds might let that through their lines."

"Well, if we haven't the car, we've got the crosses, said another officer, producing four big Red Cross labels. He pasted them on the front, sides and back of an auto. At once it looked like a Red Cross car.

Two officers took the front seat. One at the wheel, the other with his hand on the auto pocket and a revolver in his hand. A haggard man, half crazed with fear, the father of one of the Yunkers, climbed into the rear.

"Jump in and come along," said the officers to me. The Whites always took it for granted that anyone in bourgeois dress was on the bourgeois side. Even many who knew of the revolutionary activity of men like John Reed, for example, and myself, assumed it was only a ruse to get the confidence of the Bolsheviks.

I climbed into the car and the hood was pushed through the archway. At sight of the Red Cross the firing of the Red Guard ceased. Slowly and anxiously we drove up to the Red lines. The soldiers, sailors and workmen received us, guns in hand.

"Well, what do you want?" they glowered.

"Many of our men are badly wounded. No bandages, no medicines," the officer at the wheel explained. "We want to go to Red Cross quarters and get supplies. Our men are suffering terribly."

"Let 'em suffer," growled one of the sailors with an oath. "Haven't they made our men suffer? And we had just paroled them—the damned liars."

To this, one of the other sailors cried, "No, *tovarish.*" To us in the car they said, "All right. Pass through. Hurry."

We swept on up the street, while behind us the fusillade against the telephone station began again.

"Not bad fellows after all, those Red Guards," I interjected.

"Fools! (Doorake). What you call in English 'damn fools,' eh?" They laughed hysterically again.

We ran down the French Quay[5] at terrific speed, making a wide detour in order to throw possible pursuers off our track. A sharp turn brought us up before the Engineers' Castle.[6] The big gates opened to let us in and a minute later we were in a salon filled with officers—Russian, French and British. The staff heard the report on the crisis at the telephone station and ordered the immediate dispatch of an armored car and reinforcements. There were a few other details, some words with a Czarist general, and we turned to go.

"Wait a minute," interrupted the general, "let me give you something useful to take back with you." He sat down at a table and laid out some papers, in size and shape like credentials of the Soviet. Picking up a stamp he brought it down sharply on the first credential. There were the magic words *"War Revolutionary Committee"* in form and letter just like the seal of the Soviet. If that was not a stolen Soviet stamp it was an exact replica. No one could detect the imitation. In Russia this sort of forgery is a fine art.

"Trotsky himself couldn't give you a better credential than that," the general remarked, handing it over. "In uncertain times like these, one always carries the proper kind of papers," he continued facetiously, imprinting the Soviet seal on two more credentials. "There you are! Ready for any emergency. Fill it out with bad writing and misspelled words and you have a first-class Bolshevik pass for any place you want to go. And by the way," he added, passing over some black iron globes about the size of baseballs, "a few of these will come in handy."

"Hand grenades?" I queried.

"No," the general answered. "They are pills. Capsules. Medicine for Reds. Give a Red Guard one of these in the right place and it's a sure cure for Bolshevism, Rev-

---

[5] The French Quay, which runs along the Neva River in St. Petersburg, is also known as the Quay with Sphinxes for its giant stone sphinx statues.

[6] The Engineers' Castle is a nickname for St. Michael's Castle, built in St. Petersburg for Emperor Paul between 1797 and 1801.

olution, Socialism, and everything else that ails him. What, eh?" he cried, tremendously pleased with his wit. "A Red Cross car full of pills!"

Again our car was headed back to the telephone station. But in the last half hour the streets had changed. Red sentries were posted on nearly every corner. They were largely peasants whom fate had torn from the country quiet and thrown down into this city, all agog with Revolutionists and Counter-Revolutionists and no mark to tell the two apart.

They were puzzled as we bore down on them waving our papers, pointing to the Red Cross sign on our car and yelling out, "Aid to the wounded *tovarishe.*" While they were trying to collect their wits we went sweeping past. One after another was rushed off his feet, until we came to a big peasant standing guard in the center of the Millionaya.[7] With rifle raised he barred the way and brought us up with a sudden halt.

"Idiot!" shouted the officers. "Don't you see that this is a Red Cross car? Don't waste time while the *tovarishe* are dying."

"Are you *tovarishe* too?" asked the peasant, eyeing the officers' uniforms suspiciously.

"Of course we are. Too long have the bourgeoisie drunk the people's blood! Down with the traitor Counter-Revolutionists," said the officers, mouthing shibboleths of the Revolution.

"And do I live to see the day when officers come over to the help of the dark people?" said the old peasant half to himself. It was too much. He couldn't quite believe it and asked for our papers.

With his finger tracing the lines he painfully spelled out each word. As the peasant read the officer's paper the officer, hand on pistol, read the peasant's face. That peasant never knew how close he stood to death. If he had said "No. You cannot pass," the officer would have blown out his brains. His permit to let us go was his own permit to live. He didn't know the seal on our paper was forged. He only saw it was like his own, so he said, "Yes!" and we were off again.

Once more we came to the Red cordon around the telephone station. It was a nervous moment for the officers. Under pretense of bringing life and succor to wounded Whites they were bringing death and wounds to the Reds. These Reds did not know that. Though they had had a taste of the treachery of the Counter-Revolution, they did not suspect that it would flout all moral laws and violate its own codes. So when these officers begged quick passage for their car in the name of humanity, the Red Guards answered, "All right, Red Cross. Hurry through."

The lines opened and a minute later our car with its load of hand-grenades slipped under the archway of the station, hailed by shouts of joy from the imprisoned Whites. They were glad for the hand-grenades and for the latest military information. But they were gladdest of all to learn of the armored car coming to their relief.

---

[7] Millionaya Street runs through central St. Petersburg, ending in Palace Square near the Winter Palace.

Chapter 10
MERCY OR DEATH TO THE WHITES?

It was a black outlook for the White Guards hemmed inside the telephone station. But now comes this jubilant news that an armored car is hurrying to their rescue. They gaze intently down the street for the first glimpse of it.

As it comes swinging in from the Nevsky, they hail it with cheers. Like a great iron steed it lumbers along and stops before the barricades. Cheers again from the Whites. Ill-starred cheers! They do not know that they are cheering their end. They do not know that this is not their car; it has passed into the hands of the Reds. It is a Trojan horse, within whose armored belly are concealed the soldiers of the Revolution. It slews about until its muzzle is pointed through the archway. Then suddenly it spouts a stream of lead as a garden hose spouts water. Screams now instead of cheers! Tumbling over boxes and one another, the officers, in one shrieking, tangled mass, go crashing through the hallway and up the stairs.

Poetic justice! Here where a few hours earlier these Counter-Revolutionists pressed their revolvers against the temples of the Revolution, the Revolution presses its machine guns against their temples.

The White Guards in a Funk

At the top of the stairway the Whites disentangle themselves, not to make a stand, but to run better. Ten resolute men could have held this stairway against a thousand. But there are not ten men to do it. There is not one. There is only a panic-stricken pack, in the clutch of a fear that drains the blood from their faces, the reason from their brains. All courage gone. All prudence gone. Gone even the herd-instinct of unity in the face of common peril.

"*Sauve qui peut*" (let him save himself who can) becomes the cry of the older officers.

They fling away caps, belts and swords; insignia of honor now become badges of shame and death. They rip off shoulder straps, gold-braid and buttons. They plead for a workman's costume, a cloak, an overcoat—anything to disguise their rank. An officer coming upon a greasy blouse hanging on a peg becomes a maniac with joy. A captain finding the apron of a cook puts it on, plunges his arms in flour and already white from terror becomes the whitest White Guard in all Russia.

But for most of them there is no cover save the darkness of closets, booths and attic corners. Into these they crawl like hunted animals in collapse. To treachery against their enemies these officers now add treason to their allies. They had led the Yunkers into this trap. Now the trap is closing, and the officers abandon them.

First to rally their wits, the Yunkers begin to cry out, "Our officers! Where are our officers?" No answer to their cries. "Damn the cowards!" they shout. "They have deserted us."

Rage at this betrayal fuses the Yunkers together. Their best tactics would be to hold the stairway, but they shrink away from it. Red vengeance crouching at the foot fills them with dread. It will not let them move forward. They fall back into a thick-walled room with a narrow entrance. There, like rats clustering in a hole, they wait the onrush of the Red tide that may come rising up the stairway, flooding the corridors, drowning them out.

To some of these young fellows, sprung from the middle class, this is a doubly tragic ending. Death at the hands of peasants and workers with whom they have no quarrel! But, caught in this camp of the Counter-Revolution, they must share its doom. They know how richly they deserve it. This sense of guilt unnerves them. Their guns fall from their hands. They slink down on chairs and tables, moaning, their eyes fixed on the entrance through which the Red tide is to come crashing in. They listen for the swirl of the first wave flinging itself on the stairway; hammering on the door.

Save their own hammering pulses there is not a sound.

Reds, Whites and Girls Petrified by Fear

There is another chamber of torture in this building. It holds Antonov, the Red sentries, and all captives bagged by the Whites during the day. They sit helpless, locked in their prison, while outside rages the battle sealing the fate of their Revolution, and their own fate. No one comes to tell them how the battle goes. Only through the thick walls comes the muffled crackle of rifles, the crash of falling glass.

Now all these noises abruptly cease. What does it mean? The triumph of the Counter-Revolution? The Whites victorious? What next? The opening of the door? The firing-squad lining them up before a wall? Bandages tied round their eyes? The report of rifles? Their own death? The death of the Revolution? So they muse, heads sunk in hands, while the clock above the door pitilessly tells off the seconds. Each stroke may be the last. Awaiting that last, they sit straining to hear the tread of the firing-squad coming down the corridor. But save for the ticking clock, not a sound.

Still another torture chamber, this one filled with women. It is the top floor, with hundreds of telephone girls huddled around the switch-boards. The eight-hour bombardment, the stampede of the officers, their frenzied cries for help, have shattered the nerves of these girls and their minds run wild. They run to wild stories of Bolshevik atrocities, the rape of the Women's Battalion, crimes imputed to these Red hordes swarming into the court-yard below.

In their fevered imagination they are already victims of a like brutality, writhing in the arms of these monsters. They break into tears. They write frantic little last farewells. They cling together in white-faced groups, listening for the first yells of the ruffians, the thumping of their boots along the hall. But there are no thumping boots—only their own thumping hearts.

The building becomes quiet as a tomb. It is not the quiet of the dead, but tense and vibrant, the silence of hundreds of living beings paralyzed with terror. The silence is contagious. It passes through the walls and lays hold of the Red throngs outside. They in turn become still, stricken by the same paralysis of fear. They shrink away from the stairway lest it belch out clouds of gas, a fusillade of bombs. Hundreds outside in terror of the Whites within! Hundreds inside in terror of the Reds without! Thousands of human beings torturing each other.

Inside the building this ordeal by silence becomes unendurable. I, at least, can endure it no longer. For relief I run forward, not knowing where; anywhere to get away from the silence. Opening a side-door by accident I catapult into the chamber filled with Yunkers. They jump as though it is the crack of doom.

"American correspondent," they gasp. "O! Help us! Help us!"

"How can I?" I falter. "What shall I do?"

"Something—anything!" they implore. "Only save us."

Some one says, "Antonov." The others catch up the name, repeating it like an incantation. "Antonov. Yes, Antonov. Go to Antonov. Downstairs—Antonov. Quick, before it is too late—Antonov!" They point the way.

In a minute I make another headlong entrance before another astounded audience—the captive Reds and Antonov.

"You are all free. The officers have fled. The Yunkers surrender. They beg you to save them. Any terms. All they ask is their lives. Only hurry, hurry."

In a moment this prisoner Antonov awaiting death becomes the arbiter of death. The condemned is asked to be the judge. A startling change! But the face of this little, tired overworked Revolutionist did not change. If the thought of revenge flashed into his mind, it as quickly flashed out again. "So I am not to be a corpse but a commander," he said wanly. "Next thing is to see the Yunkers, is it? Very well." He put on his hat and walked upstairs to the Yunkers.

"Antonov! *Gospadeen* Antonov![1] Commander Antonov! " they wailed. "Spare our lives. We know we are guilty. But we throw ourselves on the mercy of the Revolution."

Sorry ending to a gay adventure! In the morning sallying out to kill Bolsheviks and in the evening begging Bolsheviks for their own lives. Saying *"Tovarish"* as one might say "swine," then breathing it reverently as a term of honor.

---

[1] *Gospodin* is Russian for "mister."

"*Tovarish* Antonov," they implored, "give us your word as a Bolshevik, a true Bolshevik. Give us your word for our safety."

"My word," said Antonov. "I give it."

"They may not take your word, *Tovarish* Antonov," muttered one poor wretch. "They may kill us anyhow."

"If they kill you," assured Antonov, "they must first kill me."

"But we don't want to be killed," whimpered the poor fellow.

The Mob Decrees Death to the White Guards

Antonov, could not conceal his contempt. Turning into the hall, he started down the stairs. To the taut nerves every step sounded like the detonation of a gun.

The Red throng outside heard the steps and raised their rifles, expecting a fusillade. And then this surprise! Antonov, their own leader,

"*Nash! Nash!*" (Ours! Ours!) acclaimed a hundred voices. "Antonov! Long live Antonov!" rose from another hundred throats. The shout raised in the courtyard was caught up in the street and the crowd surged forward crying, "The officers, Antonov? Where are the officers and the *Yunkers*?"

"Done for," announced Antonov. "Their arms are down."

Like the bursting of a dam came the roar from a thousand throats. Yells of triumph and howls of rage proclaiming "Death to the officers! Death to the Yunkers!

Good reason for the Whites to tremble! At the mercy of those to whom they had forfeited all claims for mercy. Not by fighting, but by fighting foully they had roused this volcano of wrath. In the eyes of these soldiers and workmen the Whites were murderers of the Red comrades, assassinators of the Revolution, miscreants to be exterminated like vermin. Fear only had kept the Reds from plunging up the stairway. Now all cause for caution was gone. The infuriated men stormed forward filling the night with their cries, "Wipe out the butchers! Kill the White Devils! Kill every one of them!"

A torch here and there in the blackness lit up the bearded faces of peasants, soldier-faces, the faces of city artisans grimed and thin, and in the front rank the open, alert countenances of the big sailors from the Baltic fleet. On all of them, in flashing eyes and clenched jaws vengeance was written, the terrible vengeance of the long-suffering. Pressed from the rear, the mass lunged forward against the stairway where Antonov stood, calm and impassive, but looking so frail and helpless before this avalanche of men.

Raising his hand and voice, Antonov cried out, "*Tovarishe*, you cannot kill them. The Yunkers have surrendered. They are our prisoners."

The throng was stunned. Then in a hoarse cry of resentment it found its voice. "No! No! They are not our prisoners," it protested. "They are dead men."

"They have given up their arms," continued Antonov. "I have given them their lives."

"You may give them their lives. We don't. We give them the bayonet!" bawled a big peasant turning to the crowd for approval.

"The bayonet! Yes, we give them the bayonet!" they howled in a blast of approbation.

Antonov faced the tornado. Drawing a big revolver, he waved it aloft, crying out, "I have given the Yunkers my word for their safety. You understand! I will back my word with this."

The crowd gasped. This was incredible.

"What's this? What do you mean?" they demanded.

Clutching his revolver, finger on the trigger, Antonov repeated his warning: "I promised them their lives. I will back that promise with this."

"Traitor! Renegade!" a hundred voices thundered at him. "Defender of the White Guards!" a big sailor flung in his face. "You want to save the rascals. But you can't. We'll kill them."

"The first man who lays his hands on a prisoner *I will kill him on the spot!*" Antonov spoke slowly, with emphasis on each word. "*You understand! I will shoot him dead!*"

"Shoot us?" queried the affronted sailors.

"Shoot us! Shoot us!" bellowed the whole indignant mob.

For it was just that—a mob, with all the vehement passions of the mob. A mob with every primitive instinct inflamed and ascendant: cruel, brutal, lusting for blood. In it flamed the savagery of the wolf, the ferocity of the tiger. A huge beast drawn out of the jungles of the city, stirred up by these White hunters, wounded, and bleeding from its wounds, all day exasperated and tormented, at last, in a paroxysm of joy and rage it was about to pounce upon its tormentors and tear them to pieces. At this moment this little man stepped between it and its prey! To me the most emotional thing in the whole Revolution is this little man standing in that stairway, so unemotionally looking that mob in the eye; rather, in its thousand glaring eyes. There was pallor in his face, but no tremor in his limbs. And no quaver in his voice, as he said again slowly and solemnly, "The first man who tries to kill a Yunker, I will kill him."

The sheer audacity, the impudence of it took their breath away.

"What do you mean?" they yelled. "To save these officers, Counter-Revolutionists, you kill us workmen-Revolutionists?"

"Revolutionists!" retorted Antonov, derisively. "Revolutionists! Where do I see Revolutionists here? You dare call yourselves Revolutionists? *You*, who think of killing helpless men and prisoners!" His taunt went home. The crowd winced as though struck by a whip.

"Listen!" he went on. "Do you know what you are doing? Do you realize where this madness leads? When you kill a captive White Guard you are not killing the Counter-Revolution, you are killing the Revolution. For this Revolution I gave twenty years of my life in exile and in prison. Do you think that I, a Revolutionist, will stand by and watch Revolutionists crucify the Revolution?"

"But if they had us there would be no quarter," bellowed a peasant, "they would kill us."

"True, they would kill us," answered Antonov. "What of that? They are not Revolutionists. They belong to the old order, to the Czar and the knout, to murder and death. But *we* belong to the Revolution. And the Revolution means something better. It means liberty and life for all. That's why you give it your life and blood. But you must give it more. You must give it your reason. Above the satisfaction of your passions you must put service to the Revolution. For the triumph of the Revolution you have been brave. Now, for the honor of the Revolution be merciful. You love the Revolution. I only ask you not to kill the thing you love."

He was aflame, his face incandescent, his arms and voice imploring. His whole being, focussing itself in that last appeal, left him exhausted.

"Speak to them, comrade!" he entreated.

Four weeks earlier I had spoken to these sailors from the turret of their battleship *The Republic*. As I stepped to the front they recognized me.

"The American *tovarish*," they shouted.

Loudly and fervently I spoke about the Revolution, about the battle waged throughout Russia for land and freedom, about their own betrayal by the White Guards and the justice in their wrath. But the eyes of the world turned to them as the fighting vanguard of the Social Revolution. Would they take the old bloody path of retaliation or blaze the way to a nobler code? They had shown themselves daring for the preservation of the Revolution. Would they show themselves magnanimous for its glory?

It was an effective speech at the outset. But not because of its content. The recitation of the Lord's Prayer or Webster's Oration[2] would have been almost as effective. Not one in a hundred understood what I was saying. For I spoke in English.

But these words—strange and foreign—crackling out in the dark held them and made them pause—precisely what Antonov was working for—that this hurricane of passion might subside a little, to gain time for another impulse to get the upper hand.

The Mob Disciplined by the Revolution

For while this was a mob, it was a revolutionary mob. Deep-rooted in the hearts of at least half this workman-soldier crowd was one powerful abiding loyalty—the Revolution. The word was a fetish. Their dreams and hopes and longings were all woven around "The Revolution." They were its servants. It was their master.

---

[2] Daniel Webster (1782–1852), U.S. Senator, gave the first commemoration of the Declaration of Independence on July 4, 1800, in Hanover, New Hampshire, known as Webster's Oration.

True, at this moment another master held them, displacing every idea of the Revolution. Revenge was in the saddle, recklessly lashing the mob along. But this was temporary. The permanent allegiance of their lives was to the Revolution. Given the chance it would rise up, expel the usurper, assert its authority, and again control its followers. Antonov did not stand alone against a multitude. In that mob, there were a thousand Antonovs, sharing with him the same high zeal for the Revolution. Antonov was just one unit of that mob, flesh of its flesh, spirit of its spirit, sharing its antagonism to the Yunkers, and officers, aflame with its same hot passions.

Antonov happened to be first of this mob to rein in his passions, the first in whose consciousness the Revolution replaced revenge. The change made in his heart by the concept of the Revolution would likewise be wrought in the hearts of the soldiers and workers. This Antonov knew. By repeating the magic word "Revolution" he sought to bring them to their revolutionary selves; he sought to evoke revolutionary order out of chaos. And he did.

Before our eyes we saw again the ancient miracle of the Word—the stilling of the tempest. The howling and the raging died away, save for here and there an angry voice still persisting. But as Woskov interpreted my words, and Antonov spoke again, these centers of dissent subsided. Chastened and in a receptive mood, these soldiers and sailors were substituting for their own will to revenge the will of the Revolution. Only let them understand that will.

"What is it, Antonov?" they cried. "What do you want us to do?"

"To treat the Yunkers as prisoners of war," said Antonov. "To carry out the terms of surrender. I have pledged these Yunkers their lives. I ask you to back my pledge with yours."

The mob became a Soviet. A sailor spoke; then two soldiers and a workingman. The vote was taken by show of hands. A hundred battle-stained hands went up, and another hundred until nearly a thousand hands were lifted. A thousand clenched fists threatening death to the officers now raised in an open-handed promise of life.

At this juncture arrived a delegation from the Petrograd Duma commissioned "to liquidate the civil strife with the shedding of as little blood as possible." But the Revolution was liquidating its own affairs without the shedding of any blood at all. It ignored these gentlemen, and detailed a squad to enter the building and bring the White Guards down. First came the Yunkers, and then the officers, ferreted out of their hiding places, one of them dragged out by his heels. Hustled out upon the elevated stone steps, they stood blinking in the torch-light, facing the muzzles of a thousand guns, the scorn of a thousand hearts, the grilling of a thousand pairs of eyes.

There were a few jeers, cries of *"Assassins of the Revolution!"* and then silence—the solemn silence of a court. For this was a court—the tribunal of the disinherited. The oppressed sitting in judgment on their oppressors. The new order passing sentence upon the old. The grand assizes of the Revolution.

"Guilty! All guilty!" was the verdict. Guilty as enemies of the Revolution. Guilty as retainers of the Czar and the exploiting classes. Guilty as violators of the Red Cross and the laws of war. Guilty on all counts as traitors to the workers of Russia, and to the workers of the world.

The wretched prisoners in the dock shrank before the blast and bowed their heads. Some of them would have found it easier to stand up to a volley from the guns. But the guns were there to guard them.

Five sailors shouldering rifles took their stand at the foot of the steps. Antonov seized the hand of an officer and placed it in the hand of a sailor.

"Number one," he said. "A helpless, disarmed prisoner. His life is in your hands. Guard it for the honor of the Revolution." The squad encircled the prisoner and marched through the archway.

With a like formula the next prisoner was handed over, and the next, and the next; each one entrusted to a detachment of four or five. "The end of the rubbish," muttered an old peasant as the last officer was delivered to his escort, and the procession filed out into the Morskaya.

Near the Winter Palace infuriated mobs fell upon the Yunkers and tore them from the hands of their convoys. But the revolutionary sailors, charging the mobs, rescued the prisoners and brought them safely to the prison Fortress of Peter and Paul.

The Revolution was not everywhere powerful enough to check the savage passions of the mobs. Not always was it on time to allay the primitive blood-lusts. Unoffending citizens were assaulted by hooligans. In out-of-the-way places half-savages, calling themselves Red Guards, committed heinous crimes. At the front General Dukhonin[3] was dragged from his carriage and torn to pieces despite the protesting commissars. Even in Petrograd some Yunkers were clubbed to death by the storming crowds; others were pitched headlong into the Neva.

The Workers' Respect for Life

The attitude of the revolutionary working-classes toward human life, however, is not reflected in these mad, sporadic deeds of the hot-blooded and the irresponsible, but in one of the first laws the Soviet made as it entered into power.

As the ruling-class the workers were now in a position to take vengeance on their former exploiters and executioners. When I saw them rise up and take the govern-

---

[3] Nikolai N. Dukhonin (1876–1917) was a general and the last commander of the Imperial Army after Kerensky fled Russia. He was killed by sailors in early December 1917 by order of the Bolsheviks.

ment in their own hands, and at the same time take in their grasp those who had lashed them, jailed them, and betrayed them, I feared a savage outburst of revenge.

I knew that thousands of the workmen now in authority had been sent with clanking chains across the snows of Siberia. I had seen them pallid and tottering from long years in those coffins for the living—the stone sacks of Schlusselburg.[4] I had seen the deep scars cut in their backs by the Cossacks' *nagaika*[5] and I recalled the words of Lincoln: "If for every drop of blood drawn by the lash another shall be drawn by the sword, the judgments of the Lord are pure and righteous altogether."

But there was no dreadful blood-bath. On the contrary, the idea of reprisals seemed to have no hold on the minds of the workers. On November 30 the Soviet passed the decree declaring the Abolition of Capital Punishment. This was not merely a humanitarian gesture. The workers turned to their enemies not only to guarantee their lives but in many cases to grant them freedom.

Many sinister figures of the old régime had been incarcerated by Kerensky in the bastion of the Peter-Paul Fortress. There we met Biletsky,[6] the chief of the Czar's Secret Service, who in his day had railroaded countless victims into these dungeons. Now the old grizzled rat was getting a taste of his own medicine. Here also was the ex-War Minister Sukhomlinov,[7] whose intrigue with the Germans had sent tens of thousands of Russian soldiers to death in the trenches. These two arch-villains received us with the most engaging manners, proclaiming their innocence and protesting against their "inhuman persecution."

"But the Bolsheviks are more human than Kerensky," they said. "They give us the newspapers."

We visited also the ministers of the fallen Provisional Government in their cells and found them taking their misfortunes with good grace. Tereshchenko, handsome as ever, received us sitting cross-legged on his cot, smoking a cigarette.

"This is not the life *de luxe*," he said in faultless English. "But the commandant is not to blame. Suddenly he had to provide for hundreds of extra prisoners and no extra rations. So we are hungry. But we get the same as the Red Guards; though they scowl at us they share their bread with us."

The young Yunkers we found recounting their telephone-station adventures, opening packages from friends, or stretched out on mattresses playing cards.

A few days later these Yunkers were released. A second time they were paroled and a second time they broke faith with their liberators—they went south and joined the White Guard armies mobilizing against the Bolsheviks.

---

[4] Schlusselburg is a fortress at the mouth of the Neva River on Lake Ladoga.

[5] A *nagaika*, or *nagyka*, is a thick whip used by the Cossacks.

[6] Leonid Biletsky was the head of the tsar's secret police, the Ohkrana.

[7] Vladimir A. Sukhomlinov (1848–1926) was chief of staff and minister of war in the Russian Imperial Army.

With like acts of treachery thousands of Whites repaid the Bolsheviks for their clemency. Over his own signature General Krasnov[8] solemnly promised not to raise his hand against the Bolsheviks, and was released. Promptly, he appeared in the Urals at the head of a Cossack army destroying the Soviets. Burtsev[9] was liberated from the Peter-Paul prison by order of the Bolsheviks. Straightway he joined the Counter-Revolutionists in Paris and became editor of a scurrilous anti-Bolshevik sheet. Thousands, who thus went forth to freedom by mercy of the Bolsheviks, were to come back later with invading armies to kill their liberators without ruth or mercy.

Surveying battalions of comrades slaughtered by the very men whom the Bolsheviks had freed, Trotsky said: "The chief crime of which we were guilty in those first days of the revolution was excessive kindliness."

Sardonic words! But the verdict of history will be that the Russian Revolution—vastly more fundamental than the great upheaval in France in 1789—was no saturnalia of revenge. It was to all intents a "bloodless revolution."

Take the most exaggerated estimates of the shootings in Petrograd, the three days' battle in Moscow, the street-fighting in Kiev and Irkutsk, and the peasants' outbreaks in the provinces. Add up the casualties and divide it into Russia's population—not the 3,000,000 involved in the American Revolution, nor the 23,000,000 of the French Revolution, but the 160,000,000 of the Russian Revolution. The figures will show that in the four months it took the Soviet to establish and consolidate its power—from the Atlantic to the Pacific, from the White Sea on the north to the Black Sea on the south—less than one in 3,000 Russians were killed.

Sanguinary enough to be sure!

But look at it in the perspective of history. Rightly or wrongly, when the fulfillment of the national destiny of America demanded that we cut out the cancer of slavery, vast property rights were confiscated, and in doing this we did not stop until we had killed one in every 300 people. Rightly or wrongly, the peasants and workers feel it essential to cut out of Russia the cancer of Czarism, landlordism, and capitalism. Such a deep-seated and malign disease called for a major surgical operation. Yet it was performed with comparatively little letting of blood. For, like children, the nature of a great folk is to forgive and forget—not to retaliate. And vindictiveness is alien to the spirit of working-people. In those early days they strove hard to conduct a civil war in a civil manner.

In a large measure they succeeded. The death-toll of both Whites and Reds together was not equal to the casualties in a single big battle of the World War.

---

[8] Peter N. Krasnov (1869–1947) was a Don Cossack General who led White armies in the Russian Civil War.

[9] Vladimir L. Burtsev (1862–1942) was a revolutionary activist and publisher of several magazines. He helped expose the fraud of the *Protocols of the Elders of Zion* and died in Paris in 1942.

"But the Red Terror!" someone interjects. That was to come later when the Allied armies were to come to Russia, and under their protecting wing the tsarists and Black Hundreds were to loose upon peasants and workers the White Terror of the Counter-Revolution—a hideous orgy of butchery and lust in which helpless women and children were to be massacred in droves.

Then in defense the workers, goaded to desperation, were to strike back with the Red Terror of the Revolution. Then capital punishment was to be restored and the White conspirators were to feel the swift chastising hand of the Revolution.

There are furious charges and counter charges about Red and White Terrors. Out of the controversy four facts emerge and may be stated here.

The Red Terror was a distinctly later phase of the Revolution. It was a defensive measure, a direct reply to the White Terror of the Counter-Revolution. Both in number and fiendishness the outrages of the Reds pale before the atrocities committed by the Whites.* Had not the Allies intervened in Russia and again stirred up civil war against the Soviets, in all probability there would have been no Red Terror and the revolution would have continued as it began—practically a "bloodless revolution."

* Appendix II. "The Train of Death," from the *American Red Cross Magazine*.

Chapter 11
THE WAR OF THE CLASSES

Upstarts, adventurers, impostors!

Thus the bourgeoisie stigmatized the Bolsheviks, or sneered with Shatsky,[1] "How can such dogs, such *canaille* run a government!"

The idea that the Red régime would last longer than a few hours or a few days was a joke. Again and again we were told, "The hangings will begin tomorrow." But many tomorrows passed and no Bolsheviks dangled from the lamp-posts. The bourgeoisie became alarmed as the Soviet showed no sign of falling. "It is necessary to do battle and pull it down," read the appeal of the Council of the Republic. "It is the enemy of the people and the Revolution."

The City Duma became the center for all forces mobilizing against the Soviets. It was swarming with generals, priests, intelligentsia, *chinovniks* [clerks], speculators, Knights of Saint George, Boy Scouts, French and British officers, White Guards and Cadets. Out of these elements was organized the "Committee of Salvation"—the General Staff of the Counter-Revolution.

"All of Russia is represented here," boasted the old Mayor Schreider. And so it was. "All Russia"—all except her peasants and workers, her soldiers and sailors. Coming here from proletarian Smolny was like entering another world, the world of the well fed and well dressed. From here the ancient order of privilege and power struck against the new order set up by the working class. From here the bourgeoisie engineered its campaign against the Soviet, using every means to discredit, cripple and destroy it.

The Bourgeois Strike and Sabotage

By one stroke the bourgeoisie sought to bring the Soviet to its knees. It proclaimed a general strike in all departments of the new government. In some ministries the white-collared workers walked out in a body. In the Foreign Office 600 officials listened to Trotsky's appeal for translators of the Peace Decree, then resigned. A big strike-chest collected from the banks and business houses corrupted the minor officials and

---

[1] Stanislav Shatsky (1878–1934) was an important educator in late imperial Russia and the Soviet Union. He based many of his ideas on American progressive education and helped construct the idea of the "new Soviet person."

even part of the working-class. For a time postmen refused to deliver Soviet mail, the telegraph would not dispatch Soviet messages, railways would not carry troops, the telephone girls left the switchboards, huge buildings were deserted—no one was left to light the fires.[2]

The reply of the Bolsheviks to this general strike was to declare the positions and pension rights of all strikers forfeit if they did not return at once. At the same time they set to work recruiting new staffs out of their own ranks. Men in smocks and overalls occupied the vacated offices. Soldiers pored over books and figures, tongues sticking out of their mouths from the unaccustomed mental strain. Big sailors laboriously picked out keys on the typewriter with one finger. Workingmen at the switchboards in the telephone station clumsily plugged in and out while irate subscribers screamed curses and threats at them over the wires. They were pitifully heavy-handed and slow. But they were in dead earnest, and day by day their speed was increasing. Day by day the old employees came drifting back, and in the end the strike of the bourgeoisie was broken.

Sabotage was the second weapon used against the Soviets. In factories managers hid vital parts of machinery, falsified accounts, destroyed plans and formulas and, under cover of night, shipped away lead and flour to Germany. Officials misdirected freight, destroyed good food under the pretext of its being unfit for use, tied everything up in loops of red tape.

The Bolsheviks answered with a "Warning to all Saboteurs and Provocateurs, who have wormed their way into Soviet Institutions." At the same time the walls of the city were placarded with this poster addressed *To all HONEST CITIZENS*:

---

[2] [Williams's note]: Appendix, <<p. 190>>.

ВСѢМЪ ЧЕСТНЫМЪ ГРАЖДАНАМЪ!

ВОЕННО-РЕВОЛЮЦІОННЫЙ КОМИТЕТЪ ПОСТАНОВЛЯЕТЪ:

Хищники, мародеры, спекулянты объявляются врагами народа.

Лица, виновныя въ этихъ тягчайшихъ преступленіяхъ, будутъ немедленно арестовываться по спеціальнымъ ордерамъ Военно-Революц. Комитета и отправляться въ Кронштадтскія тюрьмы впредь до преданія ихъ Военно-Революціонному суду.

Всѣмъ общественнымъ организаціямъ, всѣмъ честнымъ гражданамъ Военно-Революц. Комитетъ предлагаетъ: обо всѣхъ извѣстныхъ случаяхъ хищенія, мародерства, спекуляціи немедленно доводить до свѣдѣнія Военно-Революц. Комитета.

Борьба съ этимъ зломъ—общее дѣло всѣхъ честныхъ людей. Военно-Революц. Комитетъ ждетъ поддержки отъ тѣхъ, кому дороги интересы народа.

Въ преслѣдованіи спекулянтовъ и мародеровъ Военно-Революціонный Комитетъ будетъ безпощаденъ.

Военно-Революціонный Комитетъ.

Петроградъ.
10 ноября 1917 г.

TO ALL HONEST CITIZENS!

THE WAR-REVOLUTIONARY COMMITTEE DECREES:

HOOLIGANS, PROFITEERS AND SPECULATORS ARE DECLARED TO BE ENEMIES OF THE PEOPLE.

PERSONS GUILTY OF THESE GRAVE CRIMES WILL BE IMMEDIATELY ARRESTED BY SPECIAL ORDER OF THE WAR-REVOLUTIONARY COMMITTEE AND WILL BE SENT TO THE KRONSTADT PRISONS TO REMAIN THERE UNTIL BROUGHT BEFORE THE WAR-REVOLUTIONARY COURT.

THE WAR-REVOLUTIONARY COMMITTEE URGES ALL PUBLIC ORGANIZATIONS AND ALL HONEST CITIZENS IMMEDIATELY TO INFORM THE WAR-REVOLUTIONARY COMMITTEE, OF ALL CASES OF THEFT ROBBERY AND SPECULATION.

THE FIGHT AGAINST THESE EVILS IS THE TASK OF ALL HONEST PEOPLE. THE WAR-REVOLUTIONARY COMMITTEE EXPECTS THE SUPPORT OF ALL THOSE WHO HAVE THE INTERESTS OF THE PEOPLE AT HEART.

IN THE PROSECUTION OF SPECULATORS AND PROFITEERS THE WAR-REVOLUTIONARY COMMITTEE WILL BE RELENTLESS.

War-Revolutionary Committee.

PETROGRAD,
NOVEMBER 23, 1917.

[*This is a reproduction in English of the Russian poster on the preceding page.*]

Under this threat, those speculating in the hunger of the masses took to cover. Later on, the Extraordinary Commission (*Cheka*)³ was created to deal with these offenders, and other enemies of the new Soviet order.

In classes where there was no enmity against the Soviet, the bourgeoisie fomented it. The sufferings of millions of cripples, orphans and wounded was made acute by closing down the Department of Public Welfare. Hospitals and asylums became foodless and fireless. Delegations on crutches and starving mothers, babies in arms, besieged the new Commissar, Madame Kollontai. But she was helpless. The safes were locked, and the officials had made off with the keys. The former Minister, Countess Panina,⁴ had made off with the funds.

The Bolshevik reply to this and similar acts were not the guillotine but the Revolutionary Tribunal. Behind a long semicircular table in the music room of the palace of the Grand Duke Nicholas sat the seven judges—two soldiers, two workmen, two peasants and the President, Jukov.⁵

The first prisoner was the Countess Panina. The defense recited at length her golden deeds and charities. The young workman prosecutor Naumov replied:

"Comrades: All this is true. The woman has a good heart. But she is all wrong. She has helped the people out of her riches. But where did her riches come from? Out of the exploited people. She tried to do good with her schools, her nurses and her soup-kitchens. But if the people had the money she received out of their blood and sweat, we could have our own schools, our own nurses and our own soup kitchens. And we could have them the way we want them, not the way she thinks we ought to have them. Her good deeds cannot excuse her taking funds from the Ministry."

The verdict was guilty. She was sent to prison until the money was returned, then liberated to public censure! In the beginning light sentences like this were the order of the day. But as the class conflict grew more and more bitter the penalties imposed by the Revolutionary Tribunal grew more severe.

Money is the life-blood of all governments, and all financial institutions were in the hands of the bourgeoisie. To the City Duma and the "Committee of Salvation" the

---

³ *Cheka* was an acronym for the Emergency Committee created by the Bolsheviks for state security.

⁴ Countess Sofia V. Panina (1871–1956) was vice minister of state welfare and education of the Provisional Government in 1917.

⁵ Georgy Zhukov was the president of the Revolutionary Tribunal.

banks privately paid over fifty million rubles—to the Soviets not a single ruble. All their pleas and papers were unavailing. The bourgeoisie found great mirth in the spectacle of the Government of All-Russia going to the banks cap in hand begging for funds and not getting any.

Then one morning the Bolsheviks came to the banks guns in hand. They took the funds. Then they took the banks. By the decree for Nationalization of Banks, these centers of financial power passed into the hands of the working-class.

Alcohol, Press, and Church versus the Soviets

In their efforts to befuddle the brains of the masses the bourgeoisie saw an ally in alcohol. The city was mined with wine cellars more dangerous than powder magazines. This alcohol in the veins of the populace meant chaos in the life of the city. With this aim the cellars were opened and the mob invited in to help themselves. Bottles in hand the drunks would emerge from the cellars to fall sprawling on the snow, or rove through the streets, shooting and looting.

To these pogroms[6] the Bolsheviks replied with machine-guns, pouring lead into the bottles—there was no time to break them all by hand. They destroyed three million rubles' worth of vintage in the vaults of the Winter Palace, some of it there for a century. The liquor passed out of the cellars, not through the throats of the Czar and his retainers, but through a hose attached to a fire-engine pumping into the canals. A frightful loss. The Bolsheviks deeply regretted it, for they needed funds. But they needed order more.

"Citizens," they declared, "no violation of revolutionary order! No thefts nor brigandage! Following the example of the Paris Commune, we will destroy any looter or instigator of disorder." To meet this crisis this placard was posted:

---

[6] A pogrom is usually defined as an organized massacre of a group of people, most notably Jews, with the cooperation of government officials.

ОБЯЗАТЕЛЬНОЕ ПОСТАНОВЛЕНІЕ.

1) Городъ Петроградъ объявленъ на осадномъ положеніи.

2) Всякія собранія, митинги, сборища и т. п. на улицахъ и площадяхъ воспрещается.

3) Попытки разгромовъ винныхъ погребовъ, складовъ, заводовъ, лавокъ, магазиновъ, частныхъ квартиръ и проч. и т.п. будутъ прекращаемы пулеметнымъ огнемъ безъ всякаго предупрежденія.

4) Домовымъ комитетамъ, швейцарамъ, дворникамъ и милиціи вмѣняется въ безусловную обязанность поддерживать самый строжайшій порядокъ въ домахъ, дворахъ и на улицахъ, причемъ ворота и подъѣзды домовъ должны запираться въ 9 час. вечера и открываться въ 7 час. утра. Послѣ 9 час. вечера выпускать только жильцовъ подъ контролемъ домовыхъ комитетовъ.

5) Виновные въ раздачѣ, продажѣ или пріобрѣтеніи всякихъ спиртныхъ напитковъ, а также въ нарушеніи пунктовъ 2-го и 4-го будутъ немедленно арестованы и подвергнуты самому тяжкому наказанію.

Петроградъ 6-го декабря, 3 часа ночи.

Комитетъ по борьбѣ съ погромами при Исполнительномъ Комитетѣ Совѣта Рабочихъ и Солдатскихъ Депутатовъ.

OBLIGATORY ORDINANCE

1) The city of Petrograd is declared to be in a state of siege.

2) ALL ASSEMBLIES, MEETINGS AND CONGREGATIONS ON THE STREETS AND SQUARES ARE PROHIBITED.

3) ATTEMPTS TO LOOT WINE-CELLARS, WAREHOUSES, FACTORIES, STORES, BUSINESS PREMISES, PRIVATE DWELLINGS, ETC., ETC., WILL BE STOPPED BY MACHINE-GUN FIRE WITHOUT WARNING.

4) HOUSE COMMITTEES, DOORMEN, JANITORS AND MILITIAMEN ARE CHARGED WITH THE DUTY OF KEEPING STRICT ORDER IN ALL HOUSES, COURTYARDS AND IN THE STREETS; AND HOUSES, DOORS AND CARRIAGE-ENTRANCES MUST BE LOCKED AT 9 O'CLOCK IN THE EVENING, AND OPENED AT 7 O'CLOCK IN THE MORNING. AFTER 9 O'CLOCK IN THE EVENING ONLY TENANTS MAY LEAVE THE HOUSE, UNDER STRICT CONTROL OF THE HOUSE COMMITTEES.

5) THOSE GUILTY OF THE DISTRIBUTION, SALE OR PURCHASE OF ANY KIND OF ALCOHOLIC LIQUOR, AND ALSO THOSE GUILTY OF THE VIOLATIONS OF SECTIONS 2 AND 4, WILL BE IMMEDIATELY ARRESTED AND SUBJECTED TO THE MOST SEVERE PUNISHMENT.

PETROGRAD, 19TH OF DECEMBER, 3 O'CLOCK IN THE NIGHT.

COMMITTEE TO FIGHT AGAINST POGROMS, ATTACHED TO THE EXECUTIVE COMMITTEE OF THE SOVIET OF WORKERS AND SOLDIERS' DEPUTIES.

[This is a reproduction in English of the Russian poster on the preceding page.]

If liquor might not poison the minds of the people, there was the press. The lie-factories ground out their daily grist of papers and posters telling of the imminent fall of the Bolsheviks; of Lenin's flight to Finland with thirty millions of gold and platinum stolen from the State Bank; of the massacres of women and children by the Reds; of German officers in command at Smolny.

The Bolsheviks replied to this by the suspension of all organs "appealing to open revolt or inciting to crime."

"The wealthy classes," they declared, "holding the lion's share of the public press seek to befuddle the brains and consciences of the people with a stream of slander and lies.... If the first Revolution, which overthrew the monarchy, had the right to suppress the monarchist press, then this Revolution, which has overthrown the bourgeoisie, has the right to suppress the bourgeois press."

The opposition press, however, was not wholly suppressed. Papers suspended one day came out the next under a new name. *Speech* became *Free Speech*. *The Day* appeared as *Night*, then *In The Dark Night, Midnight, Two A.M.*, and so on. In picture and verse *Satire* went on merrily and mercilessly lampooning the Bolsheviks. The American Committee on Public Information carried on its propaganda unhindered, publishing the words of Samuel Gompers[7] under the headline "Socialists Support the War." But the Bolshevik measures were effective enough to prevent wholesale lying to the masses.

The Czar had used the priests of the Greek Orthodox Church as his spiritual police making "Religion the opiate of the people." With threats of hell and promises of heaven the masses had been bludgeoned into submission to autocracy. Now the church was called to perform the same function for the bourgeoisie. By solemn proclamation the Bolsheviks were excommunicated from all its rites and services.

The Bolsheviks made no direct assault upon religion, but separated Church from State. The flow of government funds into the ecclesiastical coffers was stopped. Marriage was declared a civil institution. The monastic lands were confiscated. Parts of monasteries were turned into hospitals.

The Patriarch thundered his protests against these sacrileges, but with little effect. The devotion of the masses to the Holy Church proved to be almost as mythical as their devotion to the Czar. They looked at the Church Decree giving them hell if they sided with the Bolsheviks. Then they looked at the Bolshevik Decree giving them land and factories.

---

[7] Samuel Gompers (1850–1924) was an English-born American labor leader. He founded the American Federation of Labor (AFL), but he strongly opposed socialists.

"If we must choose," some said, "we choose the Bolsheviks." Others chose the Church. Many merely muttered *"Neechevo"* (it doesn't matter much), and walked in the church procession on one day and in the Bolshevik parade on the next.

Peasants, Anarchists, and Germans Pitted against the Soviets

The cities were the stronghold of the Bolsheviks. The bourgeoisie sought to play the country against them.

"Look!" they said to the peasants, "The cities work but eight hours a day, why should you work sixteen? Why deliver your grain to the cities when you get nothing in return?"[8] The old Executive Committee of the Peasants' Soviet flatly refused to recognize the new government at Smolny.

Over their heads, however, the Bolsheviks called a new congress of peasants. Here the old guard with Chernov made furious assaults upon the Bolsheviks. But two stubborn facts could not be downed. First: The Bolsheviks had given the peasants land—not promises. Second: The Bolsheviks were now inviting the peasants to participate in the new government.

After days of stormy debate an agreement was concluded. The peasants streamed out into the night lit with torches, the band of the Pavlovsky Regiment crashed into the Marseillaise, workmen rushed in upon the peasants, clasping them in their arms and kissing them. Behind the huge peasant Soviet banner with its inscription: *"Long Live the Union of the Toiling Masses,"* the procession passed through the snow-covered streets to Smolny. Here the formal "wedding" of the peasants with the soldiers and workers was consummated. In exaltation an old mujik cried out, "I came here not walking on the ground but flying through the air." The new government became in reality a Soviet of Workmen, Soldier and Peasant Deputies.

In their efforts to break the Soviets the bourgeoisie struck out right and left—as far left as the Anarchists. Hundreds of officers and monarchists filtered into the anarchist organizations and under the black flag became anarchists of deed.

They entered hotels and at revolver-point "requisitioned" the pocket-books of the guests. In Moscow they "nationalized" thirty-four palaces by dumping the inmates into the streets. They found the American Red Cross automobile of Colonel Robins[9] standing by a curb and "socialized" it by jumping in and driving off. They justified

---

[8] [Williams's note]: Appendix VII, <<191>>. Soviet Appeal to Peasants: "Dear Brothers."

[9] Raymond Robins (1873–1954) was an economist and writer who headed the American Red Cross in Russia and worked for American recognition of the Soviet Union for many years.

everything by saying: "We are the real revolutionists—more radical than the Bolsheviks."

The Bolsheviks delivered an ultimatum to the genuine Anarchists to clean house. At the same time they raided the "Anarchist" centers and found great stores of provisions, jewelry, and machine-guns fresh from Germany. They restored the stolen property to the owners and arrested all reactionaries masquerading as ultra-revolutionists.

For help the bourgeoisie turned to their former enemies—the Germans. Again and again they told us that next week we would see the German armies marching into Moscow.

The Bolsheviks had then no Red Armies to oppose the Germans, no batteries of guns. But they had batteries of linotypes; and printing presses, which sprayed the German ranks with the deadly shrapnel of propaganda. In the *Torch* and the *People's Peace*, in all languages, flamed the appeal to the German soldiers to use their guns—not to destroy the workingmen's republic in Russia, but to set up a workingmen's republic in Germany.

In the Soviet offices John Reed and I made up an illustrated sheet. Picture No. 1 showed the German Embassy in Petrograd, a big banner on its front. Underneath this picture these sentences:

> See the great banner. It is the word of a famous German. Was it Bismarck? Was it Hindenburg? No. It is the call of the immortal Karl Marx to international brotherhood—"Proletarians of all lands, unite!"
>
> This is not merely a pretty decoration of the German Embassy. In all seriousness the Russians have raised this banner, and to you Germans they hurl back the same words that your Karl Marx gave to the whole world seventy years ago.
>
> At last a real proletarian republic has been founded. But this republic cannot be secure until the workers of all lands conquer the power of government.
>
> The Russian peasants, workers and soldiers will soon send a Socialist as ambassador to Berlin. When will Germany send an internationalist Socialist to this building of the German Embassy in Petrograd?

Picture No. 3 showed a soldier prying the Russian imperial eagles off a palace, the crowd below burning them. Underneath these words:

> On the roof of a palace, a soldier is tearing down the hateful emblem of autocracy. Below the crowd is burning the eagles. The soldier in the crowd is explaining that the overthrow of autocracy is only the first step in the march of social revolution.

It is easy to overthrow autocracy. Autocracy rests on nothing but the blind submission of soldiers. The Russian soldiers merely opened their eyes and autocracy disappeared.

These pictures, papers and leaflets were flung up into the air to be blown by favorable winds into the German trenches. They were dropped from aeroplanes and smuggled across in shoes and boxes and on prisoners returning to Germany.

All this disintegrated the German armies and made for revolution. General Hoffman said: "It was Lenin and the Bolsheviks that broke our morale and gave us defeat and the revolution you now see ruining us." Probably the propaganda was not so effective as this. But it did prevent the German troops from coming to overwhelm the Soviet. The Russian bourgeoisie began scheming for intervention by the Allies.

The Debacle of the Constituent Assembly[10]

On January 18, 1918, at the height of the struggle between the classes the Constituent Assembly convened. It reflected an earlier phase of the Revolution—a viewpoint now discarded. It was elected from antiquated lists—lists in which one Soviet Party—the Left Socialist Revolutionists,[11] did not appear as a party at all. The masses were indifferent to this institution coming like a ghost out of the past. But the bourgeoisie loudly acclaimed it. In reality the bourgeoisie had no zeal for the Constituent Assembly and for months had done everything to postpone or kill it. How often had I heard them say: "The Constituent Assembly—we spit upon it." Now it was their last hope, the last screen behind which they could operate, they became its ardent champions.

For the opening day a big demonstration was organized. About 15,000 officers, *chinovniks* and intelligentsia paraded through the streets. Fur-clad ladies of leisure arrayed in scarlet colors, old monarchists carrying banners of red, large-bellied landlords lustily singing "We starved and bled in the people's cause" all tried their best to look like a revolutionary procession. But only the songs and banners were red. The marchers were largely White Guards and Black Hundreds—scarcely a peasant or worker. The masses stood aside and greeted the paraders with jeers or contemptuous silence.

The Constituent Assembly came too late. It was still-born. In the swift pace of Revolution the allegiance of the revolutionary masses had passed wholly to the Soviet. For the Soviet they had marched 500,000 strong and they were ready, not only to march for it, but to fight and die for it. The Soviet was precious to the working-classes

---

[10] The Constituent Assembly was elected in late 1917, but only met for a few hours on January 18–19, 1918, before the Bolsheviks disbanded it.

[11] Left Socialist Revolutionaries were a left faction of the Socialist Revolutionary Party that split from the main portion of the party to support the Bolsheviks rather than the Provisional Government.

because it was their own institution, born in their own class and admirably fitted to realize their own ends.

Every dominant class fashions the kind of state-apparatus that will best secure its power, through which it can govern in its own interests. When kings and nobles were in power the state apparatus through which they functioned was the Autocracy, the Bureaucracy. When the bourgeois-capitalist classes rose to power in the 18th century they scrapped this old state apparatus and created a new one adapted to their purposes—the Parliament, Congress.

In like manner the working-classes rising to power in Russia brought with them their own state-apparatus—the Soviet. They had tried and tested it in thousands of local Soviets. They were familiar with its workings. It was part of their daily experience. Through it they had achieved the desires of their hearts—land, factories, and the proffers of peace. They had marched to victory with it. They had made it the government of Russia.

And now this belated Constituent Assembly refused to recognize the Soviet as the government of Russia. It refused to accept the Soviets' Declaration of the Rights of the Working and Exploited Peoples—"the Magna Carta of the Russian Revolution."[12] It was as if the French Revolution refused to accept the Declaration of the Rights of Man.

Accordingly it was dissolved. In the morning of January 19, 1918, the sailor guards said they were sleepy and that the remaining delegates must stop talking and go home. Thus after one session the Constituent Assembly expired, making a great furor in the Western world, but in the life of Russia hardly a ripple. It had no hold on the people. By the manner of its dying it showed that it had no right to live.

The chief mourners for the Constituent Assembly were the bourgeoisie. It was their last hope. Now it was gone their rage against the Revolution and all its works was implacable. This was quite natural. The Revolution was a catastrophe to them. It declared: "If a man does not work, neither shall he eat." "No one shall have cake until everybody has bread." It dynamited the whole basis of their lives. It took the great estates away from the landlords, the gilt-edged jobs away from the office-holders, the control of banks and factories away from the capitalists. Nobody likes to have things taken away from him. No leisure class gracefully steps down from the roof-garden and goes to work. No privileged class voluntarily resigns any of its privileges. No class steeped in tradition discards the old and gladly embraces the new.

There are of course exceptions to this rule—in Russia some striking ones. The old Czarist general, Nikolayev, declared himself a Bolshevik and took command in the Red Army. Later captured by the Whites at Yamburg he was called upon to deny his faith. He refused. He was tortured—a red star burned upon his breast. Still he refused to recant. He was led to the scaffold and a noose placed around his neck.

---

[12] [Williams's note]: Appendix VI, <<p. ?>>.

"I die a Bolshevik. Long live the Soviet," he cried as he was swung out into space.

There were others like him—men whose hearts had been touched by the teachings of Tolstoy and the long line of Russian humanitarians, men who saw the iniquity of the old order and the justice of the new.

But these were exceptions. As a class the Russian bourgeoisie looked at the Revolution with horror and hate. Their only thought was to kill it. Blinded with vengeance they cast aside all codes of honor, chivalry and patriotism. They cried for foreign bayonets to strike it down. Every weapon was sanctified—even assassination. The civilized veneer dropped away. The primitive fang and claw appeared. Men of parts and culture became savages.

Chapter 12
BUILDING THE NEW ORDER

THE conduct of the Russian upper-classes in their efforts to regain the power of the state shows nothing new or unusual in history. The unprecedented thing is the determination of the Russian working-class to hold that power. They clung to their course with dogged tenacity, meeting thrust with counter-thrust, striking back blow for blow, steel for iron. They developed unexampled discipline and solidarity.[1]

It is said that the rank and file were held in line by the iron will of their leaders, that their resolution was just the reflex of the resolution of the men above. The opposite is nearer the truth.

It was the leaders who were irresolute. Three Bolshevik Commissars left their posts at a critical moment. Five others (Zinoviev, Kamenev, Milyutin, Nogin, Rykov)[2] tendered their resignation to the Central Committee of the Bolshevik Party. Lunacharsky,[3] believing all the tales of Moscow's destruction, cried out, "My cup is full. I am unable to endure this horror. It is impossible to work under the pressure of thoughts that drive me mad. I can bear no more. I resign."

"Shame upon these men of little faith, who hesitate and doubt, capitulating to the cries of the bourgeoisie," cried Lenin. "Look at the masses. In them there is not a shadow of hesitation." The names of the deserters were pilloried through Russia. Before the blast of indignation from the proletarians, the commissars scurried back to their posts never to waver again.

---

[1] [Williams's note]: Appendix VII, 190–91: "To All Workers of Petrograd."

[2] Lev B. Kamenev (1883–1936), whose real name was Rozenfeld, was a Bolshevik revolutionary and one of the first members of the Politburo. After Lenin's death in 1924, he fell out of favor with Stalin and would be executed as part of the Purges. Nikolai A. Milyutin (1889–1942) was a trade union and Bolshevik activist. He would eventually reach the position of commissar of finance. Victor P. Nogin (1878–1924) was a key Moscow Bolshevik who held many positions in the revolutionary era. Aleksei I. Rykov (1881–1938) was a prominent Bolshevik politician who held many positions in the Soviet government, including commissars of interior and justice.

[3] Anatoly V. Lunacharsky (1875–1933) was a Marxist revolutionary and Bolshevik who was an influential commissar of public enlightenment. Under Stalin, he lost his position. He died in France in 1933.

But they could never quite shake off the haunting fear of defeat. Even Lenin was not immune. "Ten days more and we shall have lived seventy days—as long as the Paris Commune," he exclaimed, surprised at so far escaping disaster. At times the leaders saw their venture ending in certain death.

"We did our best," said Peters[4] dolefully one day, "but it is all over for us shortly."

"Perhaps tomorrow," said Pokrovsky,[5] "we shall get a sleep—a long one."

These forebodings never assailed the minds of the Bolshevik rank and file. They drove ahead in full confidence and assurance, infusing their leaders above with fresh courage and determination, and inspiring the broad masses below with the will to victory.

How Many Bolsheviks in Russia?

To what extent did these masses support the new government set up by the Bolsheviks? How wide a following did the Revolution find in the people? The *People's Business* (*Dielo Narodo*) said: "A revolution is a rising of all the people. But what have we here? A handful of poor fools deceived by Lenin and Trotsky."

True, the membership of the Bolshevik Party was a "handful" among the great populations of Russia—not more than 1 or 2 percent. If that was all, the new government might well be stigmatized as "the tyranny of an infinitesimal fraction over the great majority." But one fact must be borne in mind, viz.: Bolshevik sentiment is not to be gauged by the Bolshevik Party. For every Bolshevik in the official Bolshevik Party there were 30 to 50 Bolsheviks in the general population.

The high standard of admission, the hard duties and drastic discipline of the Bolshevik Party, made the masses unwilling to join it. But they voted for it.[6*7]

---

[4] Yakov Kh. Peters, also known as Jacob Peters (1886–1938), was one of the founders of the Cheka. He was executed during the Purges of the 1930s.

[5] Mikhail N. Pokrovsky (1868–1932) was a Marxist historian who was very influential in the 1920s.

[6] Socialist voters are always 10 to 50 times as numerous as Socialist Party members. New York in 1920 had 12,000 Socialist Party members. This election showed 176,000 Socialist Party voters. In Vladivostok in 1918, the Bolshevik Party members were 300. In the June election there were 12,000 Bolshevik Party voters. This election was held under Allied auspices with the Bolshevik papers suppressed and their leaders imprisoned, yet more citizens voted for the Bolsheviks than for the other 16 parties combined. Yet propagandists for the tsarists Kolchak and Denikin—like John Spargo—tried to focus all attention on the membership, which is utterly misleading.

[7] Alexander V. Kolchak (1874–1920) was a key military leader in Siberia for the Whites during the Russian Civil War. Anton I. Denikin (1872–1947) was a key military leader for the Whites during the Russian Civil War. John Spargo (1876–1966) was born in England but was very active in the Socialist Party of America in the early twentieth century.

In the elections to the Constituent Assembly in Northern and Central Russia, Bolsheviks got 55 percent of the vote—not 1 or 2 percent. In Petrograd the Bolsheviks and their allies, the Left Socialist-Revolutionists, received 576,000 votes—more than the 17 other parties combined.

It is said that there are three grades of lies: "Lies, damned lies, and statistics." Revolutionary statistics are particularly unreliable. For in time of revolution public opinion moves like a tidal wave. The people vote one way today. A few weeks hence they will vote quite differently.

When the Constituent Assembly was *elected* in November 1917, about one-third were for the Bolsheviks (including their allies, the Left Socialist-Revolutionists). When the Constituent Assembly *convened* in January, 1918, possibly two-thirds were for the Bolsheviks. In the few weeks' interim the Bolshevik ideas swept from the cities into the villages, and out into the provinces. The peasants, finding that the Soviet Land Decree had actually given them the land, rallied behind the Bolshevik banners in millions.

A fair estimate of the growth of Bolshevik adherents in the adult population would go like this:

March 1917—at the fall of the Czar	1,000,000
July 1917—after the armed demonstration	5,000,000
November 1917—Constituent Assembly election (official returns)	9,000,000
January 1918—3rd Congress of Soviets representing	13,000,000

The Bolsheviks had not merely numbers but all the strategic positions. The big cities were Bolshevik—so were the railwaymen, the miners, the workers in basic industries. And the bayonets were overwhelmingly on their side. The Bolsheviks had the mandate of the essential forces of Russia to carry on the Revolution in the Bolshevik way.

Apathy of the Masses

It is a grave error to minimize the following the Bolsheviks had in the masses. It is an equally grave error to say that these masses were all zealots of the Revolution, all filled with a high and holy enthusiasm. On the contrary great numbers were quite indifferent. The Revolution was only "skin-deep."

One winter morning I set out in a sleigh with Charles Kuntz,[8] a New Jersey farmer and philosopher, who had come to Russia for a scientific study of the Revolu-

---

[8] Charles Kuntz (born 1870) was born in Kiev but immigrated to New Jersey with his parents. He returned to Austria and Switzerland for education before he finished at Columbia Uni-

tion. On finding that we were Americans, our driver, a lad of fifteen, was all excitement.

"Oh, Americans!" he exclaimed. "Tell me did Buffalobill and Jessejams really live?"

We said "Yes" and at once leaped to glory in the eyes of our driver. The exploits of these Western daredevils he knew by heart. Now this great joy—he was driving two countrymen of his heroes. He gazed long at us in big blue-eyed admiration while we tried hard to look like Buffalo Bill and Jesse James themselves.

"Oh! Ho!" he shouted. "I'll show you how to drive." He loosed the reins, cried *"B-r-r"* to his horse and with a jerk struck out into a breakneck gallop, the sleigh bounding over the ice-hummocks like a stage-coach on a Rocky Mountain road. Shouting with delight, he stood up in his box, cracking his whip, the sleigh slewing fearfully from side to side while Kuntz and I clung desperately to our seats and begged him to stop.

We told him that Buffalo Bill at his best never did better—but not to do it again. He plied us with incessant questions about the West while we tried to get him to talk about Russia. But in vain. The Russian Revolution was in eclipse. The deeds done in his books with glaring paper covers were so much more blood-stirring and important than those done in the streets of Petrograd.

Not all indifference to the Revolution was so picturesque. The energies of multitudes were absorbed by routine, and the sheer details of finding food and clothes. Others sordidly saw in the Revolution their chance for loot and laziness. They had toiled like slaves, now they would loaf like lords. The Revolution meant to them not freedom *for* work but freedom *from* work. They lounged all day on the corners, their sole contribution to the new order being to spit the husks of sun-flower seeds on the pavement. Soldiers became "State boarders," doing nothing in return for the food, clothes and lodging they got from the government. The nights they spent in card playing, their days in sleeping. Instead of drilling they became hawkers peddling rubbers, cigarettes and gew-gaws in the streets.

There was venal criminal indifference, too, to the interests of the Revolution. In positions deserted by the intelligentsia, adventurers and careerists saw their chance for plunder and glory. When John Reed and I visited the Petrograd Prefect of Police he flung his arms around us, crying: "Welcome, dear comrades. I will commandeer for you the best apartments in the city. We must sing the *Marseillaise* together. Ah! Our Magnificent Revolution," he exclaimed ecstatically. There was no doubt about his inspiration. The sources of it stood in a dozen bottles on the table. Under their influence he grew eloquent:

---

versity in the early twentieth century. At the time of the Bolshevik Revolution, he returned to Russia. He was employed as a translator in the Bureau of Propaganda of the Foreign Ministry.

"Danton and Marat ruled Paris in the French Revolution. Their names have gone down in history. I rule Petrograd today. My name shall go down in history." Short-lived glory! Next day he was jailed for accepting a bribe.

Another romantic buccaneer in some way received an appointment as military commissar. His self-importance mounted with every verst that took him away from Moscow. He sent word to a local Soviet that his coming would be announced by the booming of a cannon and the delegates were forthwith to assemble. Revolver in hand he strode upon the platform and in stentorian voice read his commission to the astounded auditors, punctuating each sentence by firing a bullet into the ceiling. There was short shrift for such adventurers.

But for the broad masses the Bolsheviks had infinite tolerance. They knew that the state had stupefied their brains, the church had deformed their consciences, famine had racked their bodies, alcohol had soddened their spirits. They had been exhausted by years of war and perverted by centuries of cruelty and deceit. For these masses the Bolsheviks had patience—and education.

A New Creative Spirit

"Whatever other expenses are cut down," the Bolsheviks declared, "the expenditures on public instruction must stay high. A generous budget for education is the honor and glory of every people. Our first aim must be the struggle against ignorance."

Everywhere schools were opened—even in palaces, barracks and factories. Over them was blazoned the legend "Children are the hope of the world" (*Detye nadezhde meera*). Into them marched millions of children, some of them forty and sixty years of age—old *babas* and grey-bearded peasants. A whole nation was learning to read and write.

Alongside the revolutionary proclamations and bills for the opera, appeared on the boardings biographies of great men, screeds on health and art and science. Workmen's theaters, libraries and lecture-courses sprang up on all sides. Doors to culture hitherto tight-closed to the masses were unlocked. Peasants and workers flocked into the museums and galleries.

The Bolsheviks aimed not only at better brains but better bodies. To this end many decrees were issued, such as the eight-hour law. The right of every child to be well-born was proclaimed. The stigma of illegitimacy was removed. Each industry was to provide one maternity bed for each two hundred workwomen. For eight weeks before and eight weeks after childbirth the mother was exempted from work. A Palace of Motherhood was established in different centers. The children instead of the wealthy were given the first claim upon such "luxuries" as milk and fruit. By the housing law the rich man lost his right to ten or twenty rooms or as many dwellings. On the other hand a dozen families gained for the first time the right to fresh air, light and decent dwellings. Not only was their health better, but they gained in self-respect and dignity. The Dictatorship of the Proletariat, basing itself on the multitudes, sought to nourish multitudes of sound, clean bodies, brains and consciences. The Bolsheviks were working for the future.

Having destroyed the main foundations of the old bourgeois order, they now faced the infinitely more trying task—the construction of a new order. They had to build it anew in every department, to build it from the bottom up, to build it out of the ruins of the past, to build it while beset and bedeviled on every side.

No one can exaggerate the magnitude of the task of reorganizing a new society. Some of the obstacles I glimpsed in one department—the military. Trotsky had just flung into the face of General von Hoffman his "You are writing with the sword on the bodies of living nations" and had refused to sign the First Treaty of Brest-Litovsk. The Germans then started a sudden drive on Petrograd. I joined the Red Guards for the defense of the city. Hearing this, Lenin suggested that I form a foreign detachment. *Pravda* printed our "call" in such English type as they could muster. (See reproduction of this opposite.)

About sixty men joined the detachment. Amongst them was Charles Kuntz, heretofore a Tolstoyan with scruples against killing even a chicken. Now that the Revolution was in peril, he threw over his pacifism and took up a gun. A tremendous change, to convert a fifty-year old philosopher into a soldier. In target practice his rifle would get tangled in his beard, but once his bullet hit the bull's-eye and his eyes glistened with joy.

We were a motley crowd and our fighting-strength really amounted to little. But the spirit of it had a good moral effect upon the Russians. It gave them the feeling that they were not utterly alone. And on a tiny scale it gave us an insight into the difficulties the Bolsheviks must struggle with on a colossal scale. We saw the thousand obstacles that must be overcome before any organization could function.

British and French agents on the one hand, and German agents on the other, tried to worm their way into our detachment. The Whites tried to get hold of it for counter-revolutionary purposes. Provocators stirred up jealousy and dissent. After we got the men, it was almost impossible to get the equipment. Military stores were in a hopeless tangle. Rifles in one place, bullets in another; telephones, barbed-wire, and sappers' tools in one vast jumble; and officers trying their best to make it more jumbled. When the sabotagers were removed, raw incompetent men took their places. We entrained two miles below Petrograd and, after a horrible ordeal in a box-car, we got up to find ourselves four miles on the other side of the city. We had lost six miles during the night and were stalled in a yard full of cursing troops, trains, broken-down engines. Exasperated commissars were shoving papers and fists into the faces of railway officers, who were frantically protesting they could do nothing.

This was a reflex of the chaos that prevailed all over Russia. To bring order out of it seemed a sheer impossibility. Yet the impossibility was being accomplished. In the welter of confusion was rising the great Red Army destined to amaze the world by

24 (11) февраля 1918 г.

The First International Detachment of the Red Army.

The Section for the formation and drilling of troops of the All-Russian College for the Organization and Administration of the Red Army notifies herewith that authorization has been obtained by it for the formation of a First International Detachment of the Red Army to be attached to one of the military units of Petrograd. This detachment will consist of foreigners, the general language to be English. The members are to be enrolled as volunteers. The conditions of life of the volunteers to be the same as those of the members of the Red Army. The persons wishing to enroll are to present themselves at the Mariinsky Palace 3rd floor entrance Vznesensky prospect, where a Bureau for the enrollment of foreigners of all nationalities has been organised. It is proposed to attach the detachment to the Grenadier Guard Regiment (Petrogradskaia Storona, Bolshoi Wulfova street).

The Section gives herewith a translation of the Call of the initiators of the formation of the detachment Comrades American Socialist Albert Williams and Samuel Agursky, who are at the head of the Bureau for the enrolling of volunteers.

Members of College of the Section for the Formation and Drilling.

CALL.

In this terrible world war democracy has been threatened; the international force have been split asunder, and the working classes have been ridden into the shambles by the imperialist of all countries. In the darkness there rose the Russian Revolution evoking the mighty hopes of all man-

Интернациональный отряд красной армии.

Отдѣлъ формированія и обученія при Всероссійской Коллегіи организаціи и управленія Красной Арміей объявляетъ, что имъ разрѣшено формированіе при одной изъ воинскихъ частей Петрограда, перваго Революціоннаго Интернаціональнаго отряда Красной Арміи изъ иностранцевъ (разговорный языкъ англійскій).

Запись производится на добровольческихъ началахъ. Условія жизни волонтеровъ общія съ условіями жизни красноармейцевъ. Организовано бюро по записи иностранцевъ различныхъ національностей. Отрядъ предположено формировать при Гвардіи Гренадерскомъ полку (Петроградская стор., Б. Вульфова улица).

При семъ отдѣлъ прилагаетъ переводъ воззванія иниціаторовъ формированія отряда, товарищей американскихъ соціалистовъ — Альберта Вильямса и Самуила Агурскаго — стоящихъ во главѣ бюро по записи волонтеровъ.

Члены: Коллегія Отдѣла Формированія и Обученія.

ВОЗЗВАНІЕ!

Въ эту страшную мировую войну, всей демократіи угрожала опасность, интернаціональныя силы были разрознены и рабочій классъ поведенъ сломать империалистами всѣхъ странъ. Изъ всеобщей тьмы возникла загадка свѣтъ русской революціи, пробуждая великія надежды человѣчества. Со-

Citizens! Comrades! Internationalists!

Russia is in prison. Even so, above the clangor of the world — war her voice cries out loudest for justice and humanity — for the poor and the oppressed.

Russia has enemies inner and outer, strong and cunning. And Russia needs not your words and pious wishes. She needs work, discipline, organisation and

guns in the hands of fearless fighters.

Do you believe in the Revolution, in the International, in the Soviet power? Then join the International Legion of the Red Army. It is formed for those speaking foreign languages and to it are coming the fighting revolutionists from around the world.

Are you a free man? Then enlist at once

Are you working in shop or office? Then give your spare time to drill, rifle practice and the military courses.

Headquarters: 2 Nijni Lesnoy Pereooluk — near the Temple of the Saviour.

Bürger! Genossen! Internationalisten!

Rußland ist im Gefängnisse. Jedoch über all den Klängen des Weltkrieges erschallt seine donnernde Stimme um Gerechtigkeit und Humanität für die Armen und Unterdrückten. Rußland ist von mächtigen Feinden belagert, inneren und äußeren. Rußland braucht nicht eure Worte und fromme Wünsche; es braucht Tat, Disziplin, Organisation, Gefechte in den Händen unerschrockener Kämpfer. Habt ihr festen Glauben an die Revolution, an die Internationale und die Sowjet-Macht? Dann schließt euch der

Internationalen Legion der Roten Armee

an. Dieselbe wird für diejenigen gebildet, die fremde Sprachen sprechen, und an ihr reihen sich die revolutionären Kräfte der ganzen Welt. Bist du ein freier Mann? Dann schließe dich sogleich an. Schaffst du in Werkstätten oder Kontor? Dann widme deine freie Stunden dem Drillen, der Schießübung und dem Militärstudium.

Hauptquartier: Nischni-Lesnoi Pereulok Nr. 2 — nahe dem Tempel des Heilandes.

Citoyens! Camerades! Internationalistes!

La Russie est en captivité. Mais même captive elle domine le grondement de la guerre mondiale et on entend sa voix criant le plus haut pour la justice et l'humanité pour les pauvres et les opprimés. La Russie n'a pas seulement des ennemis extérieurs, elle en a aussi au dedans du pays qui sont forts et rusés. La Russie n'a pas besoin de vos paroles, ni de vos souhaits, elle a besoin du travail, de l'organisation et des combattants sans peur. Si vous avez de la confiance dans la Revolution, l'International, et dans la puissance du Soviet enrôllez vous dans la Legion Internationale de l'Armée Rouge. Celle-ci est formée pour ceux qui parlent des langues étrangères, et de toutes parts du monde arrivent des combattants révolutionnaires pour la renforcer. Etes-vous libre? Enrollez-vous alors tout de suite. Si vous travaillez dans l'usine ou dans le bureau sacrifies votre temps libre aux exercises militaires, au tir, à la discipline militaire.

Adressez-Vous au Quartier: Nijni Lesnoy Pereulok 2 — auprès du Temple de Jésus Christ.

Граждане! Товарищи! Интернационалисты!

Россия въ тискахъ, но ея голосъ, покрывая шумъ міровой войны, призываетъ человѣчество и правду и справедливость для бѣднѣйшихъ угнетенныхъ. У Россіи много другихъ внутреннихъ и внѣшнихъ, сильныхъ и хитрыхъ. Она не нуждается в словахъ и пустыхъ пожеланіяхъ. Ей нужна работа, дисциплина, организація и безстрашные бойцы.

Вѣрите ли вы в революцію, в Интернаціоналъ, в Совѣтскую власть? Если да, то немедленно присоединяйтесь в Интернаціональному боевому Красной Арміи. Онъ теперь формируется из товарищей, говорящихъ на иностранныхъ языкахъ; в немъ соберутся боевые революціонеры со всего свѣта.

Если ты свободный человѣкъ, присоединяйся безотлагательно. Если ты работаешь за станкомъ или в конторѣ, то посвяти свои свободные часы военнымъ упражненіямъ и стрѣльбѣ.

Обращаться для записи и по справкамъ: Нижній Лѣсной пер. д. № 2, кв. 7 — близъ Храма Христа Спасителя.

Москва, 16 (3) апрѣля 1919 г.

Cittadini! Compagni! Internazionalisti!

Russia è in prigione. Nell'odierno sopra il clamore della guerra universale la sua voce proclama il più alto giustizia ed umanità pei poveri e soppressi. La Russia non nemici, interiori ed esteriori, forti e cauti. E la Russia non ha bisogno delle vostre parole o dei vostri buoni auguri. Essa ha bisogno della vostra azione disciplinata, della vostra organizzazione e di fuvili nelle mani di intimorditibili lottanti. Credete voi nella rivoluzione, nell'Internazionale, nella forza del Sovieti? Allora unitevi alla Legione Internazional dell'Esercito Rosso. Esso è formato per quelli che parlano le lingue estere e vengono con lui i rivoluzionarii lottanti di tutto il mondo. Siete liberi? Allora unitevi all'istante. Lavorate nelle fabbriche oppure negli uffici? Allora dedicate il vostro tempo libero all'esercizio, alla pratica del fucile ed ai corsi militari!

Quartiere Generale: Nisnij Lesnoi Pereulog 2 — presso il Tempio de Salute.

[*This is the Moscow appeal of the International Legion as it appeared in five languages.*]

187

its organization, discipline and effectiveness. And not only in the realm of war but in the cultural and economic fields were appearing the results of the powerful directing spirit begotten of the Revolution.

Always there were tremendous latent energies in the Russian masses. But they had never found expression. They had been locked up by the grim jailer—Autocracy. The Revolution came as their releaser, and with the pent-up fury of centuries they burst forth and smashed the old bourgeois order to pieces.

We had seen the Revolution unloose the tremendous powers of the people for destructive ends. Now we were seeing the Revolution evoke their creative powers and direct them to constructive ends. *"Order. Work. Discipline."* are the new watchwords of the Revolution.

But is this new spirit being born only in these great centers? Or is a like process at work out in the provinces and the vast populations of Russia. Presently we are to find out for ourselves. After nearly a year in the midst of the Revolution Kuntz and I are going home. Our eyes are turned to the East—toward America. Our journey is to take us through the two continents over which Russia spreads herself, across 6,000 miles of Trans-Siberian Railway to the Pacific.

PART III

THE OUTREACH OF THE REVOLUTION ACROSS SIBERIA ON THE EXPRESS

Chapter 13
THE STEPPES RISE UP

It is the end of April, 1918. Kuntz and I are saying goodbye to the Red Commune of Petrograd. The snow-flakes are falling, the night descending. Stormy, hungry old city, but dear to us, with its thousand lights and shadows of the Revolution, for nearly every street and prospekt has staged some act in the colossal revolutionary drama.

The square we gaze upon from the steps of the Nicholas Station has been sprinkled red by the first sacrifices of the Revolution, and we have helped to sprinkle it white with a shower of Soviet posters, flung from a plunging truck at midnight. It has rumbled beneath the tread of marching columns chanting their funeral hymn, bearing away their dead; and we have heard it ring with triumphant shouts proclaiming: *"All Power to the Soviets."* It has witnessed the rush of Cossack horses thru the ranks of workingmen, felling them to the cobbles. And it has seen the return of these workers, welded together in the iron battalions of the proletariat—the invincible Red Army of Russia.

A multitude of memories bind us to the city. But steam is up in the engine of the Trans-Siberian Express, and it does not wait on sentiment. Every week it starts on its 6,000-mile journey to the Pacific, heeding only the clanging signal-bell, whether rung by order of the Czar or by order of the Bolsheviks. On the third stroke we climb aboard and are off on our long journey to the distant East.

What will this East unfold to us? Shall we find that the spirit of the revolutionary centers carries out far toward the circumference or not?

The Émigrés' View of the Revolution

Already our fellow passengers are stretched out in their compartments, sipping tea and smoking cigarettes. In our car are about twenty landowners, speculators, war-profiteers, ex-officers in mufti, evicted officials, and three overpainted ladies—all members or retainers of the old privileged class.

Their ancient privileges are gone. But life still has its glamor. Even now, are they not engaged in the thrilling adventure known amongst their fellow-émigrés as "Escaping out of the bloody clutches of the Bolsheviks"? And before them, a few weeks hence, lies another thrilling adventure in the salons of Paris, London and Washington, recounting the terrors and perils of their escape.

That it was an escape *de luxe* in an International sleeper, with excellent beds, dining-car and porter inclusive, will be omitted from their tales. Other details will be inserted however—little figments about Bolshevik murders, rapes and robberies. Every émigré must have his atrocity. At all costs his escape must be harrowing and dramatic. Otherwise no thrill for the jaded palates of the Western democracies.

Supplied with Bolshevik passports, stamped with a Bolshevik seal, these émigrés were driven to the station by Bolshevik cabmen; aided by Bolshevik porters they boarded this train, whose conductor, brakeman and engineer belonged to the Bolshevik faith. Riding now over a track tended by Bolshevik laborers, guarded by Bolshevik soldiers, guided by Bolshevik switchmen, and fed by Bolshevik waiters, they while away their hours in cursing these self-same Bolsheviks as bandits and cutthroats. A curious spectacle! Damning, reviling, execrating the very ones upon whom they depend for food, shelter, travel—for the very breath they draw. For every member of this train-crew is a Bolshevik—all except the porter (*provodnik*).

He had the soul of a flunkey, and the creed of a monarchist. Tho of peasant origin, he was more Czaristic than the Czar himself. All the émigrés he still addressed as "my lords!" (*barin*).

"You see, my lords!" he said, "we dark people are a lazy, shiftless lot. Give us a bottle of vodka and we are happy. We don't need more freedom. We need a club over us to keep us at work. We need a Czar."

The émigrés were delighted with him. He was to them a perpetual source of comfort—a flaming light in the Bolshevik darkness.

"In this honest *mujik*," they declared, "you see the soul of the millions of Russian peasants, content to serve their master, to obey the church and love the Czar. True, a few have been misled by Bolshevik fantasies, but only a few. What have these millions of patient, plodding folks to do with that madness festering back there in Moscow and Petrograd?"

This seemed plausible. For out here it is hard even for us to sustain our interest in the Revolution at high pitch. Great concerns, political and personal, are dwarfed by the vastness of the panorama unfolding before our eyes on this, the longest railway journey in the world.

We pass over the wide stretching grain-fields of Central Russia, across the vast bridges spanning the broad rivers flowing north to the Arctic, thru the winding passes of the Urals, into the shadows of the giant virgin forest (*taiga*), almost unblazed by man, then out again upon the steppelands of Siberia.

Thru the day we watch on the horizon the peasant huts, huddled together for protection against wolves, and winds blowing from the frozen *tundras*; or take our places in the long lines that obtain hot water for tea from the tanks, buying bread and eggs and fish from the peasant women. At evening we watch the wood-burning locomotive flinging spark showers from its stack like a comet. Night after night we go to sleep with the wheels grinding beneath our car, and every morning we wake to see the track in two glistening ribbons of steel, still unrolling itself before the eastward plunging engine.

Slowly these immensities steal over us with mesmeric influence, creating the feeling the Russians call *prostor*, a sense of space and vastness. Under its spell things once mighty and imperative, become trivial and unimportant. Even the Revolution relaxes its grip upon us. May it not after all be a ferment confined to railwaymen and the industrial workers of the cities?

Back there the Revolution was an insistent fact, assailing us in eye and ear with banners and battle-cries, parades and assemblages. Out here on the Siberian steppes we see no evidence of it. We see woodsmen with axes, drivers with horses, women with baskets, a few soldiers with guns; but beyond a few tattered remnants of red flags flapping on poles there are no marks of the Revolution.

"Is the revolutionary spirit as frayed out as those faded flags?" we ask. "Are the émigrés right in summing up the aspirations of the Russian peasant as love and service to his master, his church and the Little Father? Is this after all 'Holy Russia'?"

In the midst of our ruminations—Crash! Bang! The brakes clutch the wheels, grinding and grating, sending a shiver thru the car and hurling us out of our seats. The train comes abruptly to a standstill.

Everybody stares out of the window, asking excitedly: "Washout? Cave-in? Bridge gone?" But nothing appears save the same sere, level steppe-land with drifts of snow, relics of the winter.

A Bolshevik Hold-up!

Suddenly from behind a snow-bank a figure shoots up, waves a signal behind him, and comes running violently towards the train. From behind a copse another form darts out and follows after. From other snow-piles and bushes and from the far horizon, more and more figures keep emerging, until the whole plain is dotted with men racing headlong toward the train. Like the ground sown with dragon-teeth, in a trice these dead waste-lands spring to life, and teem with men in arms.

"My God! Look! Look!" exclaimed one of the painted ladies. "Guns! They carry guns!" The phantasies of her imagination have materialized. Here in flesh and blood are the Bolsheviks of her tales. They have become realities, carrying in their hands guns and grenades, and on their faces a most unpleasant look. The foremost runner checks his steps, cups his hands to his mouth, and bellows out to us, "Windows down."

No one argues the point. Along the whole train the windows go banging down. So do the spirits of the émigrés, finding little cheer in the faces of these oncoming men. They are a harsh, determined lot. Many of them are grimy, nearly black. All of them have black looks for the train. By mien and gesture they clearly indicate that their weapons have a distinct bearing upon our case.

We have no inkling of our offense. We only know that some thunderbolt has stopped our train, and on all sides we face a cordon of violent-talking men. We catch wild words about "killing the bloody tyrant" and, as the face of the florid lady appears at the window, jeering cries of "Hey! Mrs. Rasputin!" She is certain that the ruffians are debating whether to take us out and murder us one by one, or destroy us *en masse* by burning or blowing up the train.

The suspense is racking. I volunteer to investigate the situation, and start to raise a window. When half way open, I gaze into the muzzle of a gun thrust up into my face. A big peasant at the other end of the gun growls, "Put the window down quick or I'll shoot." He looks as though, he would shoot, but my year in Russia has taught me that he won't; that the peasant is uncivilized enough to retain an aversion to killing a human being. So I do not shut my window, but thrust my head out and address the big peasant as *"Tovarish."*

"Don't you *tovarish* me, you Counter-Revolutionist!" he snorted back. "You drinker of the people's blood! You monarchist, you Czarist!"

Such were the usual epithets bestowed upon the enemies of the Revolution. But I had never heard them rolled into one broadside and shot forth with such malice. Hastily I produced a Soviet credential vouching for me and bearing the signature of Chicherin.[1] But reading was not this peasant's forte. The next man, a heavy set, scowling fellow, took it and scanned it critically.

"Forged!" was his instant verdict.

I passed out a credential signed by Trotsky. "Forged!" he repeated. I followed up with a document issued by the Bolshevik Railway Commissar. The same laconic comment "Forged!" Still obdurate, was he? As a climax I would play my trump card. I produced a letter signed by Nikolai Lenin. Not only his signature but all the letter was written out in full by Lenin's own hand. My inquisitor scrutinized it intently, while I watched to see the magic name of Lenin transform the thunder-cloud on his face into a smile. I was certain that this would settle the matter. And it did. Not in my favor, however, but against me, as I discerned by the set of his jaw. I had overplayed myself in this matter of credentials.

In his mind my case was clear. Here is a plotter up to some deviltry against the Revolution. To ingratiate himself with the Bolsheviks, he displays a grand array of Soviet documents pretending to come from even Lenin himself. This marks him as no ordinary spy. We must act at once!

He carried my sheaf of papers over to a tall man dismounting from his horse. "That's Andrey Petrovich. He will know all about these papers," declared the big peasant who had run the muzzle of his gun into my face. "He just got back from

---

[1] Georgy V. Chicherin (1872–1936) was the Soviet commissar of foreign affairs.

Moscow. He knows all the Bolsheviks and how they write their names. He knows the Counter-Revolutionists, and all their tricks. Those devils can't fool Andrey Petrovich."

Kuntz and I sincerely prayed that Andrey Petrovich would prove as wise as his reputation. And happily for us he did. He did know the leaders of the Bolsheviks. He knew their signatures. In a few questions he tested our knowledge. Satisfied, he shook hands with us heartily, greeted us as *tovarishe*, invited us to come outside where he would ask us a hundred questions.

"But we have a hundred questions to ask *you*," we rejoined, opening up on him forthwith. "Where did all these men suddenly spring from? Why is this train held up? What do you mean by this display of arms?"

"One question at a time," he replied, laughing. "First: These men are miners from the great coal mines less than half a mile away, and peasants from the villages. Thousands more will be along directly. Second: We grabbed up these guns and grenades fifteen minutes ago, not for display but for immediate use. Third: We held up this Trans-Siberian Express to take off of it the Czar and the Royal Family."

"Czar and Royal Family! On this train? Here?" we shouted.

"We don't know that for sure," replied Andrey Petrovich, "all we know is that about twenty minutes ago came a telegram from Omsk saying: *Release of Nicholas just effected by clique of officers. Probably escaping with staff on Express. Plan to set up Czardom at Irkutsk. Stop him dead or alive.*"

(So it was the Czar whom the crowd meant by "bloody tyrant" and the Czarina whom they were calling "Mrs. Rasputin!")

The Czar's Surprise Party Disappointed

"We sent two men running to the villages and two to the mines, shouting the telegram," continued Andrei Petrovich. "Every man dropped his tools, snatched up his gun, and rushed for the train. A thousand here now, and they won't stop coming till night. You see how deeply we feel for our Czar! Only twenty minutes advance notice and we got this nice big reception party ready for him. He likes military displays. Well, here it is. Not in regulation style, but quite impressive, is it not?"

It was! Never have I seen such a beweaponed set of men. They were like moving arsenals. In their hands were missiles enough to blow a thousand Czars into eternity, and in their hearts and eyes vengeance enough to annihilate ten thousand.

But there seemed to be no Czar to annihilate.

"Just as I thought," Andrey Petrovich went on, "another ruse of the Counter-Revolution. That telegram is an act of provocators against the Soviet. They want it to demoralize the workings of the mines. And it will. Our men are too excited now to do anything more today. There will be other telegrams like this in the days to come. By crying out: 'The Czar is escaping, the Czar is escaping,' they think the men will get disgusted with false alarms. Then, when we have become careless they will try to slip the Czar through. But they don't know our men here. For a chance to get a pot-shot at the Czar they will turn out every day in the year."

The zest with which the searching party went through the cars left no doubt as to their attitude towards the Little Father. They combed the train from end to end, opening trunks, ransacking beds, even shifting the logs on the engine tender to see if by chance His Imperial Majesty might be hidden in the woodpile.

There were two white-bearded old peasants who did a little investigating on their own account. They would run their guns up under a sleeper, ram their bayonets around and then withdraw them, shaking their heads sadly. The Czar of all the Russias they hoped to find riding the bumpers. Each time disappointed, they would hope for better luck at the next car and repeat the prodding. But there was no Czar, and so their bayonets did not puncture him.

But something else they did puncture—the hoary old tradition about the deep love and devotion of the Russian *mujik* to the Little Father. That pleasant myth could not survive the spectacle of these two devout, benign old peasants, plunging their bayonets into dark corners, and drawing them out again, aggrieved that on them were no fatal signs of the Little Father.

We Substitute for the Czar

Andrey Petrovich was a man of resources. Having no Czar for his men, he used Kuntz and me as substitutes.

"It is a strange world, *tovarishe*, full of strange surprises," he said, addressing his comrades. "We came down here to get the greatest criminal in history. Not a man here but has known pain or misery through the Czar. But instead of finding our worst enemy, we find here our best friends. This train, instead of carrying the ideas of our autocracy, is carrying the ideas of our Revolution—and carrying them to America. Long live the Revolution! Long live our American comrades!"

There was a riot of cheer-giving, hand-shaking and picture-taking and we were off again. But not for long. Again we were halted by a storming mass. And again and again. It was in vain to protest that the Czar was not aboard. Even the documents attesting this they waved aside as counter-revolutionary forgeries. Each crowd must reassure itself thru its own search. Thus the fastest express upon the Trans-Siberian became the slowest.

At Marinsk, the Commissar of Transport gave a new turn to events, by despatching this telegram:

To all Soviets:

Kuntz and Williams, General Organizers of the Red Army, are on Train Two. I ask that representatives of the Soviets meet with them for consultation.
Sadovnikov.

The telegram was read to the crowds assembling at every station to meet the express. With their appetites and implements whetted for a Czar, suddenly two comrades were handed them. It called for a swift reversal of their emotions, but they did nobly. We rode into each station in a storm of greetings. The new detachments of the Red Army saluted, the commissars solemnly laid before us their problems, the throngs pushed forward to gaze upon us as military geniuses.

It was embarrassing but illuminating. We got a glimpse of a new civilization in the making, the future in the act of being born. In one town the foundations had just been laid—the peasants marching over had joined the workers in one central Soviet. In another they had scarcely got to the foundations—the intelligentsia were all on strike. In many centers the new structure was well along, the Soviet schools were filled, the peasants were bringing the grain to market, the factories were turning out goods, as well as oratory. The exhibits, tho often crude and incomplete, testified to the release of real creative forces in the masses.

We pointed this out to the émigrés, but they were busy weaving fictions for the Western democracies, and the facts irritated them. Some became sullen and suspicious, treating us as apostates and traitors to our class. Others fatuously returned to their usual themes: the golden days of Czardom, the "darkness" of the Russian masses, the sheer idiocy of the Bolsheviks.

Chapter 14

THE RED CONVICTS OF CHERM

The émigrés on our train had many points of conflict. But on one point they agreed: the grave danger lying ahead of us in Cherm, the great penal colony of Siberia.

"Fifteen thousand convicts in Cherm," they said.

"Criminals of the worst stripe—thugs, thieves and murderers. The only way to deal with them is to put them in the mines and keep them there at the point of the gun. Even so, it is too much liberty for them. Every week there are scores of thefts and stabbings. Now most of these devils have been turned loose, and they have turned Bolshevik. It always was a hell-hole. What it is now God only knows."

It was a raw bleak morning on the first of May, when we rode into Cherm (Chermkhovo). A curtain of dust, blown up by a wind from the north, hung over the place. Curled up in our compartment half asleep, we woke to the cry, "They're coming! They're coming!" We peered thru the window. Far as we could see nothing was coming but a whirling cloud of dust. Then thru the dust we made out a glint of red, the gray of glittering steel, and vague, black masses moving forward.

Behind drawn curtains, the émigrés went frantically hiding jewels and money, or sat paralyzed with terror. Outside, the cinders crunched under the tread of the hob-nailed boots. In what mood "they" were coming, with what lust in their blood, what weapons in their hands, no one knew. We knew only that these were the dread convicts of Cherm, "murderers, thugs and thieves"—and they were heading for the parlor-cars.

Slowly they lurched along, the wind filling their eyes with dust and soot, and wrestling with a huge blood-red banner they carried. Then came a lull in the wind, dropping the dust screen and bringing to view a motley crew.

Their clothes were black from the mines and tied up with strings, their faces grim, and grimy. Some were ox-like hulks of men. Some were gnarled and knotted, warped by a thousand gales. Here were the cannibal-convicts of Tolstoy, slant-browed and brutal-jawed. Here was Dostoevsky's "House of the Dead." With limping steps, cheeks slashed and eyes gouged out they came, marked by bullet, knife and mine disaster, some cursed by an evil birth. But few, if any, were weaklings.

By a long, gruelling process the weak had been killed off. These thousands were the survivors of tens of thousands, driven out on the gray highroad to Cherm. Thru sleet and snow, winter blast and summer blaze they had staggered along. Torture-chambers had racked their limbs. Gendarmes' sabers had cracked their skulls. Iron fetters had cut their flesh. Cossacks' whips had gashed their backs, and Cossacks' hoofs had pounded them to earth.

Like their bodies their souls, too, had been knouted. Like a blood-hound the law had hung on their trail, driving them into dungeons, driving them to this dismal outpost of Siberia, driving them off the face of the earth into its caverns, to strain like beasts, digging the coal in the dark, and handing it up to those who live in the light.

Now out of the mines they come marching up into the light. Guns in hand, flying red flags of revolt, they are loose in the highways, moving forward like a great herd, the incarnation of brute strength. In their path lie the warm, luxurious parlor-cars—another universe, a million miles removed. Now it is just a few inches away, within their grasp. Three minutes, and they could leave this train sacked from end to end as though gutted by a cyclone. How sweet for once to glut themselves! And how easy! One swift lunge forward. One furious onset.

But their actions show neither haste nor frenzy. Stretching their banners on the ground they range themselves in a crescent, massed in the center, facing the train. Now we can scan those faces. Sullen, defiant, lined deep with hate, brutalized by toil. On all of them the ravages of vice and terror. In all of them an infinitude of pain and torment, the poignant sorrow of the world.

But in their eyes is a strange light—a look of exaltation. Or is it the glitter of revenge? A blow for a blow. The law has given them a thousand blows. Is it their turn now? Will they avenge the long years of bitterness?

The Comrade Convicts

A hand touches our shoulder. We turn to look into the faces of two burly miners. They tell us that they are the Commissars of Cherm. At the same time they signal the banner bearers, and the red standards rise up before our eyes. On one in large letters is the old familiar slogan: *Proletarians, arise! You have nothing to lose but your chains.* On another: *We stretch out our hands to the miners in all lands. Greetings to our comrades throughout the world.*

"Hats off!" shouts the commissar. Awkwardly they bare their heads and stand, caps in hand. Then slowly begins the hymn of the International.

> Arise, ye prisoners of starvation!
> Arise, ye wretched of the earth!
> For justice thunders condemnation,
> A better world's in birth.
> No more tradition's chains shall bind you;
> Arise, ye slaves! No more in thrall.

The world shall rise on new foundations.
You have been naught: you shall be all.

I have heard the streets of cities around the world, ringing to the "International,"[1] rising from massed columns of the marchers. I have heard rebel students send it floating through college halls. I have heard the International on the voices of 2,000 Soviet delegates, blending with four military bands, go rolling through the pillars of the Tauride Palace. But none of these singers looked the *"wretched of the earth."* They were the sympathizers or representatives of the wretched. These miner-convicts of Cherm were the wretched themselves, most wretched of all. Wretched in garments and looks, and even in voice.

With broken voices, and out of tune they sang, but in their singing one felt the pain and protest of the broken of all ages: the sigh of the captive, the moan of the galley-slave lashed to the oar, the groan of the serf stretched on the wheel, the cries from the cross, the stake and the gibbet, the anguish of myriads of the condemned, welling up out of the long reaches of the past.

These convicts were in apostolic succession to the suffering of the centuries. They were the excommunicate of society, mangled, crushed by its heavy hand, and hurled down into the darkness of this pit.

Now out of the pit rises this victory-hymn of the vanquished. Long bludgeoned into silence, they break into song—a song not of complaint, but of conquest. No longer are they social outcasts, but citizens. More than that—Makers of a New Society! Their limbs are numb with cold. But their hearts are on fire. Harsh and rugged faces are touched with a sunrise glow. Dull eyes grow bright. Defiant ones grow soft. In them lies the transfiguring vision of the toilers of all nations bound together in one big fraternity—The International.

"Long live the International! Long live the American workers!" they shout. Then opening their ranks, they thrust forward one of their number. He is of giant stature, a veritable Jean Valjean[2] of a man, with a Jean Valjean of a heart.

"In the name of the miners of Cherm," he says, "we greet the comrades on this train! In the old days how different it was! Day after day, trains rolled thru here, but we dared not come near them. Some of us did wrong, we know. But many of us were brutally wronged. Had there been justice, some of us would be on this train and some on this train would be in the mines.

"But most of the passengers didn't know there were any mines. In their warm beds, they didn't know that way down below were thousands of moles, digging coal to put heat in the cars and steam in the engine. They didn't know that hundreds of

---

[1] The *Internationale* is a popular left-wing anthem that dates back to 1864.

[2] Jean Valjean is the main character in Victor Hugo's *Les Miserables*.

us were starved to death, flogged to death or killed by falling rock. If they did know, they didn't care. To them we were dregs and outcasts. To them we were nothing at all.

"Now we are everything! We have joined the International. We fall in today with the armies of labor in all lands. We are in the vanguard of them all. We, who were slaves, have been made freest of all.

"Not our freedom alone we want, comrades, but freedom for the workers thruout the world. Unless they, too, are free, we cannot keep the freedom we have to own the mines and run them ourselves.

"Already the greedy hands of the imperialists of the world are reaching out across the seas. Only the hands of the workers of the world can tear those clutches from our throats."

The range and insight of the man's mind was amazing. So amazed was Kuntz that his own speech in reply faltered. My hold on Russian quite collapsed. Our part in this affair, we felt, was wan and pallid. But these miners did not feel so. They came into the breach with a cheer for the International, and another for the International Orchestra.

The "Orchestra" comprised four violins played by four prisoners of war; a Czech, a Hungarian, a German and an Austrian. Captured on the eastern front, from camp to camp they had been relayed along to these convict-mines in Siberia. Thousands of miles from home! Still farther in race and breeding from these Russian masses drawn from the soil. But caste and creed and race had fallen before the Revolution. To their convict-miner comrades here in this dark hole they played, as in happier days they might have played at a music festival under the garden lights of Berlin or Budapest. The flaming passion in their veins crept into the strings of their violins and out into the heart-strings of their hearers.

The whole conclave—miners, musicians and visitors, Teutons, Slavs and Americans—became one. All barriers were down as the commissars came pressing up to greet us. One huge hulking fellow, with fists like pile drivers, took our hands into his. Twice he tried to speak and twice he choked. Unable to put his sentiments of brotherhood into words, he put it into a sudden terrific grip of his hands. I can feel that grip yet.

For the honor of Cherm he was anxious that its first public function should be conducted in proper fashion. Out of the past must have flashed the memory of some occasion where the program of the day included gifts as well as speeches. Disappearing for a time, he came running back with two sticks of dynamite—the gifts of Cherm to the two Americans. We demurred. He insisted. We pointed out that a chance collision and delegates might disappear together with dynamite—a total loss to the International. The crowd laughed. Like a giant child he was hurt and puzzled. Then he laughed, too.

The second violinist, a blue-eyed lad from Vienna, was always laughing. Exile had not quenched his love of fun. In honor of the American visitors he insisted upon a *Jazze-Americane*. So he called it, but never before or since have I heard so weird a melody. He played with legs and arms as well as bow, dancing round, up and down to the great delight of the crowd.

Our love-feast at last was broken in upon by the clanging signal-bell. One more round of hand-clasps and we climbed aboard the train as the orchestra caught up the refrain:

> It is the final conflict,
> Let each stand in his place;
> The Internationale—
> Shall be the human race.

There was no grace or outward splendor in this meeting. It was ugliness unrelieved—except for one thing: the presence of a tremendous vitality. It was a revelation of the drive of the Revolution. Even into this sub-cellar of civilization it had penetrated, into these regions of the damned it had come like a trumpet-blast, bringing down the walls of their charnel-house. Out of it they had rushed, not with bloodshot eyes, slavering mouths and daggers drawn, but crying for truth and justice, with songs of solidarity upon their lips, and on their banners the watchwords of a new world.

The Émigrés Unmoved

All this was lost upon the émigrés. Not one ray of wonder did they let penetrate the armor of their class-interest. Their former fears gave way to sneers:

"There is Bolshevism for you! It makes statesmen out of jail-birds. Great sight, isn't it? Convicts parading the streets instead of digging in the mines. That's what we get out of Revolution."

We pointed to other things that came out of Revolution—order, restraint and good will. But the émigrés could not see. They would not see.

"That is for the moment," they laughed. "When the excitement is over they'll go back to stealing, drinking and killing." To these émigrés it was at best a passing ecstasy that would disappear with our disappearing train.

Leaning out from the car steps we waved farewell to the hundreds of huge grimy hands waving farewell to us. Our eyes long clung to the scene. In the last glimpse we saw the men of Cherm with heads still bared to the cutting wind, the rhythmic rise and fall of the arms of "Jean Valjean," the red banner with *"Greetings to Our Comrades throughout the World,"* and a score of hands still stretched out towards the train. Then the scene faded away in the dust and distance.

* * *

Two years later Jo Redding came back to Detroit after working in Cherm and watching the Revolution working there. He reports its permanent effects. Thefts and murders were reduced almost to zero. Snarling animals became men. Tho just released from irons, they put themselves under the iron discipline of the Soviet armies. Lawless under the old law, they became the writers and defenders of a new law. Men who had so many wrongs of their own to brood over now assumed the wrongs of the world. They had vast programs to release their energies upon, vast visions to light their minds.

To the rich and the privileged, to those who sit on roof-gardens or ride in parlor- cars, the Revolution is a thing of terror and horror. It is the Antichrist. But to the despised and disinherited, the Revolution is like the Messiah coming to "preach good tidings to the poor; to proclaim release of the captives and to set at liberty them that are bruised." No longer can Dostoevsky's convict mutter, "We are not alive, though we are living. We are not in our graves, though we are dead." In the House of the Dead, Revolution is Resurrection.

Chapter 15

THE VLADIVOSTOK SOVIET AND ITS LEADERS

THE limits of the Revolution—what were they? We had seen this Revolution, loosed by the city-workers, drive deeper and deeper down, taking ever lower and lower strata of the people within its grip. When it laid hold of the convicts of Cherm it reached bottom. It could go no further vertically. How far could it reach horizontally? Would it prove the same power here in these far-flung outposts on the Pacific that it was back there upon the Atlantic? Would the Revolution show the same strong pulse-beat in these extremities as it did in the heart of Russia?

In a world of Soviets we had moved across the great, slow, north-flowing rivers, the Urals, the *taiga* forests, and the steppes. Trainmen and miners had spoken of their Soviets, peasants and fishermen had greeted us with red banners in the name of theirs. We had conferred with the Soviet of Central Siberia and the Far East Soviet. This whole Amur district was dotted with Soviets. Now, as we stepped from the train at Vladivostok, we were to find a replica of the Soviet we had left at Petrograd, seven thousand miles away.

In six months the Soviet had struck its roots deep into the Russian soil, crowded out all rivals, resisted the shock of every attack, and now held undisputed sway from the Arctic Ocean on the north to the Black Sea on the south, from Narva looking upon the Atlantic all the way to Vladivostok here on its promontory looking into the Pacific.

Vladivostok is a city built on hills, with streets as steep as Alpine paths. But with an extra horse attached to the *droshky's*[1] shafts, we rattled over the cobbles as swiftly as we did along the level wood-paved prospekts of Petrograd. The main highway, *Svetlanskaya*, lies folded up and down across the hills, flanked by the commercial houses of the French and English, the International Harvester, and the buildings of the new rulers of Russia—the Red Fleet and the Soviet of Workmen's Deputies.

Massive fortresses frowned from all the hills around, but they were harmless as dove-cotes. In the first days of the war they had been dismantled, and the great guns shipped to the Eastern Front. A defenseless city, into which extends a peculiar tongue of water called the *Golden Horn*. Here the Allied battleships, uninvited, rode at anchor. Their flags were a welcome sight to the fleeing émigrés at the end of the long Siberian

---

[1] A *droshky* is a light, four-wheeled carriage.

journey. With a sigh of relief here they settled down. Soon, they believed, the Revolution would be over. Then they would return and take up their old life again in Russia.

A City of Refuge for the Émigrés

The city was thronged with evicted landowners dreaming of their estates, their retinue of servants, and the idle feasting of bygone days; officers telling of the former discipline, when soldiers jumped into the gutter at their presence and stood rigid in salute while beaten in the face; speculators longing for the return of the good old times of war profiteering and patrioteering, to the tune of 50, 100, and 500 percent. Gone are all those gilded fabulous fortunes. The Revolution wrecked them along with the arbitrary power of the officers and the dreams of the landowners.

As a port of exit, Vladivostok was full of Russian émigrés coming out. As a port of entry, it was full of Allied capitalists going in. It was a key to the El Dorado[2] beyond. With its vast unexploited natural riches and labor power, Siberia was a loadstone drawing the agents of capital from around the world. From London and Tokyo, from the Paris Bourse and Wall Street, they came flocking hither, lured by dazzling prospects.

But between them and the fisheries, gold-mines, and forests they found a big barrier. They found the Soviet. The Russian workingman refused to be exploited by the Russian capitalist. At the same time he refused to allow his blood and sweat to be minted into bonanza dividends for the benefit of foreign bankers. The Soviet was the instrument of this refusal to all exploiters.

Meeting the same obstacles as the Russian bourgeoisie, the Allied exploiters had the same reaction. They lent a ready ear to the cursings and ravings of their Russian brethren, who saw the Soviet and its members as the very spawn of hell.

It was in this circle that the Allied consuls, officers, YMCA, and intelligence men largely lived, moved and had their being. They rarely got outside of it. They were in revolutionary Russia, but out of touch with the Revolution. And quite naturally. Peasants and workers knew little French or English or how to dress well or order dinner.

Not that Allied society was without "information." Their Russian bourgeois friends and their own prejudices gave it to them. Very direct and dogmatic, it passed current in phrases like:

"The Soviet is made up mainly of ex-criminals."
"Four-fifths of the Bolsheviks are Jews."
"These Revolutionists are just ordinary robbers."
"The Red Armies are mercenary and will run at the first shot of a gun."

---

[2] This is a reference to the ideal place in Voltaire's *Candide*.

"The dark, ignorant masses are swayed by their leaders, and their leaders are corrupt."

"The Czar may have had his faults, but Russia needs an iron hand."

"The Soviet is tottering, and will not last longer than two weeks at the outside."

The most cursory investigation would reveal the falsehood of these phrases. One needed but to parrot them, however, to be acclaimed a man of deep insight.

The man who could add, "I don't give a damn what others say about Lenin and Trotsky, I know they are German agents," was hailed as a fellow of spirit, a true soldier of democracy.

There were some honest seekers after light. The genial commander of the Asiatic Squadron was indiscreet enough to invite me to dinner on his flagship the *Brooklyn*. The American Consul also tried hard to break through the circle of lies. Awaiting word from Washington, however, he withheld visé to my passport. So I was marooned for seven weeks in Vladivostok.

As I grew more and more outspoken in my sympathies with the workers and peasants, the bourgeoisie grew ever more hostile towards me. Thrown now into close contact with the Soviet I had opportunity to observe and share its work, and to count many of its members as my friends.

A Few Students Aid the Soviets

First among these was Constantin Sukhanov.[3] When the March Revolution broke out, he was a student of Natural History in the University of Petrograd. He hastened back to Vladivostok, a Menshevik. After the Kornilov adventure he became a Bolshevik, and an ardent one. He was small in stature, but great in energy. Night and day he toiled, snatching an occasional wink of sleep in a small room above the Soviet, ready at a moment's notice to spring to the saddle or the typewriter. While his face was habitually drawn tight in lines of thought, he would often explode in a contagious burst of laughter. His speech was terse, on occasion flaming. But a bare fire-brand would never have done in such a powder-magazine as Vladivostok. By skill and tact he pulled the Soviet out of many ugly positions, into which its enemies had jockeyed it.

Respected by everybody, even by his bitter political opponents, Sukhanov was chosen President of the Soviet. He was thus the tip of the spearhead that the Bolshevik movement thrust out into the Pacific and the eastern world. He found himself, at 24, facing tasks that would have taxed the resources of a veteran diplomat.

But statecraft was in his blood. His father was a functionary of the old régime, charged with the arrest of Revolutionists. Among those he had found plotting against

---

[3] Konstantin A. Sukhanov (1894–1918) was a very active Bolshevik official in Vladivostok in 1917 and 1918. He was captured by the Whites and executed.

the Czar were his own daughter, and this son, Constantin. Constantin was arrested. Bitter and cynical, the father had faced his son across the table of the tribunal.

It was by grace of his Imperial Majesty, Czar Nicholas II, that the elder Sukhanov had sat in the magistrate's place, with the white, blue, and red flag of the autocracy behind the dais. When we arrived in Vladivostok the red flag of the Revolution had replaced it. Yet we found a Sukhanov sitting in the judgment seat. This time it was the son, Constantin, now President of the Vladivostok Soviet by grace of their Republican Majesties, the worker, peasant and sailor citizens of the Russian Soviet Republic.

Curious reversal of the Revolution! Just as the younger Sukhanov had been caught conspiring against the rule of the Czar, now Sukhanov, the elder, was found plotting against the rule of the Soviet. Once more across the tribunal the two men faced each other: father against son, Counter-Revolutionist against Revolutionist, Monarchist against Socialist. But this time the son was the judge, the father the culprit. Once only was Constantin Sukhanov derelict in his revolutionary duties. He refused to imprison his father!

Sukhanov's constant aide was the student Sebertsev. There were also three girl-students *(kursists)*, Zoya, Tanya and Zoya, respectively, secretaries of the Bolshevik Party, the Finance Department, and the Soviet organ *The Peasant and Worker;* and respectively daughters of an officer, a priest and a merchant. Their bourgeois life they entirely renounced. They became one with the proletarians. With proletarian incomes they thought in proletarian terms. They lived like proletarians. Their home now was two bare rooms which they called "the Commune." For beds they had soldier-cots, straw-pallets laid on planks instead of springs.

These students fitted the picture of the Russian student of tradition. One night, when the strain of trying to talk in the Russian language was tying my tongue and brain into knots, Sebertsev said: "We have all been to the university, we can talk in Latin!" But how many American college graduates can read even the Latin on their diplomas? These Russian students not only talked Latin but submitted Latin verses for my approval. I made a strategic retreat upon Russian!

Leaders Out of the Rank and File

Outside of these students the members of the Vladivostok Soviet were workingmen—mechanics, longshoremen, railwaymen, etc. But they were Russian workingmen; while using the hammer, the sickle and axe, they had used their brains. For this the heavy hand of the Czar had fallen on them. Some had been jailed, others driven out as wanderers over the earth.

From exile they returned at the call of the Revolution. Utkin[4] and Jordan came back from Australia, speaking English; Antonov from Naples, speaking Italian. Melnikov,[5] Nikeferov[6] and Preminsky emerged from their prison-cells speaking French. This trio had turned their jail into a university. They had specialized in mathematics, and now were experts in calculus, plotting graphs as well as they had plotted revolution.

Seven years they were bound together in jail. Now they were free, each to go his own way. But the long hard years had forged around their hearts ties more binding than the iron chains around their limbs. They were together in death, and now in life they could not be divided. In mind, however, they were much divided, expounding their rival creeds to each other with terrific energy. Yet, however wide afield they went in theory, in action they were a unit. Melnikov's party did not then support the Soviet, but his two comrades did. So he followed them into the service of the Soviet, as Commissar of Post and Telegraph.

In the soul of Melnikov had been waged some big battle, which put furrows deep in his face, and left deep in his eyes the marks of pain. But in that face victory and a great serenity were written. His eyes sparkled, and a smile always flickered on his lips. When things grew blacker he smiled the more.

Little help the Soviet got from the intelligentsia. They declared a boycott against the Soviet until the workingmen should completely change their program. In open meeting they proclaimed a policy of sabotage.

Bitter and sarcastic was the retort shot back by a miner: "You pride yourselves on your knowledge and skill! But where did you get it? From us. At the price of our sweat and blood. In school and university you sat at your desks while we slaved in the dark of the mines and the smoke of the mills. Now we ask you to help us. And you say to us: 'Give up *your* program and take our program: then we will help you.' And we say to you: 'We will not give up our program. We shall get along without you.'"

Supreme audacity in these workingmen, tyros in government, taking over the administration of a territory large as France and rich as India, beset by hordes of scheming imperialists, challenged by a thousand tasks!

---

[4] Pyotr Vasilyevich Utkin was a revolutionary who had learned English in Australia and who would later be killed by the Whites in the Russian Civil War.

[5] Konstantin Melnikov (1890–1974) was a Bolshevik revolutionary who would later be a notable architect in the Constructivist movement.

[6] Pyotr Nikeforov was a returning revolutionary émigré who later wrote a book about Vladivostok.

Chapter 16

THE LOCAL SOVIET AT WORK

The Vladivostok Soviet had taken power without shedding a drop of blood. That was easy. But the task now facing it was hard—terribly hard and complex.

The first problem to grapple with was the economic. The dislocation of industry through war and Revolution, the homecoming of the soldiers, and the employers' lockouts, filled the streets with the workless. The Soviet saw the menace of these idle hands and started to open the factories. The management was placed in the hands of the workingmen themselves, and credit was furnished by the soviet.

The leaders voluntarily limited their own wages. By decree of the Central Russian Soviet the maximum salary of any Soviet official was fixed at 500 rubles a month. The Vladivostok commissars, pointing out the lower cost of living in the Far East, scaled theirs down to 300 rubles a month. After this, when anyone felt the itching desire for a fatter pay envelope, he was liable to be asked: "Do you want more pay than Lenin or Sukhanov?" This was unanswerable.

Soviet Organizes Industry

As soon as the workmen found the factories in their hands there came a change in their morale. Under Kerensky the tendency was to elect lenient foremen. Under their own government, the Soviet, they elected foremen who put discipline into the shop and raised production. The first time I met Krasnoshchekov, the head of the Far East Soviet, he was pessimistic.

"For every word I say to the bourgeoisie against their sabotage," he said, "I say ten to the workingmen against their slackness. But I believe a change is coming."

When I saw him at the end of June, 1918, he was in a happy mood. The change had come. Six factories, he said, were producing more than ever before.

In the so-called "American Works," the wheels, frames and brakes of cars, shipped from the United States, were assembled, and the cars sent out over the Trans-Siberian Railway. These shops had been hotbeds of trouble, one disturbance following on the heels of another. The 6,000 workmen on the payroll had been turning out but 18 cars a day. The Soviet Committee closed the plant and reorganized the shops, reducing the force to 1,800 men. In the underframe section, instead of 1,400 there were now 350; but by means of short-cuts introduced by the workers themselves, the output of that department was increased. Altogether, the 1,800 men on the new payroll were now turning out 12 cars a day—an efficiency increase of more than 100 per cent per man.

One day I was standing with Sukhanov on the hills overlooking the shops. He was listening to the clank of cranes and the stamp of trip-hammers ringing up from the valley.

"That seems to be sweet music to your ears," I said.

"Yes," he replied, "the old Revolutionists used to make a noise with bombs. This is the noise of the new Revolutionists, hammering out the new social order."

The strongest ally of the Soviet was the Union of Miners. It organized the unemployed into little Soviets of 50 and 100, equipped them, and sent them out to the mines along the great Amur. These enterprises were highly successful. Each man was panning out from 50 to 100 rubles of gold a day. The question of pay arose. One of the miners unearthed the slogan: "To every man the full product of his labors." It at once achieved tremendous popularity with the miners, who declared their loyalty to this basic Socialist principle. Nothing, they said, could induce them to depart from it.

The Soviet held a different view. There was a deadlock. Instead of using the historic method of settling the dispute by bombs and troops, the workingmen fought it out on the floor of the Soviet. The miners capitulated to the logic of the Soviet. Their wages were fixed at 15 rubles per day, with a bonus for extra production. In a short time 26 *poods* (there are 36 pounds in a pood) of gold were accumulated at headquarters. Against this reserve the Soviet issued paper money. The seal was a sickle and a hammer, and the design showed a peasant and a worker clasping hands, with the riches of the Far East streaming out over the world.

The Soviet fell heir to a white elephant in the shape of the *"Military Port."* This was a huge plant built for military and naval purposes—a monument to the inefficiency of the old régime. It had carried on its payroll as fine a line of grafting officials and favorites as ever decorated an establishment of the Czar. The barnacles on the ships of the Volunteer Fleet were a consequence of those on the payroll. The Soviet immediately scraped off these eminent barnacles but retained the old manager as chief technician. The proletarians recognized the necessity of experts and not finding them in their own ranks, they were ready to pay big salaries for them. The working class set out to buy brains just as the capitalists had always done.

The committee shifted the production of the *Military Port* to implements of peace. They introduced a system of strict accounting. This showed that the new plows and rakes were being produced at higher cost than the same articles could be imported from abroad. They then set to work to change the machinery and speed it up. Machines and ships were brought in for repairs. When a contract was not completed at the end of the eight-hour day, the foreman would state the condition of the work, and the extra hours required. The men, taking new pride in fast work, often voted to stick by the job, even if it took all night. With this went a vote of increase of pay to the foreman.

Under the old administration most of the workers lived from one to three hours' journey from the factory. The Committee started the building of new workers' quarters. Numerous devices were introduced to save time and energy. The long line of employes waiting in turn to receive their pay envelopes was abolished by appointing one man to receive the pay for every two hundred.

Unfortunately among the men elected was one who could resist everything but temptation. Having received the two hundred pay envelopes, he started out to distribute them. Then he thought better of it. No one knows how it happened. Some of the men said that some bourgeois devil must have whispered into the ears of this weak comrade, and driven from his mind all thought of his family, his shop, and the Revolution. At any rate he was found later beside some empty vodka bottles with his pockets empty, too. When he recovered from his happiness he was brought before the Shop Committee and charged with breach of revolutionary honor and treason to the *Military Port*.

The Grand Session of the Revolutionary Tribunal was held in the main shop, with 150 men on the jury. The verdict was "Guilty!" The jury was asked to vote on one of the three following sentences: (1) summary dismissal; (2) dismissal, with wages to his wife and children continued; (3) pardon and reinstatement.

Proposition number two was carried, thus attaching a definite stigma to the culprit's dereliction, but at the same time saving his family from hardship. This did not bring back the money to the unfortunate two hundred, so the fifteen hundred voted to divide among themselves the loss of the two hundred.

In their new experiments the workingmen made many costly blunders. But their verdict upon the Soviet as a whole was that it had made good. Toward the mistakes of the Soviet they took the same attitude a man takes toward his own mistakes—a very lenient one.

Out of their experience the workers gained confidence. They found that they could organize industry; they found they could increase production, and with the Soviet daily entrenching itself in the economic field, they began to feel a sense of elation. They would have been still more elated had it not been for their enemies, constantly launching fresh attacks against the Soviet.

The Soviet Organizes an Army

As soon as the shops were running well, the men would have to drop tools and take up rifles; the railroads, instead of carrying food and implements, had to carry ammunition and troops. The workmen, instead of strengthening the new institutions, had to rally to defend the ground on which they stood.

Raids were continually directed against the frontiers of the workingmen's republic. As soon as the enemy broke thru the cry went up "The Socialist Fatherland is in danger!" Into every village and factory hurried the call to arms. Each formed its little detachment, and along the roads and trails they marched up into the Manchurian Mountains, singing revolutionary hymns and folk songs of the village. Poorly equipped and poorly fed, they advanced to pit themselves against a merciless, well-equipped foe. Just as Americans today cherish the memory of the tattered barefoot troops of Washington, who left their blood-stained prints on the snows of Valley Forge, so in the future Russians will thrill to the story of those first ragged groups of Red Guards who, at the call of danger, grasped their guns and went forth to the defense of the Soviet Republic.

Beside the Red Guards were rising the units of the new Red Army. It was an International Army. All peoples were represented, including platoons of Czechs and Koreans. Around the camp-fire the Koreans would say: "We will fight for you now, for your liberty: some day you will fight with us against Japan for our liberty." Among the officers were the Czech Captain Murovsky, Lenin's nephew Popov, and Abramov, who had served two years with the British.

In discipline the Red troops were inferior to the regular national armies. But they had an *élan* which the others lacked. I talked much with these peasants and workers, who for weeks had been lying out on the rain-drenched hillsides.

"Who made you come, and what keeps you here?" I asked.

"Well—millions of us dark people had to go out and die for the government of the Czar in the old days," they replied. "Surely we should be cowards if we didn't go out and fight for a government that is all our own!

There were certain gentlemen who didn't have this view of the Soviet. Quite the opposite. They wanted the Russian peasants and workers to have a very different sort of government. In fact they themselves claimed to be the one true and only government of Russia.

In grandiose phraseology they laid claim to sovereignty over the territory extending from the Golden Horn of the Far East to the Finnish Bay in the West, and from the White Sea in the north to the Black Sea on the south. While these gentlemen were not very modest, they were most discreet. They did not set foot upon any of their vast domains. Had they ventured to do so they would have been locked up as common criminals, by the government really functioning—the Soviet.

From the safe confines of Manchuria they issued their glowing manifestos. There all the conspiracies against the Soviet were hatched. After the defeat of Kaledin, the Counter-Revolutionists, egged on by foreign capital, put their hopes in the Cossack

Semyonov.[1] Under him were organized regiments of Hun-Huz bandits, Japanese mercenaries, and monarchists rounded up from ports down along the Chinese coast.

Semyonov declared that with an iron fist he was going to drive decency and common sense into the Bolsheviks. He announced his objective as the Urals, 4,000 miles away, then a descent upon the Muscovite plain, with Petrograd opening its gates, and the whole countryside rising up to welcome him.

Raising his standards amid great plaudits from the bourgeoisie, he crossed over into the Siberian border twice, and twice came hurtling back again. The people did rise up to meet him. Not with flowers, however, but with guns and axes and pitchforks.

The Vladivostok workers helped in this defeat of Semyonov. After five weeks they came back bronzed, tattered, and foot-sore. But they came back victors. The working-class turned out to acclaim their fellow-proletarians in arms. There were flowers, speeches and a triumphal march through the city. This victory put great elation in their hearts. But not in the hearts of the bourgeois and Allied onlookers. It was evident that in the military field the Soviet was growing stronger.

The Soviet Educates the People

In the realm of culture the creative force of the Revolution succeeded in establishing a People's University, three workmen's theaters and two daily papers. The *Peasant and Worker* was the official Soviet organ. It featured an English department edited by Jerome Lifschiz, a young Russian-American. The *Red Banner*, the Communist Party organ, carried long academic articles. Neither was a masterpiece of journalism, but both were voices of the inarticulate masses, reaching out for the things of the mind and spirit.

While the Revolution was primarily a drive for land, and bread, and peace, it was more than that. I remember a session of the Vladivostok Soviet, when one of the Right was making a furious attack upon the Soviet, scoring the cutting down of food rations:

"The Bolsheviks promised you lots of things, but they didn't give them to you, did they? They promised you bread, but where is it? Where is the bread that...?" The words of the speaker were drowned in a storm of whistles and hisses.

Man does not live by bread alone. Neither does the Soviet live by satisfying merely the hunger of the stomach, but the hunger of the spirit.

All men crave fellowship. "For fellowship is heaven, and lack of it is hell," said John Ball to the English peasants in the fourteenth century. The Soviet was like a great family in which the lowest man was made to feel his human worth.

---

[1] Grigory M. Semyonov (1890–1946), a leader of the White movement in the Transbaikal region with the support of the Japanese.

All men crave power. In the Soviet, workingmen felt the joy of being arbiters of their own destiny, masters over a vast domain. A workingman is like any other human being. Having tasted power he is loth to let it go.

All men crave adventure. In the Soviet men embarked upon a supreme adventure—the quest for a new society based on justice, the building of the world anew.

All men have a spiritual passion. It needs only to be aroused. The Revolution stirred up even the dull, complacent peasant. It gave him the impulse to read and write. One day an old *mujik* appeared in the Children's School.

"Children, these hands cannot write," he said, holding them up, toil-worn and calloused, "they cannot write because the only thing the Czar wanted them for was to plough." As the tears flowed down his cheeks he said, "But you, the children of a new Russia, you can learn to write. Oh, that I might begin again as a child in our new Russia!"

Workingmen as Diplomats

The workingmen had captured the ship of state. Now they had to steer it along a labyrinthine channel, through uncharted waters, the Allies constantly striving to sink it on the rocks.

Rebuffed by the Allied consuls, the Soviet turned to China with overtures of friendship. The Chinese had been so atrociously treated by the Czar that they could not understand any Russian government addressing them in a kindly manner. They thought it was a new species of trickery. But the Soviet backed its fair words with fair deeds. Chinese citizens were placed upon the same footing as other foreigners. Chinese boats were allowed to ply upon the rivers. The Chinese began to feel that a Russian government looked upon them not as an inferior race, to be cursed and bled, but as human beings. They sent their emissaries to the Red Army, saying:

"We know that we have no right to allow the cut-throats and adventurers of Semyonov to mobilize upon our territory. We know that the Allies have no right to make us put an embargo against you. We want our foodstuffs to go to Russian workmen and peasants."

A general conference was held in June at the frontier in Grodekovo. The Chinese were greeted in their own language by Tunganogi, a daring brilliant lad of 21, the incarnation of the spirit of young, revolutionary Russia. The delegates of these two races, representing one-third of the population of the globe, sat down together to work out the problem of living together in peace and co-operation.

It was not a Versailles Conference of old men cooped up in a gilded chamber: crafty, suspicious, duelling with words and phrases. These were young men, open-minded and open-hearted, meeting under the open sky in brotherhood. Yet it was not a welter of emotion in which reality was lost. They faced the issues squarely: the danger of swamping Russia with a yellow tide, the lower standard of coolie labor, etc.

But it was all done frankly, generously, fraternally. As Krasnoshchekov, chairman of the Russian delegation, said:

"The Chinese and Russian masses are true children of Nature, uncorrupted by the vices of Western civilization, unversed in diplomatic deceit and intrigue."

Yet, on this very day, while delegates from these two great child races were reaching out to one another in an effort for mutual understanding, the foreign diplomats—behind their backs—in Harbin and Vladivostok, were plotting to hurl these two peoples at each other's throats. They were planning to use Chinese troops in a raid upon Siberia, and to smash the Soviets.

PART IV

THE TRIUMPH OF THE REVOLUTION: THE SOVIETS AGAINST THE CAPITALIST WORLD

Chapter 17
THE ALLIES CRUSH THE SOVIET

WHY this animus of the Allies against the Soviets? Why not regard Russia as a vast laboratory experiment?" someone once asked an American banker. "Why not let these visionaries try out their socialistic schemes? When their dream becomes a nightmare, when their Utopia collapses, you can point to it always as an example of the horrible failure of Socialism."

"Very good," was the reply, "but supposing it isn't a failure? Then where are we?"

Failure is what the Allies prayed for, and eager-eyed, they watched for Soviet collapse. But it did not come. It was precisely this that enraged the Allies. The Soviet was showing signs of success. It was creating not disorder, but order—not chaos, but organization. It was entrenching itself in the economic and military fields. In the cultural and diplomatic fields it was pressing forward. Everywhere it was consolidating its gains.

The Soviet stood straight across the pathway of the Imperialists. If it continued to grow in power their plans would be completely shattered. They could no longer hope for a free hand in the exploitation of the immense resources of Russia.[1]

So the crushing of the Soviet was decreed. Now, before it should become too strong and lusty, it must be smashed.

Counter-Revolution Uses the Czechs

The Czecho-Slovaks were the instrument chosen to administer the death-blow. Unwittingly they were being groomed by their French officers for this job. Regiments of these seasoned troops were strategically strung out along the Trans-Siberian line. Vladivostok held 17,000 of them armed, fed, and transported hither by grace of the Soviets.

---

[1] [Williams's note]: "What we are witnessing now in Russia is in the opening of a great struggle for her immeasurable raw materials." *Russia*, the magazine of Anglo-Russian finance, May 1918.

"In the city events are shaping more and more towards an international suzerainty over Russia modeled on the British plan in Egypt. Such an event would transform Russian bonds into the cream of the international market." *London Financial News*, November 1918.

The French said that transports were coming to take them to the Western battle-front. Week after week it was announced that the boats were on the way. But no ships came. The French had never intended to ship the Czechs away. They intended to use them here in Siberia to smash the Soviet.

The Czechs were already restless, fretting with inaction. They had a deep hereditary hatred of the Austro-Germans. The French told them that there were tens of thousands of Austro-Germans in the Red Army. Adroitly playing upon their patriotism, the French pictured the Soviets as friends of the Austro-Germans, and enemies of the Czechs. So they engineered friction, and got them ready for the assault upon the Soviets. The methods of attack were adapted to the place.

Here in Vladivostok surprise was deemed essential. The plan was to get the Soviet off guard, and then spring a sudden *coup*. To do this the Soviets must be hoodwinked with a show of friendship. This business was delegated to the British. Dropping their hostile front, they assumed toward the Bolsheviks an attitude of amiability.

With frank, engaging air the Consul confessed to a former antagonism to the Soviets, and the backing of Semyonov. Now that the Soviet had proved its right to live, the British would lend their aid. To begin with, they would cooperate in the importation of machinery. Following this, on Friday afternoon, June 28th, 1918, two genial officials called to present their respects to Sukhanov, bringing the information that wireless messages received on *H. M. S. Suffolk* would be daily handed to the Soviet for publication in its papers.

The editors, particularly Jerome, were jubilant. They came down to Russian Island, urging me to come up and celebrate the capitulation of the Allies. Good reason for their rapture! It had been a hard up-hill pull, plodding through the murk and the night. Now suddenly the clouds break, and the sky shines blue.

Next morning at eight-thirty a thunderbolt comes out of the blue! It strikes Sukhanov, sitting in his Soviet office. It is an ultimatum in the name of the Czechs. It calls for the unconditional surrender of the Soviet. All offices are to be evacuated. All soldiers are to proceed to the High School field, and lay down their arms. The time limit is thirty minutes.

Sukhanov, rushing to Czech headquarters, begs for permission to call the Soviet together.

"Certainly, if you can do it in half an hour," coolly replies the Czech commander.

As Sukhanov turns to leave, he is placed under arrest.

All this goes on behind the scenes. The city remains in the dark. One or two commissars only have a hint of the tragedy now so imminent. On Svetlanskaya, near the Red Fleet Building, I meet Preminsky having his shoes blacked.

"Getting all shined up early in the morning," I say.

"Yes," he replies casually, lighting a cigarette. "In a few minutes I may be dangling from a lamppost, and I want to be as nice looking a corpse as possible." I stare at him wondering, quizzical.

"Our days are done for," he explained, still nonchalant and smiling, "The Czechs are taking over the city."

Even as he speaks the end of the street is filling with troops. So are the side-streets. In all quarters soldiers are moving, in boats from across the bay, in launches from the battleships. Down from the hill above and up from the piers below, like a dense fog the army of Interventionists rolls in upon the city. The open spaces are seething with soldiery, heavily armed, loaded with grenades, huge ominous-looking things. Enough explosives to pulverize the whole city!

The occupation proceeds swiftly, like clock-work, according to plan.

The Japanese seize the powder-magazine, the British the railroad station. The Americans throw a cordon around the consulate. The Chinese and others take up lesser points. The Czechs converge upon the Soviet building. They encircle it from all sides. With a loud "Hurrah,"—they rush forward, and go crashing through the doors. The Red Flag of the Socialist Republic is pulled down, and the red, white and blue flag of autocracy is run up. Vladivostok passes into the hands of the Imperialists.

"The Soviet has fallen," a hoarse shout goes up in the street, and runs like wildfire through the city. The patrons of the Olympia Café, rushing out into the street, burst into yells, flinging up their hats, cheering the Czechs. The Soviet and all its works is a cursed thing to them. It is fallen. But that is not enough. They would obliterate every trace of it.

Before them, wrought out in flower-beds edged with stone, is the design which spells SOVIET OF WORKMEN'S DEPUTIES. Vaulting the iron fence, they kick away the stones, stamp through the flowers, plunging their hands deep into the soil in order to extirpate the last root and vestige of the odious symbol.

Their blood is up now. Their appetites are whetted. They want something animate to vent their rage upon.

The Bourgeois Cry for Reprisals

Spying me in the throng, they raise a great hue and cry:

"Immigrant! Swine!" *(Amerikanskaya Svoloch)* they yell. "Kill him! Choke him! Hang him!" The mob of speculators converges on me, brandishing fists and cursing.

But the ring of men forming next to me makes no attempt to lay hands on me. Why, I wonder? They are partisans of the Soviet. Seeing my peril, they have wormed their way in between me and these would-be lynchers, forming a kind of protective pocket.

A low voice whispers, "Head for the Red Fleet building. Walk, don't run." Pushed and jostled by the crowd behind, I steer my course toward the Red Fleet building. Opposite its portal I hear the word "Run!" I slip thru the door, and escape in its labyrinths, leaving my pursuers disputing with the Czechs below.

In the front of the building I find a third-story window that overlooks the city. From this vantage-point I can see and still be unseen. Up and down below me stretches Svetlanskaya, boiling now like a cauldron. This street, which twenty minutes earlier had been so placid in the shining morning sun, is now a riot of people and color and sound. Blue-jacketed Japs in white puttees, English marines with the Union Jack, khaki-clad Czechs, with green and white, marching and counter-marching, cut currents through the eddying throng, each moment growing greater.

Through the bourgeois quarters the glad tiding "The Soviet has fallen" spreads with magic swiftness. From boudoir, café, and parlor, in silks and smiles, they hasten forth to celebrate. Svetlanskaya becomes a grand promenade, brightly splashed with gay plumes and petticoats and parasols.

Some of the toilettes are elaborate. Fortunate ladies! Tipped off in advance they had time to adorn themselves. The officers, too, blossom out in full regalia—gold braid and epaulets, jangling spurs—and much saluting. They make escorts for the ladies, or form into marching squads. There are hundreds of them. One wonders how Vladivostok could have held so many.

And so many bourgeois! Well-kept, rotund gentlemen with avoirdupois enough to qualify as cartoons of themselves. They hail each other, faces beaming, clasping one another's hands, embracing and kissing, exclaiming "The Soviet is fallen" as tho it were an Easter greeting. Two big fat *chinovniks*, almost apoplectic with joy, try to fall upon one another's bosom, but their expansive abdomens are in the way. In their efforts to embrace, clutching at one another, they bid fair to burst themselves.

With incredible swiftness a complete change passes over this city of the proletarians. It becomes a city of the well-fed and well-groomed, their shining faces exultant, congratulating one another, praising God and the Allies, and cheering the Czechs.

Poor Czechs! These cheers embarrass and mortify them. Their heads hang in shame, meeting a Russian workingman. Some indeed refuse point-blank to go into this garroting of a workingman's government. None of them relish the job of crucifying other workmen to make a carnival for the bourgeoisie. And the bourgeoisie want more than a holiday with bands and streamers. They want a Roman holiday with blood and victims. They want vengeance and retribution on these workmen who have forgotten their station in life.

"Now, we will put them in their proper places," they exclaim. "We will put them on the lamp-posts. It's red these birds admire, is it? Very well, we shall give them all they want of their favorite color. We'll draw it from their veins!"

They urge the Czechs to violence. They want a part in it themselves. They point out the foremost workmen and denounce them. They know where the commissars are to be found, and lead the way into office and workshop.

Very busy also is a crew of rat-faced, swart-faced creatures—spies, provocators and pogromists of the old régime. Swarming out of their holes and now come into their own again, they seek by excesses against the Bolsheviks to ingratiate themselves with the bourgeoisie. Like weasels they penetrate everywhere, even into the building where I am.

Suddenly screams, curses, and the sound of pounding feet break out on the stairs above. Four men invading the party-offices on the top-floor have laid hold of Zoya. Single-handed she resists them, fighting back every inch of the way. By twisting her arms, pummeling and pushing her, they drag her down into the street and march her off to prison.

Such scenes are repeated thruout the city. Commissars and workmen are busy at their tasks in office, shop and bank. The doors are flung open. They are pounced upon, and dragged out into the highway.

Thru the center of the highway a narrow lane is opened. Thru this channel, the captives, manacled or gripped by their captors, are prodded along by revolver-butt, and bayonet-point. Hoots, jeers and catcalls ring in their ears. Clenched fists are thrust in their faces. Some are spat upon and beaten by the mob which surges into the passageway blocking their progress.

An extra outburst of rage breaks on the head of the Commissar of Banks. He has touched them directly in their vital center—their pocket-nerve. They yell, and hoot, and would tear him limb from limb. A white-flannelled gentleman, red-faced with fury, breaks thru the Czech guards, brandishing a revolver, grabs the commissar by his arms, and stalks on beside him, howling like an Indian.

One by one the commissars are shoved along this corridor of scowling faces, derisive and hate-contorted. Their own faces by contrast are strangely serene and calm. Some are pallid, but on the whole they are dauntless, almost debonair. They are alert, terribly interested in everything. These men have tasted life. They have run its gamut, from prison-dungeons to high affairs of state. So many adventures have been theirs. What new surprise lies before them around the turning? The most thrilling of all, perhaps the final one. If so, let it come. Death has little terror for them. Long ago when they gave themselves to the Revolution, that matter was disposed of. Then they put all they had, their lives included, into its keeping.

They were conscripts of the Revolution. When it called—they came. Where it sent them—they went. What it exacted—they performed, obedient, unquestioning. Under the Czar, the Revolution had called them to the task of agitators. Under the Soviet it drafted them to the post of commissars. At the call of the Revolution they had yielded up leisure, comfort, health, and found joy therein. Now they were being summoned to yield up their lives. In the supreme sacrifice might they not find the supreme joy?

All this was certainly written upon the face of Melnikov. Thru this thunderstorm of foes—hissing, roaring, and howling—he came smiling thru like a shaft of sunshine. *Svetlanskaya* means "The Lighted Way." Always for me it will be lit with the countenance of this workingman. About him there was something celestial, transcendent. Climbing up the hill, buffeted, jeered and spat upon, he was strangely like the figure of another Workingman, toiling thru another hostile multitude, up another hill—long ago.

Only this was no "Via Dolorosa." It was a "Way of Triumph," with Melnikov coming up like a conqueror. His face was wreathed in smiles. His sparkling eyes were still more sparkling, his features more radiant than ever. A hoarse voice shouted "Scoundrel! Hang him!" Melnikov only smiled. A heavy fist struck him in the cheek. He smiled again. It was the smile of one lifted above the base passions of the mob, far beyond reach of its blows and jeers. It was a smile of pity for the haters. Could Melnikov have been aware of the power in that smile? The silent conquests it made that day in the hearts of his beholders? It was a magnet drawing the hesitant and wavering into the camp of the Revolution. At the same time it was a sword, wreaking havoc in the camp of the Counter-Revolutionists.

They could not abide this smile of Melnikov and the laugh of Sukhanov. They were irritated and haunted by them. The bourgeoisie would have liked to strike these young men dead in the streets. But they did not dare do it—yet. The commissars were not killed but jailed.

The Soviet Is Submerged

The Allies for the present are against any wholesale massacre of the workers. They are anxious to make intervention appear in the guise of a crusade for democracy, welcomed by all the people. Not yet has it unmasked itself as stark Czaristic reaction. Vladivostok, in the Allied plan, is to be the foothold for the spring upon Siberia. They do not want that foothold too slippery with blood. In the hinterland, in the back regions of Siberia, peasants' and workers' blood may flow in torrents. But not in this seaport town, exposed before the eyes of the world. A few Red Guards and workers are shot down in their tracks. But there is no general blood-spilling. The suddenness of the onslaught, the overwhelming masses of troops, have smothered the soviet.

At one point only did the Soviet forces have a chance to rally. That was near the water-front, the rendezvous of the *gruzchiki* [longshoremen], stevedores, coal-heavers, loaders of ships. They were of peasant origin, huge shaggy fellows, heavy muscled for their heavy work.

The intricate problems of state and politics they did not comprehend. But one simple fact they did comprehend. Whereas once they were slaves, now they were free! From the status of beasts they had been raised to the status of men. And they knew that the Soviet had done this.

Now they see the Soviet in peril. Rushing into the nearby Red Staff Building, they bolt and bar the doors, and barricade the windows, taking their posts, rifles in hand, ready for the assault. At all costs they will hold this ground for the Soviet.

The odds against them are one hundred to one. Two hundred freight-handlers pitted against twenty thousand seasoned troops. Revolvers against machine-guns.

Rifles against cannon. But on the side of this garrison of *gruzchiki* is the flame of the Revolution. It has fired the spirits of these coal-heavers, outwardly so gross and sluggish. They grow fearless, swift, and daring. All afternoon the ring of steel and flame around them grows denser and closer. They watch it undaunted, refusing every call to capitulate. And as night begins to fall, their guns are still blazing from the windows.

In the shadows a Czech crawls close up, and hurls an incendiary bomb thru a window of the building, setting it afire. The citadel of the longshoremen threatens now to become a funeral-pyre.

Enveloped in flame and smoke they grope and stumble into the street, hands raised in surrender. Some are slaughtered, some are clubbed into insensibility. The rest are marched away to prison.

Resistance is crushed. The Soviet is annihilated. The Allies congratulate themselves upon the success of the *coup*. The bourgeoisie are in transports of delight. Lights flame from the windows of the great houses and restaurants. From the cafés come snatches of song, and the throb of the orchestra. The merrymakers are laughing, dancing, cheering the Allied uniforms. From the churches breaks forth the clanging, chiming, pealing, booming music of the bells—the priests within offering up prayers for the Czar. From the decks of the battleships the bugles call across the waters of the bay. The city gives itself up to revelry and rejoicing.

But not in the workingmen's quarters. There is silence, broken only by the sobbing of women. Behind drawn curtains they are laying out their slain. From a nearby shed comes the sound of hammering. The men are joining rough planks together, making coffins for their comrade dead.

Chapter 18
THE RED FUNERAL

IT was the Fourth of July—I was standing on the Kitaiskaya looking down upon the holiday flags on the *Brooklyn*, the American battleship in Vladivostok Bay. Suddenly I heard a faraway sound. Listening, I caught the strains of the revolutionary hymn:

With hearts heavy and sad we bring our dead,
Who shed their blood in the fight for freedom.

Looking up, I saw on the crest of the hill the first lines of some vast procession. It was the funeral of the *gruzchiki* (longshoremen) killed four days before in the siege of the Red Staff building.

Today the people, rising out of their grief and terror, were coming forth to bury these defenders of the fallen Soviet. Out of the workmen's quarters they streamed, jamming the street, not from curb to curb, but from wall to wall. They came billowing over the hilltop by thousands until the whole long slope was choked with the dense, slow-moving throng, keeping time to the funeral march of the revolutionists.

Up thru the gray and black mass of men and women ran two lines of white-bloused sailors of the Bolshevik fleet. Above their heads tossed a cloud of crimson standards with silvered cords and tassels. In the vanguard, four men carried a huge red banner with the words: *"Long Live the Soviet of Workmen's and Peasants' Deputies! Hail to the International Brotherhood of the Toilers!"*

A hundred girls in white, carrying green wreaths from forty-four unions of the city, formed a guard of honor for the dead *gruzchiki*. The coffins with the red paint still wet upon them, were borne upon the shoulders of their comrades. The music crashed out by the Red Fleet Band was lost in the volume of song that rose from the seventeen thousand singers.

Here was color and sound and motion. But there was something else, a something which compelled fear and awe. I had seen a score of the great processions of Petrograd and Moscow, peace and victory and protest and memorial parades, military and civilian, impressive as only Russians could make them.

But this was different.

From these defenseless poor, stripped of their arms, and with sorrowing songs bearing off their dead, there came a threat more menacing than that from the twelve-inch guns of the Allied Fleet, riding in the harbor below. It was impossible not to feel it. It was so simple, so spontaneous and so elemental. It came straight out of the heart of the people. It *was* the people, leaderless, isolated, beaten to earth, thrown upon its own resources, and yet, out of its grief, rising magnificently to take command of itself.

The dissolution of the Soviet, instead of plunging the people into inactive grief and dissipating their forces, begot a strange, unifying spirit. Seventeen thousand separate souls were welded into one. Seventeen thousand people, singing in unison, found themselves thinking in unison. With a common mass will and mass consciousness, they formulated their decisions from their class standpoint—the determined standpoint of the revolutionary proletariat.

The Czechs came, offering a guard of honor. *"Ne noozhno!"* (It is not necessary!) the people replied. "You killed our comrades. Forty to one you fought against them. They died for the Soviet and we are proud of them. We thank you, but we cannot let the guns which shot them down guard them in their death!"

"But there may be danger for you in this city," said the authorities.

"Never mind," they answered. "We, too, are not afraid of death. And what better way to die than beside the bodies of our comrades!"

Some bourgeois societies came, presenting memorial wreaths.

"Ne noozhno" (it is not necessary), the people answered. "Our comrades died in a struggle against the bourgeoisie. They died fighting cleanly. We must keep their memory clean. We thank you, but we dare not lay your wreaths upon their coffins."

The procession poured down the Aleutskaya Hill, filled the large open space at the bottom, and faced up toward the British Consulate. Nearby, on the left, was a work car with a tower for repairing electric wires. Whether it was there by design or accident I do not know. Presently it was to serve as a speaker's rostrum.

The band played a solemn dirge. The men bared their heads. The women bowed. The music ceased and there was a silence. The band played a second time. Again there was the bowing and baring of heads and again the long silence. And yet there was no speaker. It was like a huge Quaker meeting in the open air. And just as a sermon has no place in Russian public worship, so here a speech was not essential to this act of public devotion. But should some one from the people feel the impulse to speak there was the platform awaiting him. It was as if in the pause the people were generating a voice.

At last out of the crowd one came and climbed upon the high platform. He had not the gift of oratory but his frequent iteration, "They died for us. They died for us," touched others to utterance.

First came a peasant, bronzed and bearded and in peasant costume. He said: "All my life has been one of toil and fear.... Pain and torture and killing without end we had in the dark days of the Czar. Then the morning of the Revolution came and these terrors passed away. Workingmen and peasants were very happy and I was happy too. But suddenly in the midst of our rejoicing came this blow. Once more all is night around us. We can not believe it; but here before our eyes, dead and cold, lie our brothers and comrades who fought for the Soviet. And in the north other comrades are falling before the guns. We listen and strain to hear the sound of the peasants and workers of other lands coming to the rescue. But it is in vain. All we can hear is the sound of the guns in the north."

As he finished, against the blue sky appeared a figure in white. A woman had climbed upon the platform. At the behest of the crowd she began to speak:

"All through the past we women have seen our men led off to the wars while we wept at home. Those who ruled told us that it was right and for our glory. Those wars were far away and we did not understand. But our men here were killed before our eyes. This we can understand. And we understand that in it there was neither right nor glory. No, it was a cruel, heartless wrong and every child born of the mothers of the working-class shall hear the story of this wrong."

Most eloquent of all was a lad of seventeen, the secretary of a league of young Socialists. "We were students and artists and such kind of people. We held ourselves aloof from the Soviet," he said. "It seemed to us foolish for workmen to govern without the wisdom of the wise. But now we know that you were right and we were wrong. From now on we shall stand with you. What you do we will do. We pledge our tongues and pens to make known the wrongs that you have suffered the length and breadth of Russia and thruout the world."

Suddenly the word went thru the throng that Constantin Sukhanov had been paroled until five o'clock and that he was coming with counsels of peace and moderation.

While some were affirming his coming and others were denying it, he himself appeared. He was quickly passed along upon the shoulders of the sailors. In a storm of cheers he climbed the ladder and came out upon the platform-top, smiling....

Twice his eyes swept across that field of upturned faces filled with trust and love, awaiting the words of their young leader.

As if to avert the flood of tragedy and pathos that beat suddenly upon him from every side, he turned his head away. His eyes fell for the first time upon the red coffins of the men who had been slain in defense of his Soviet. That was too much. A shudder passed through his frame, he threw up his hands, staggered, and would have fallen headlong into the crowd, but a friend caught him. With both hands pressed to his face, Sukhanov, in the arms of his comrades, sobbed like a child. We could see his breath come and go and the tears raining down his cheeks. The Russians are little given to tears. But that day seventeen thousand Russians sobbed with their young leader on the public square of Vladivostok.

A Pledge to the Dead

Sukhanov knew that many tears were an indulgence, and that he had a big and serious task to perform. Fifty feet behind him was the British Consulate, and fifty rods before him were the waters of the Golden Horn with the frowning guns of the Allied Fleet. He wrenched himself away from his grief and gathering himself together began his message. With an ever mounting passion of earnestness he spoke, closing with words destined to become the rallying cry for the workers in Vladivostok and the Far East:—

"Here, before the Red Staff Building where our comrade *gruzchiki* were slain, we swear by these red coffins that hold them, by their wives and children that weep for them, by the red banners which float over them, that the Soviet for which they died shall be the thing for which we live, or, if need be, like them die. Henceforth the return of the Soviet shall be the goal of all our sacrifice and devotion. To that end we shall fight with every means. The bayonets have been wrested from our hands, but when the day comes and we have no guns, we shall fight with sticks and clubs, and when these are gone, then with our bare fists and bodies. Now it is for us to fight only with our minds and spirits. Let us make them hard and strong and unyielding. The Soviet is dead. Long live the Soviet!"

The crowd caught up the closing words in a tremendous demonstration, mingled with the strains of the "International." Then that haunting *Funeral Hymn of the Revolution* at once so plaintive and triumphant:

> You fell in the fatal fight
> For the liberty of the people, for the honor of the people.
> You gave up your lives and everything dear to you.
> The time will come when your surrendered life will count.
> The time is near when tyranny falls, the people arise, great and free.
> Farewell, brothers, you chose a noble path,
> At your grave we swear to fight, for freedom and the people's happiness.

A resolution was read proclaiming the restoration of the Soviet, the objective of all the future struggles of the revolutionary proletariat and peasants of the Far East. At the call for the vote seventeen thousand hands shot into the air. They were the hands which had built the cars and paved the streets, forged the iron, held the plough, and swung the hammer. All kinds of hands they were: the big, rough hands of the old *gruzckiki*, the artisans', deft and sinewy, the knotted hands of the peasants, thick with callouses, and thousands of the frailer, whiter hands of the working women. By these hands the riches of the Far East had been wrought. They were no different from the scarred, stained hands of labor anywhere in all the world. Except in this regard: for a time they had held the power. The Government had been within their grasp. Four days ago it had been wrested from their grasp, but the feel of it was still within their hands—these hands raised now in solemn pledge to take that power again.

"The Americans Understand"

A sailor striding down from the hilltop pushed through the crowd and climbed upon the platform.

"Comrades!" he cried joyously, "we are not alone. I ask you to look away to the flags flying over there on the American battleship. You cannot see them down there where you stand. But they are there. No, comrades, we are not alone today in our grief. The Americans understand and they are with us!"

It was a mistake, of course. This was July the Fourth. Those flags had been hung out in celebration of our Day of Independence. But the crowd did not know that. To them it was like the sudden touch of a friend's hand upon a lonely traveler in a foreign land.

With enthusiasm they caught up the cry of the sailor: "The Americans are with us!" And the vast conclave of workers lifting up their coffins, wreaths, and banners were once more in motion. They were going to the cemetery, but not directly. Tired as they were from long standing in the sun, they made a wide detour to reach the street that runs up the steep hill to the American Consulate. Then straight up the sharp slope they toiled in a cloud of dust, still singing as they marched, until they came before the Stars and Stripes floating from the flagstaff. And there they stopped and laid the coffins of their dead beneath the flag of America.

They stretched out their hands, crying, "Speak to us a word!" They sent delegates within to implore that word. On the day the great Republic of the West celebrated its independence, the poor and disinherited of Russia came asking sympathy and understanding in the struggle for their independence.

Afterward, I heard a Bolshevik leader bitterly resentful at this "compromise with revolutionary honor and integrity."

"How stupid of them," he said. "How inane of them! Have we not told them that all countries are alike—all imperialists? Was this not repeated to them over and over again by their leaders?"

Truly it had been. But with this demonstration of the Fourth of July the leaders had little to do. They were in prison. The affair was in the hands of the people themselves. And, however cynical many leaders were about the professions of America, the people were not so. In the hour of their affliction, these simple trusting folk, makers of the new Social Democracy of the East, came stretching forth their hands to the old Political Democracy of the West.

They knew that President Wilson had given his assurance of help and loyalty to the "people of Russia." They reasoned: "We, the workers and peasants, the great majority here in Vladivostok, are we not the people? Today in our trouble we come to claim the promised help. Our enemies have taken away our Soviet. They have killed our comrades. We are alone and in distress and you alone of all the nations of the earth can understand." No finer tribute could they offer than to come thus, bringing their dead, with the faith that out of America would come compassion and understanding. America, their only friend and refuge.

But America did not understand. The American people did not even hear a word about it. These Russian folk do not know that the American people never heard about it. All they know is that a few weeks after that appeal came the landing of the American troops. They united with Japanese troops, marching into Siberia, shooting down peasants and workers.

And now these Russian folk say to one another: "How stupid we were to stand there in the heat and the dust stretching out our hands like beggars!"

Chapter 19
EXIT

The Bolsheviks will be crushed like eggshells," said the wisemen as the Allies started into Siberia. The idea of serious Soviet resistance was ridiculed. The Czar's government, then Kerensky's, had tumbled like a house of cards. Why should not the Soviet government go the same way?

The American Major Thacher[1] has pointed out, why not: The Czar's power was based on his armies; it was only necessary to disintegrate these armies and the Czar fell. The Kerensky government rested in the cabinet; it was only necessary to surround his ministers in the Winter Palace and Kerensky fell. The Soviet government, however, was rooted in thousands of local Soviets—an organism made up of countless cells; to destroy the Soviet government, every one of these separate organizations must be destroyed. And they did not relish destruction.

As the alarm was sounded thru the Far East the peasants and workers rallied against the invaders. They fought fiercely, yielding ground only inch by inch. In the two cities north of Vladivostok the Soviets had been established without the killing of a single person. In overthrowing these Soviets thousands were now killed, and not only the hospitals, but sheds and warehouses were filled with the wounded. Instead of an easy "military promenade through Siberia" the Interventionists faced a hard bloody conflict. The Vladivostok bourgeoisie were amazed at the stubborn resistance, Then enraged they turned on all partisans of the Soviet in fury.

I Get Arrested a Little

I had no hankering for martyrdom. So I avoided the main street and went out in disguise or under cover of night. I was an outcast. But that did not grieve me. I was concerned for the manuscript of my book on Russia. It was in the Soviet building—now headquarters of the new White government.

I decided that the only way to get it was to walk brazenly into the enemy's camp and ask for it. I did so and fell straight into the hands of the new Secret Service Chief.

---

[1] Thomas D. Thacher (1881–1950) worked for the American Red Cross in 1917–18. He was later a lawyer and judge.

"I've been looking for you. Thank you for coming," he said with mock politeness. "You will stay with us." I was a prisoner of the Counter-Revolution.

Fortunately among the Americans was an old classmate of mine, Fred Goodsell.[2] He negotiated in my behalf and secured my release—but not my manuscript.

Now I ventured to return to my lodgings. Some spy observing my arrival must have telephoned the Whites. I was busy arranging my papers when an automobile whirled up. Six White Guards jumped out, rushed into the room, and shoving their revolvers into my face, began yelling, "We've got you now, we've got you."

"But I've already been arrested and released," I protested.

"We're not going to arrest you, you damned swine. We're going to kill you," they shouted. Sudden noise outside again. Another motorcar dashed up. Bang! Another crash at the door! A captain and four more men with rifles careened into the room. They were Czechs declaring they had orders for my arrest.

"But we have already arrested him," said the Whites.

"No," insisted the Czechs. "We're going to take him."

"But we've got him," persisted the Whites.

It was quite thrilling to find myself a person of such sinister importance. My gratification over it was tempered a bit by the sight of the bayonets. There were too many of them—too much readiness to use them. Instead of a captive I might soon be a corpse. Happily the Czech captain had a sense of humor.

"Your wishes in the matter?" he said turning to me with a deep bow. "Whose prisoner do you prefer to be?"

"Your prisoner—the Czechs," I replied.

With magnificent noblesse oblige he turned to the Whites. "Gentlemen, he is yours," he declared magnanimously.

He appeased his own soldiers by letting them loose on my papers (they were afterwards delivered to the American Consul).

The Whites hustled me into their automobile and thru the city where a few days earlier I had ridden as a guest of the Soviet, I rode now ringed with bayonets and with two revolvers pressed against my ribs—a prisoner of the Whites.

White headquarters was surrounded by an excited bourgeois mob watching the round up of Reds and hailing each victim with catcalls and cries of "give him the rope." I was pushed through the jeering crowd into the building and by great good luck straight into the arms of Squersky, a former acquaintance. He motioned me not to recognize him and in due time secured my release. This time I came out with a document which read: *"Citizens—You are requested not to arrest the American Williams."*

---

[2] Fred Goodsell was an old friend of Williams's and worked in the YMCA in Europe and Russia during this World War I period.

Homeward Bound

But there was little protection in this paper, for black hatred against the Soviet grew from day to day. I had the feeling of a hunted animal and in ten days lost as many pounds. "At any moment you may lose your life," said the American Vice-Consul. "Two parties have sworn to shoot you down at sight."

"I am anxious to leave but I have no money to leave with," I told him. He could see my perplexity, but he could not see that it was any concern of his.

The workingmen heard of my plight and came to my rescue. They were in hard straits but they raised a thousand rubles. The men in jail smuggled out another thousand. Now I was ready to go. But the Japanese Consul refused to visé my passport. He confronted me with a list of my crimes, chief among which were articles against intervention that I had published in the Soviet papers. The Tokyo Foreign Office did not like these articles. It had cabled that in no circumstances was my presence to be allowed to pollute the sacred soil of Japan. The Chinese, however, gave me a visé and I booked on a coasting steamer bound for Shanghai.

My last night was spent with *tovarishe* in a hiding-place in the hills. The Soviet had not been destroyed. It had gone underground. In the secret retreat the leaders yet uncaptured gathered to plan and organize. In farewell they sang for me the hymn of the English Transport Workers, taught them by Jerome:

> Hold the fort for we are coming!
> Union men be strong;
> Side by side we battle onward,
> Victory will come.

With these words ringing in my ears on July 11, I sailed past the Allied battleships and out into the Pacific. I stewed in Shanghai a month before I could get passage for America. At last I got it and eight weeks after I left the Golden Horn of the Far East I sighted the Golden Gate of California.

As our steamer swung to anchor in San Francisco harbor a launch ran alongside and officers in naval uniform climbed aboard. They were members of the American Naval Intelligence sent out to welcome me to the homeland. No prodigal, returning from long rioting in a far country, could have had a warmer reception. Their solicitude for my welfare was most embarrassing. They overwhelmed me with attention, insisted on escorting me to their quarters, and tending to all details of my baggage. They assured me of their profound interest in all Soviet affairs and to prove it relieved me of every pamphlet, document, and note-book. Their appetite for Russian literature was insatiable. Lest one scrap of it should escape them they looked into my wallet, shoes, hat-band, even the lining of my coat. Likewise they looked into my pedigree, my past and my future. Then they passed me on to other authorities who looked into my ideas.

"Now you are a Socialist, Mr. Williams," said one of my inquisitors. "You are also an Anarchist, aren't you?"

I denied the charge.

"Well, what other beliefs do you hold?"

"Altruism, optimism, and pragmatism," I told him.

He duly recorded them in his note-book. More strange and dangerous Russian doctrines being imported into America!

After three days of pleasant *camaraderie*, I was sent on to Washington.

Chapter 20
RETROSPECT

IT was not the revolutionists who made the Russian Revolution. This in spite of hosts of revolutionists—who tried their best to make it. For a century gifted men and women of Russia had been agitated over the cruel oppression of the people. So they became agitators. Into the villages, the shops and the slums they went crying:

> Shake to earth your chains like dew,
> Which in sleep have fallen on you.
> Ye are many, they are few.

But the people did not rise. They did not even seem to hear. Then came that supreme agitator—Hunger. Hunger, rising out of economic collapse and war, goaded the sluggish masses into action. Moving out against the old worm-eaten structure they brought it down. Elemental impersonal forces did what human agencies found impossible.

The revolutionists, however, had their part. They did not make the Revolution. But they made the Revolution a success. By their efforts they had prepared a body of men and women with minds trained to see facts, with a program to fit the facts and with fighting energy to drive it through. There were a million of them—perhaps more, possibly less. The important thing is not their number, but the fact that they were organized to act as receivers of the bankrupt, old order, as a salvage-corps of the Revolution.

At the core of this were the Communists. H. G. Wells says, "In the vast disorganization an emergency government supported by a disciplined party of perhaps 150,000 adherents—the Communist Party—took control.... It suppressed brigandage, established a sort of order and security in the exhausted towns and set up a crude rationing system, the only possible government ... the only idea, the only solidarity."

For four years the Communists have had control of Russia. What are the fruits of their stewardship?

"Repressions, tyranny, violence," cry the enemies. "They have abolished free speech, free press, free assembly. They have imposed drastic military conscription and compulsory labor. They have been incompetent in government, inefficient in industry. They have subordinated the Soviets to the Communist Party. They have lowered their Communist ideals, changed and shifted their program and compromised with the capitalists."

Some of these charges are exaggerated. Many can be explained. But they cannot all be explained away. Friends of the Soviet grieve over them. Their enemies have summoned the world to shudder and protest against them.

When I am tempted to join the wailers and the mud-slingers my mind goes back to a conversation on the docks of Vladivostok in June, 1918. Colonel Robins, of the American Red Cross, was talking to Constantin Sukhanov, President of the Soviet.

"If no help comes from the Allies, how long can the Soviet last?"

Sukhanov shook his head ruefully.

"Six weeks?" queried Robins.

"It will be hard to hold on longer," said Sukhanov.

Robins turned to me with the same question. I, too, was dubious about the outlook.

We were sympathizers. We knew the might and the vitality of the Soviet. But we saw also the tremendous obstacles it confronted. And the odds seemed against it.

Forces Ranged Against the Bolsheviks

In the first place the Soviet faced the same conditions that had overwhelmed the Czar and Kerensky governments, i.e., the dislocation of industry, the paralysis of transport, the hunger and misery of the masses.

In the second place the Soviet had to cope with a hundred new obstacles—desertion of the intelligentsia, strike of the old officials, sabotage of the technicians, excommunication by the church, the blockade by the Allies. It was cut off from the grain fields of the Ukraine, the oil fields of Baku, the coal mines of the Don, the cotton of Turkestan—fuel and food reserves were gone. "Now," said their enemies, "the bony hand of hunger will clutch the people by their throat and bring them to their senses." To prevent supply trains reaching the cities, agents of the imperialists dynamited the railway bridges and put emery into the locomotive bearings.

Here were troubles enough to break the strongest souls. But still more were coming. The capitalist press of the world was mobilized against the Bolsheviks. They were pictured as "hirelings of the Kaiser," "red-eyed fanatics," "cold-blooded assassins," "long bearded ruffians running amuck by day, carousing in the Kremlin at night," "profaners of art and culture," "despoilers of women." As a crowning infamy the "Decree for the Nationalization of Women" was forged and broadcasted through the world. The public was called upon to transfer their hate from the Huns to the Bolsheviks.

While abroad hatred against the Bolsheviks as the new "enemies of civilization" mounted from day to day, these selfsame Bolsheviks were straining brains and sinews to rescue civilization in Russia from total collapse. Watching them at their heart-breaking, back-breaking tasks, Ransome[1] wrote:

"No one contends that the Bolsheviks are angels. I only ask that men shall look through the fog of libel that surrounds them and see the ideal for which these young men are struggling in the only way in which they can struggle. If they fail they will fail with clean shields and clean hearts, having striven for an ideal which will live beyond them. Even if they fail, they will none the less have written a page more daring than any other I can remember in the story of the human race.... When in after years men read that page they will judge your country and my country by the help or hindrance they gave to the writing of it."

This appeal was in vain.

As the monarchists of Europe combined to crush the idea loosed on the world by the French Revolution, so the capitalists of Europe and America combined to crush the idea loosed on the world by the Russian Revolution. To these famished, frozen, typhus-stricken Russians sailed no ships of good will laden with books, tools, teachers and engineers but grim ships of war and transports laden with troops and officers, guns and poison-gas. Landings were made at strategic points on the coast of Russia. Monarchists, landlords and Black Hundreds flocked to these rallying centers. New White armies were conscripted, drilled and equipped with hundreds of millions of dollars of supplies. The Interventionists started their drive on Moscow, seeking to plunge the sword into the heart of the Revolution.

Out of the East rolled the hordes of Kolchak following the trail of the Czechs across Siberia. Out of the West struck the armies of Finland, the Letts and Lithuanians. Down from the forests and snowfields of the North moved the British, French, and Americans. Up from the seaports of the South plunged the tanks, aeroplanes and Death Battalions of Denikin. From all points of the compass they came. Out of the Esthonian marshes—Yudenich.[2] Out of Poland—the veteran legions of Petlura. Out of Crimea—the cavalry of Baron Wrangel.

A million-bayonetted ring of steel closed in upon the Revolution. The Revolution staggered under the blows rained upon it, but its heart was undaunted. If it must die—it would die fighting.

---

[1] Arthur Ransome (1884–1967) was a British journalist and writer who reported on the Russian Civil War from Siberia. His reflections on Lenin were included in Williams's book *Lenin* in 1919.

[2] Nikolai N. Yudenich (1862–1933) was the head of the Russian Imperial Army and leader of the White Movement in the Russian Civil War. After his imprisonment by the Bolsheviks, he spent the rest of his life in France.

The Revolution Fights for Life

Once more in the war weary villages and destitute towns throbbed the drums beating the call to arms. Once more the worn-out lathes and looms were ordered to produce uniforms and rifles. Once more the crippled railways were freighted with soldiers and cannon. Out of the almost exhausted resources of Russia the Revolution armed, uniformed and officered 5,000,000 men and the Red Armies took the field.

Only 400 miles from Moscow they hurled themselves against Kolchak and pushed his panic-stricken forces back the 4,000 miles they had advanced across Siberia. In the pine forests of the North, clad in uniforms of white, sliding through the snow on skis, they met the Allies and pushed them back on Archangel, forcing them to ship for home across the waters of the White Sea. They stopped the headlong rush of Denikin at Tula, the smithy of Russia, "in whose red fires the red steel is welded into the bayonets of the invincible Red Army." Driven back to the Black Sea shores he escaped on a British cruiser.

Budenny's Cavalry[3] racing day and night across the Ukrainian steppes flung themselves suddenly on the Polish flanks, turned the victorious advance of the legionaries into a disastrous retreat and harried them up to the gates of Warsaw. Wrangel[4] was beaten and bottled up in the Crimea, and while the shock troops of the Soviet hurled themselves against his concrete forts, the main Red Army hurried across the frozen Sea of Azov and the Baron fled to Turkey. In the outskirts of Petrograd, under its very domes, Yudenich was cut to pieces, the armies of the Baltic States were beaten back behind their borders, and the Whites annihilated in Siberia. The Revolution triumphed all around the circle.

The Counter-Revolutionists were broken not only by the heavy battalions of the Soviet, but by the idea Incarnated in these armies of the Revolution.

They were armies with banners, red banners emblazoned with the watchwords of a new world. They advanced into battle singing the songs of justice and fraternity. They treated their captured enemies as misguided brothers. They fed them, bound up their wounds and sent them back to tell in their own ranks stories of Bolshevik hospitality. They bombarded the Allied Camp with questions:

"Why did you come to Russia, Allied Soldiers?" "Why should workmen of France and England murder their fellow-workers of Russia?" "Do you want to destroy our Workmen's Republic?" "Do you want to restore the Czar?" "You are fighting for the

---

[3] Semyon M. Budenny (1883–1973), also spelled Budyonny, was a leading Soviet general in the Russian Civil War and an ally of Joseph Stalin.

[4] Pyotr N. Wrangel (1878–1928), also spelled Vrangel, was an officer in the Russian Imperial Army and a leader of the White armies in Southern Russia. He fled to Belgium after the Russian Civil War.

bond holders of France, the land grabbers of England, the imperialists of America. Why shed blood for them?" "Why don't you go home?"[5]

Red soldiers rose up to shout these questions across the trenches. Red sentries with hands uplifted rushed forward crying them out. Red aeroplanes dropped them circling down from the skies.

The allied troops pondered over these queries and were shaken. Their morale broke down. They fought half-heartedly. They mutinied. The Whites, in tens of thousands—whole battalions and ambulance corps—came over to the Revolution. One after another the armies of the Counter-Revolution crumpled up or melted away like snow in a Russian spring. The great steel cordon tightening around the Revolution was smashed to bits.

Havoc Wrought by Intervention

The Revolution was triumphant. The Soviets were saved. But with what appalling sacrifices!

"For three years," says Lenin, "our whole energy was devoted to the tasks of war." The wealth of the nation was poured into the army. Fields were untilled, machines untended. Lack of fuel shut down the factories. Green wood under the boilers ruined the locomotives. The retreating armies tore up railway tracks, blew up bridges and depots and fired the grain fields and the villages. The Poles not only destroyed the water-works and electric-station of Kiev, but in sheer malice dynamited the Cathedral of St. Vladimir.

The Counter-Revolutionists turned their retreat into an orgy of destruction. With torch and dynamite they laid waste the land, leaving behind a black wake of ruins and ashes.

A host of other evils came out of the war—drastic censorship, arbitrary arrests, drum-head court-martials. The high-handed measures charged against the Communists were to a large extent measures of war—none the less they were casualties to the ideals of the Revolution.

Then the human casualties! The death toll at the front was large. The death lists from the hospitals were appalling. Medicines, gauze and surgical instruments could not come through the blockade. So limbs were amputated without anesthetics. Wounds were bandaged with newspapers. Gangrene and blood poisoning, typhus and cholera swept through the armies unchecked.

The Revolution could have sustained the further loss in man-power—for Russia is vast. But it could not afford the loss in brain-power and soul-power, the wholesale massacre of its directing energizing spirits—the Communists. It was these Communists who bore the brunt of the fighting. They were formed into shock battalions.

---

[5] [William's note]: Appendix IV. A Bolshevik Circular for British Soldiers.

They were rushed into gaps to stiffen the wavering lines. Captured they were always killed. In the three years' war half the young Communists of Russia were slaughtered.

A mere recital of casualties means nothing, for statistics are only unemotional symbols. Let the reader recall the young men he has met in the pages of this book. They were at once dreamers and hard workers, idealists and stern realists—the flower of the Revolution, the incarnation of its dynamic spirit. It seems incredible for the Revolution to go on without them. But it does go on. For they are dead. Nearly everyone in this book is now in his grave. Here is the way some of them died:

Volodarsky—assassinated in the general plot to kill all Soviet leaders.
Neibut—executed on the Kolchak Front.
Yanishev—bayonetted by a White Guard on the Wrangel Front.
Woskov—died of typhus on the Denikin Front.
Tunganogi—shot at his desk by White Guards.
Utkin—dragged from motor car and shot.
Sukhanov—led into the woods in the early morning and clubbed to death with rifle butts.
Melnikov—taken out of prison, shot and bludgeoned.

"They were tortured, they were stoned, they were sawn asunder, they were set wandering in deserts and in mountains, in caves and in dens of the earth."

It was a cold selective killing of the keymen of the Revolution, a massacre of its future builders. An incalculable loss to Russia—for these were men who could withstand the corruption of office and the poison of power. Men who could live as valorously as they died.

They went to their death in order that the Revolution might live. And it does live. Though crippled and compromised, out of the long ordeal of famine, pestilence, blockade and war, the Russian Revolution emerges victorious.

Is the Revolution worth these sacrifices? These are its assured results:

One. It has destroyed root and branch the State apparatus of Czarism.

Two. It has transferred the great estates of the crown, the landlords and the monastic orders into the hands of the people.

Three. It has nationalized the basic industries and begun the electrification of Russia. It has fenced off Russia from the unlimited exploitation of free-booting capitalists.

Four. It has brought into the Soviets 1,000,000 workers and peasants and given them direct experience in government. It has organized 8,000,000 workers into trade unions. It has taught 40,000,000 peasants to read and write. It has opened the doors of tens of thousands of new schools, libraries, and theaters and roused the masses to the wonders of science and art.

Five. It has broken the spell of the past over a great people. Their potential forces have become kinetic. Their fatalistic: "It was so, and it will be so," is changed to "It was so, but it will not be so."

Six. It has assured self-determination to a score of subject races formerly held in vassalage to the Russian Empire. It has given them free hand to develop their own language, literature and institutions. Persia, China, Afghanistan, and other backward countries—that is "countries with great natural resources and small navies"—it has treated as equals.

Seven. It has not paid lip-service to "open diplomacy," but has made it a reality. "It has swept the secret treaties into the ash-barrel of history."

Eight. It has pioneered the way to a new society and made invaluable laboratory experiments in Socialism on a colossal scale. It has quickened the faith and increased the morale of the working classes of the world in their battle for the new social order.

The wise men rise up to point out that these results might have been obtained in a better way. Likewise the Reformation, the Independence of America, the Abolition of Slavery might have been achieved in a more gracious, less violent manner. But history did not move that way. And only the foolish quarrel with history.

Appendix I
THE DEATH OF A RED REGIMENT

Interview of Mr. N. Shiffrin with the editor of a military paper of the Counter-Revolutionary army of the North. Published in the anti-Bolshevik daily Der Tag, *September 7, 1919:*

"As you know the Bolsheviks changed the names of the old regiments. The Moscow troops have 'K.L.' on their shoulder straps—the initials of Karl Liebknecht.[1] We captured one of these regiments and they were tried. The trial at the White front is brief, Every soldier is examined, and if he admits that he is a Communist he is immediately sentenced to death by hanging or shooting. The Reds are well aware of this.

"Lieutenant K. approached the captured regiment and said: 'Those of you who are true Communists show yourselves courageous and step forward! A painfully oppressive interval.... Slowly in closed ranks over half of the regiment steps forward. They are sentenced to be shot. But before being shot they must dig their own graves.

"It is twilight. The air is full of the odor of fragrant northern flowers. The green dome of the village church is seen, surrounded by sleepy poplars. Peasants, women, children and soldiers crowd on the field, huddling together like sheep in a storm.

"The condemned are told to take off their clothes. The front is poor and their uniforms are needed by the Whites. In order to save the clothes from being soiled with blood or torn by bullets the prisoners are ordered to undress before they are shot. Slowly the Communists take off their shirts, and tying their clothes together in a bundle, they put them aside.

"They stand there in the field, freezing, and in the moonlight their skin appears extremely white, almost transparent. Each of them is given a pick axe and they begin digging large common graves. The dew is falling like a mild drizzle and there is a tear in every eye. The naked Communists keep on digging. It is getting darker and darker. There is a chaos of restlessly moving limbs. It is hard to distinguish the naked from the dressed.

"At last the graves have the necessary depth. The condemned sigh from weariness. Many throw themselves on the soft wet ground and rest. It is their last repose. Only

---

[1] Karl Liebknecht (1871–1919) was a German socialist and co-founder of the Spartacist League, who were seen as martyrs of the socialist movement.

now I notice that many have bandages around their feet. They have already been wounded in the struggle.

"Lieutenant K. asks them to state their last wish. Two take thin rings off their fingers and give them to the Lieutenant. The others have no wishes to make, altho every one of them has a home, a wife, children, relatives. I ask one of them 'What made a Communist of you?'

"He replies: 'The accursed life! The world needs happiness.'

"The firing squads are holding their rifles ready to shoot. The naked Communists take their positions close to one another, forming a white wall in the moonlight.... There is a command, a flash and the sound of rifles.... The Communists are still standing erect. A second volley rings out. The bullets strike home in their hearts, thick blood streams leap into space. Some are only slightly wounded. And in the fraction of a second before the soldiers shoot again, I hear deep sickening groans. Volley follows volley. Now those who are still alive cry out: 'Ho there, take better aim!' One points to his heart, crying, 'Aim here!'

"Finally, all are dead. Some are lying near the edge of the graves, others have fallen into them. It is all over. Nothing disturbs the quiet."

Appendix II
THE TRAIN OF DEATH

This is part of the diary of Mr. Rudolph Bukely, a Red Cross worker, formerly a banker in Honolulu. It reveals the conditions following Allied Intervention in Siberia, and shows the atrocities of White Terrorists against Bolsheviks and even innocent people. It is abbreviated from the American Red Cross Magazine *of April 1919 which says: "Propriety has demanded the exclusion of much that is unprintable."*

"It is the eighteenth day of November, 1918. I am at Nikolsk-Ussurisk in Siberia. In the past two days I have seen enough misery to fill a life-time. I will try to set down in my own manner what I have seen.

"I have seen, through the windows of box-cars, forty animals who once were human men, women and children; faces glared at me which I could not recognize as human beings. They were like beasts' faces, of a species unknown to man. Stark madness and terror stared from their eyes, and over all the unmistakable signs of death.

"I have seen the dead lying along the roadside, and fifty or sixty men fighting like dogs for pieces of bread thrown to them by the sympathetic poor people of Nikolsk....

"This *'train of death,'* for by that name all Eastern Siberia now knows it, left Samara about six weeks ago in charge of Russian officers. It had on board at that time 2,100 prisoners of all sorts.

"Since that day 800 of these wretches have died from starvation, filth, and disease. There were, as near as we could count, 1,325 men, women and children penned up in these awful cars yesterday.

"It seems a wicked thing to say, but the thought has surely come to me that to kill these people painlessly would require perhaps three dollars' worth of poison or ten dollars' worth of ammunition; and yet for weeks this train of fifty cars has been wandering, driven on from station to station, every day a few more corpses being dragged out. Many of these people have been in box-cars for five weeks in their original clothing. There are from 35 to 40 in a boxcar, measuring say 25 by 11 feet, and the doors have seldom been open save to drag out the bodies of the dead, or some woman who might better be. I have climbed into these cars at night with my flashlight. I have seen men with the death rattle in their throat, half naked, with lice and vermin visible on them; others just lying in a semi-unconscious stupor; and others with the whining grin of imbeciles, holding out their hands for a few cigarettes or kopecks, chuckling with glee like apes upon being given them.

"The Russian officer in charge of the train has made inconsistent statements about the reasons why these people have been subjected to such awful deprivation and abuse. He tries to make the best story of it possible.... Often for days at a time there has been no one to give them even bread. Were it not for or the kindness of the poor villagers who, with tears running down their cheeks, give them what little they can afford, they would be absolutely without nourishment.

"It is impossible to tell in print the story of the unfortunate women imprisoned here. They are treated better than the men. You all know why. In one car are 11 women. On the inside of the car hangs a piece of string. On it are four pairs of stockings owned by these 11 women. The floor is covered with refuse and filth. There are no means of cleaning it, neither brooms nor buckets. They have not taken off their clothing for weeks. All around the sides of the cars run two rows of planks, on which the inmates sleep at night and sit hunched up by day. If there ever is any official food for the prisoners, these women get the first pick and their physical condition is much better.

"Since we arrived a cooking car has been put on the train, with a large iron kettle, and yesterday the guards claim to have given the prisoners a little soup. One kettle for 1,325 people, and soup passed through a window a foot by a foot and a half, by means of an old rusty can! Yesterday one of the women was taken out by a Russian officer. He will return her when the train pulls out.... As we walked past the train, a man hailed us from one of the cars and the guards were told that there were dead inside. We insisted on the door being opened and this is what we saw:

"Lying right across the threshold was the body of a boy. No coat, merely a thin shirt, in such tatters that his whole chest and arms were exposed; for trousers a piece of jute bag pinned around him, and no shoes or stockings. What agony that boy must have suffered in the Siberian cold before he died of filth, starvation and exposure!

"And yet 'diplomacy' prevents us from taking charge and giving aid. But we are holding the train!

"We climbed into the car and found two other dead lying on the second tier of bunks amongst the living. Nearly every man was sunken-eyed, gaunt, and half clad. They were racked by terrible coughing. They had the stamp of death on them. If aid does not come quickly they will die. We looked into a few cars only, but at one window we saw a little girl perhaps eleven years old. Her father, she said, had been mobilized into the Red Guard. So now father, mother and child are on that train and will die there. Dr. Rosett is one of the most beautiful characters that I have ever known. When I saw him in the car talking to these poor wretches and trying to comfort them, I could not help thinking of the Good Physician and how He, too, labored among the maimed, the halt and the blind.

"... It is a strange thing that they all look at you with an expression sorrowful in the extreme, but never with a trace of bitterness. Suffering seems to have destroyed in them the power to express anger. I have visited the train at least ten times and I have never as yet seen any expression of any kind pass over the faces of these poor, tortured, dumb creatures.

"I went into the hospital last night. Fourteen were lying on the filthiest straw imaginable. Three of them turned their dull eyes on me, recognized the Red Cross uniform and got upon their poor worn knees. One of them, an old man of sixty, had a silver crucifix hanging around his neck. They sobbed soundless, body-racking sobs, and said in Russian, 'May God and Jesus Christ bless you and keep you for what you have done for us! We felt absolutely repaid for all our work of these days, during which time I have not bathed or shaved, nor had my clothes off, for I have dropped exhausted on my bed when I have finished transcribing my notes, and it was time to sleep....

"There is no use disguising the fact that these people are nearly all going to die, for as soon as the train shall have pulled out the old conditions will return and there will be once more the corpses thrown out day by day."

Mr. Bukely's prophecy that the death train would still be a death train was fulfilled. It went on over the Trans-Siberian, first west then east, back and forth, driven from town to town, the authorities at each place refusing to allow the prisoners to be taken out of the train or the train to remain within its jurisdiction.

On and on, days and nights, weeks running into months, the wretched company ever dwindling as death takes its cruel and incessant toll. [This was but one of many trains of death run by the anti-Bolshevist governments.

Appendix III
THE BURIAL OF YANISHEV

The Moscow Izvestia *of July 15, 1920, says:*

"On July 13 the Moscow proletariat buried Comrade Mikhail Petrovich Yanishev under the Kremlin wall. The first speaker, the Chairman of the Moscow Soviet, L. B. Kamenev said:

"'Of the many men who gave all to the cause of the working-class, Comrade Yanishev was one of the truest. Wherever there was call for an honest, brave and energetic man, Yanishev was sent. Recently he was appointed Chairman of the Moscow Revolutionary Tribunal. He was ordered to leave that responsible post and sent to the front against Denikin. On the way to the Western front he was ordered to the defense of South Russia from the bands of Wrangel. Though wounded in the shoulder he did not leave his place in the front lines, but continued leading his division forward until the treacherous hand of a White Guard brought him down with a bayonet. He is dead. But the cause for which Comrade Yanishev gave his life will not die. His blood was not spilt in vain. Many others will carry on the struggle and bring it to a victorious finish!'

"Comrade Likhachev spoke and the ceremony ended with a salute of three guns."

Appendix IV
A BOLSHEVIK CIRCULAR FOR BRITISH SOLDIERS

Why have you volunteered to come to Russia?

Why? Is it that you like war so much? Do you enjoy this rolling in mud and blood? Do you get satisfaction from seeing mangled bodies, and wrecked towns and villages? You claim to be the representatives of a civilized race! Is this how you propose to bring civilization into Russia?

Or is it that you feared being out of work and came to Russia as a form of employment? Were you tempted by the increased pay and extra rations? If that is so, it is strange employment for men who have just finished a war for "lasting peace."

Does it not strike you that what you are getting for your work is sheer Blood Money? It is the kind of work that cutthroats, blackguards, thieves and hooligans undertake to do for money. If these are the reasons for which you came, it is not much use appealing to your reason and humanity. The only argument that we can effectively use against you is the bullet and bayonet, and you will find that the Red Army will give you all you want of that. You will find your job "soft" enough when you find yourself sucked in the mud, in the marshes and forests of Northern Russia.

We cannot believe, however, that the majority of you volunteered for these reasons. Probably you were induced by the lies circulated by the capitalist press about the anarchy and terror prevailing in Russia. Probably you have been induced to believe that Bolsheviks are devils, who must be destroyed in order that the peace of the world may be secured. If that is so, we are convinced that when you learn the truth about Russia, you too will refuse to be the executioners of the Russian people, just like the British troops you replaced in the Caucasus, and the French and foreign troops in other parts who have refused.

There is no anarchy in Russia except that which the capitalist governments of the Allies are creating by invading Russia. You are not allaying anarchy, you are creating it. You are not bringing order in a country which is accused of disturbing the peace of the world, you are commencing a new war.

You are simply the tools of the capitalists and landlords in your countries who have sent you here to "punish" the Russian workers and peasants for having dared to revolt against their oppressors. The Russian Soviet Republic is a Workers' and Peasants' Republic. The land and the wealth of Russia now belong to the working-people of Russia. You have been brought here to overthrow the power of the workers and restore tsarism, landlordism and capitalism. Your governments are officially supporting the Tsarist officers, Kolchak and Denikin, with arms and money for the avowed purpose of restoring the old régime. And you are not merely helping, you are doing this.

Without your aid, the counter-revolution in Russia would have been suppressed long ago, the civil war would have been ended and order restored. And the Russian people would have long ago had the opportunity of developing their agriculture and industry.

Volunteers! You are workingmen too. What interests have you in fighting for the gang of Russian counter-revolutionaries and international capitalists? As workingmen, your business should be to support your fellow workers in those places where they succeed in taking power, for the victory of the workers in one country is a step toward the emancipation of the workers in all countries.

In fighting the Russian workers, you are Scabbing; your fellow-workers at home, knowing the real reason of your being sent here, are preparing for a general strike against intervention in Russia. In continuing to do the work of your government, you are Scabbing on your fellow workers at home.

Comrades! it is dirty work you are doing. Have the courage to pitch it. Do not let it be said that English workingmen were so mean and contemptible as to suppress their own fellow-workers for the sake of a little extra money and food.

Comrades! Do not be scabs. Stand by your clan in the great world movement for the emancipation of labor.

Appendix V
YESTERDAY AND TODAY
By Maxim Gorky

Yesterday was the day of the Great Falsehood—the last day of its power.

For ages, man has, spider-like, thread by thread, diligently woven the strong cobweb of a cautious philistine life, impregnating it more and more with falsehood and greed. Man fed on the flesh and blood of his fellow men. The means of production were used to oppress men,—this cynical falsehood was regarded as immutable truth.

And yesterday this road brought mankind to the madness of the great World War. In the red glow of this nightmare the ugly nakedness of this old falsehood was brought to light. Now we see the old world shaken to its foundations. Its hidden secrets are exposed, and today even the blind have opened their eyes and see the utter ugliness of the past.

Today is the day of reckoning for the falsehood which reigned yesterday.

The violent explosion of the people's patience has destroyed the outworn order of life, and it cannot again be reestablished in its old forms. Not all of the outworn past is annihilated, but it will be—tomorrow.

Today there is a great deal of horror, but it is all natural and comprehensible. Is it not natural that people infected by the strong poisons of the old order—alcohol and syphilis—should not be generous? Is it not natural for people to steal,—if theft was the fundamental law of yesterday? Is it not natural, that tens, hundreds, thousands of men should be killed, after being accustomed for years to kill them by millions? The seed of yesterday brings the fruit of today.

We should understand that in the midst of the dust and mud and chaos of today, there has already begun the great work of liberating mankind from the strong, iron cobweb of the past. It is as painful and difficult as the pangs of a new birth; but it is the death of the evil of yesterday, going through its last hours together with the man of yesterday.

It has so happened that the peoples marching to the decisive battle for the triumph of justice are led by the least experienced and weakest fighters,—by the Russians, a people of a backward land, a people worn out by its past more than any other people. Only yesterday the whole world looked upon them as semi-barbarians, and today, almost dying from hunger, they are marching toward victory or death with the ardor and courage of veterans.

Everyone who sincerely believes that the irresistible aspiration of mankind toward freedom, beauty, and a sensible life is not a vain dream, but that it is a real force which alone can create new forms of life, the lever which can move the world,—every honest man must recognize the universal significance of the activity now carried on by the earnest revolutionists of Russia.

The revolution should be interpreted as a gigantic attempt to incorporate in life, the great ideas and watchwords created and enunciated by the teachers of mankind. Yesterday the socialist thought of Europe pointed the way to the Russian people; today the Russian worker is striving for the triumph of European thought.

If the honest Russian revolutionists, few in number, surrounded by enemies and exhausted by starvation, shall be conquered, the consequences of this terrible calamity will fall heavily on the shoulders of all the working class of Europe.

The Russian worker is confident that his brothers in spirit will not permit the strangling of the revolution in Russia, that they will not permit the resuscitation of the order, which is expiring and which will disappear,—if the revolutionary thought of Europe will comprehend the great tasks of today.

Come and go with us towards the new life, whose creation we work for without sparing ourselves and without sparing anybody or anything. Erring and suffering, in the great joy of labor and in the burning hope of progress, we leave to the honest judgment of history all our deeds. Come with us to battle against the ancient order and to labor for the new. Forth to life's freedom and beauty!

Appendix VI
DECLARATION OF THE RIGHTS OF THE WORKING AND EXPLOITED PEOPLES

(Rejected by the Constituent Assembly, January 18, 1918. Accepted by the great Third Congress of Soviets, January 27, 1918.)

I. RUSSIA is declared a Republic of Workmen's, Soldiers' and Peasants' councils. The whole central and local authority rests with the Councils (Soviets). The Russian Soviet Republic is declared a free alliance of free nations and a federation of national republics.

II. With the object of removing the exploitation of man by man, of preventing the division of society into classes, of mercilessly suppressing all exploiters, of establishing a socialist organization of society and of securing the victory of Socialism in all lands, the Great Convention (Third All-Russian Congress) makes the following declarations:

   a. With the object of realizing the socialization of land, all private property in the land is abolished, and the whole territory of the Republic is declared the property of the people and is without compensation handed over to the working population on the basis equal rights of utilization for all. All forests, natural wealth and water power of public value, all live and dead stock, model farms and agricultural stations, are declared national property.
   b. As a first step towards the complete transference of factories, mines, railways, and of the means of production and distribution to the possession of the Workers' and Peasants' Republic, the decrees concerning Workmen's Control and concerning the Supreme Council of Public Economy are hereby confirmed.
   c. As one of the conditions for the emancipation of the working masses from the yoke of capitalism, the transference of all banks to the possession of the Workers' and Peasants' Soviet Republic is confirmed.
   d. With the object of removing parasitical elements of society and of securing industrial organization on a public basis, the obligation of every citizen to work is recognized.
   e. In the interests of securing the full authority of the toiling masses and of removing all possibilities of a re-establishment of the power of the exploiters, the arming of the workers, the formation of a Red Army out

of workmen and peasants, and the complete disarming of the propertied classes is hereby decreed.

III. With the firm intention of rescuing mankind from the claws of finance, capital and of imperialism, which have flooded the earth with blood in the most criminal of all wars, the Great Convention endorses and confirms the following acts of the Soviet Commissars:

   a. The annulling of the Secret Treaties, the organization of fraternization between the workmen and peasants of the armies now opposing each other in the field, the conclusion at all costs of a democratic peace by the workers themselves, without annexations or indemnities, on the basis of the self-determination of nations through revolutionary means.
   b. The complete break with the barbarous policy of capitalist civilization, which establishes the power of the exploiters in a few select nations at the cost of the enslavement of hundreds of millions of the toiling masses in Asia, in the colonies and in all small countries.
   c. The recognition of -the complete independence of Finland, the withdrawal of the Russian armies from Persia, and the right of self-determination for Armenia.
   d. The annulling of the loans which were concluded by the government of the tsar, the foreign banks and the Russian bourgeoisie, as the first blow against international bank and finance-capital.

IV. The Great Convention believes that the time is at hand for the decisive struggle with the exploiters, for whom there is now no place in the organs of government. Power must be now wholly and exclusively in the hands of the toiling masses and of their representative organs—the Soviets of Workmen's, Soldiers' and Peasants' Deputies.

Moscow, Oct. 26th 1921—The humblest peasant may come to ask the help or advice of Kalinin, the President of the Soviet Republic, with none to bar his way.

Around him come pressing two or three score of men dressed in rough untanned sheepskin or dun-colored cloth, that hall-mark of the Russian villagers. Some are carrying a sack of food or a bedroll, token of the long journey they made to lay their case before Kalinin.

He greets his visitors simply and talks to one after another in the same peasant dialect as theirs.

It is hard to realize that here before one's eyes is the secret of the no small Bolshevist hold on the Russian people. More than any of his colleagues, more even than Lenin, Kalinin knows what the peasants think, what they love or hate and what they want.

However impossible it is for him to appease their grievance or satisfy their requests, he contrives somehow to send them away comforted and almost contented. For the man streams magnetism in every word and gesture.

"See, now, little mother," he says persuasively to an old woman who has traveled a thousand miles to ask Kalinin that her village be let off the food tax because the harvest is only half what was estimated, "your crop is only 500 poods instead of 1,000. Then you will pay only 25 poods instead of 55 on each hundred—that is your tax.

"More than that we cannot do, for we must feed our hungry brothers on the Volga, who have no crop at all—you would not have them starve."

The old woman shakes her head strongly and backs away with the evident feeling that somehow she has got the tax reduced 50 per cent, which will be good news for her fellow-villagers.

Next comes a young soldier who claims that as a veteran of the Polish war he should not pay a tax at all.

"But you are a man of Tula," says Kalinin, "and Tula folks, farm as well as they fight. Why, I hear Tula has the best crop in Russia. Surely you won't grudge help to hungry brothers not so clever or lucky as you?"

The soldier looks sheepish but sticks stubbornly to his point.

"This is, the first year I have been able to sow or reap my own harvest for seven years, Comrade Kalinin. Others reaped while I was fighting to defend them. Now let them pay the tax for me."

The President takes him up like a flash.

"What!" he cries, "Others worked to feed you while you were winning glory?"— he bends forward and touches the red star medal on the youngster's army overcoat— "well, now you, too, must give something to help those who need it."

This time he has struck home, The soldier flushes with pride, and, as he shakes the President's hand with a firm grip, he mutters:

"That's only fair, comrade. I will tell the rest of the soldiers of our village what you say, and all will help."

And so it goes. An old man from Tambov and a widow from a village near Moscow get part of their tax remitted because the former is supporting a war-broken son, and the latter, five fatherless little children. And the peasants go back to Russia's myriad villages with a message of good tidings from Kalinin, the new Little Father of the people.

WALTER DURANTY, correspondent,
in the *New York Times*, Oct. 29th, 1921

Appendix VII
PLACARDS AND POSTERS

Machine-guns played their part in the Revolution. But a bigger part was played by the printing-presses. The Soviet waged a mighty battle with ink as well as lead. Every crisis, every important event, produced its corresponding placard or poster. They were pasted on walls and *kiosks*—one on top of the other—in some places 20 and 30 deep. Arranged in order, they would tell a complete story: *The History of the Revolution in Posters from the Walls of Petrograd and Moscow.*

Six of these posters appear in the foregoing text. Five more are printed in the following pages. (On the left-hand page, a facsimile of the original Russian; on the right-hand page, in English.)

Ко всѣмъ рабочимъ ПЕТРОГРАДА!

Товарищи! Революція побѣждаетъ—революція побѣдила. Вся власть перешла къ нашимъ Совѣтамъ. Первыя недѣли самыя трудныя. Надо раздавить до конца сломленную уже реакцію, надо обезпечить полное торжество нашимъ стремленіямъ. Рабочій классъ долженъ, обязанъ проявить въ эти дни

величайшую выдержку и выносливость,

чтобы облегчить Новому Народному Правительству Совѣтовъ выполненіе всѣхъ задачъ. На этихъ же дняхъ будутъ изданы новые законы по рабочему вопросу и въ томъ числѣ однимъ изъ самыхъ первыхъ законъ о рабочемъ контролѣ надъ производствомъ и объ регулированіи промышленности.

Забастовки и выступленія рабочихъ массъ въ Петроградѣ теперь только вредятъ.

Мы просимъ васъ немедленно прекратить всѣ экономическія и политическія забастовки, всѣмъ стать на работу и производить ее въ полномъ порядкѣ. Работа на заводахъ и во всѣхъ предпріятіяхъ необходима новому правительству Совѣтовъ, потому что всякое разстройство работъ создастъ для насъ новыя затрудненія, которыхъ и безъ того довольно. Всѣ къ своему мѣсту.

Лучшее средство поддержать новое правительство Совѣтовъ въ эти дни—исполнить свое дѣло.

Да здравствуетъ твердая выдержка пролетаріата! Да здравствуетъ революція!

Петроградскій Совѣтъ Р. и С. Д.
Петроградскій Совѣтъ Профессіональныхъ Союзовъ.
Центральный Совѣтъ Фабрично-Заводскихъ Комитетовъ.

To All Workers of Petrograd!

Comrades! The Revolution is winning, the Revolution has won. All the power has passed over to our Soviets. The first weeks are the most difficult ones. The broken reaction must be finally crushed, a full triumph must be secured for our endeavors. The working-class ought to —must—show in these days

THE GREATEST FIRMNESS AND ENDURANCE

in order to facilitate the execution of all the aims of the new People's Government of Soviets. In the next few days, decrees on the Labor question will be issued. Among the very first will be the decree on Worker's Control over the production and regulation of industry.

STRIKES AND DEMONSTRATIONS OF THE WORKER MASSES IN PETROGRAD NOW CAN ONLY DO HARM.

We ask you to stop immediately all economic and political strikes, to take up your work, and do it in perfect order. The work in factories and all industries is necessary for the new Government of Soviets, because any interruption of this work will only create new difficulties, and we have enough as it is. All to your places.

The best way to support the new Government of Soviets in these days—is by doing your job.

LONG LIVE THE IRON TENACITY OF THE PROLETARIAT! LONG LIVE THE REVOLUTION!

Petrograd Soviet of W. & S. D.
Petrograd Council of Trade Unions.
Central Council of Factory-Shop Committees.

TO ALL WORKERS OF PETROGRAD. An appeal to celebrate the success of the November revolution—not by strikes and demonstrations, but by quietness and work.

Отъ Комиссіи по Народному Образованію при Центральной Городской Думѣ.

Товарищи рабочіе и работницы

За нѣсколько дней до праздника была объявлена забастовка учащими городскихъ училищъ. Учащія оказались на сторонѣ буржуазіи противъ рабочаго и крестьянскаго Правительства.

Товарищи, организуйте родительскіе комитеты и выносите резолюціи противъ забастовки учащихъ. Обращайтесь въ районные Совѣты Рабочихъ и Солдатскихъ Депутатовъ, профессіональные союзы, фабрично-заводскіе и партійные комитеты съ предложеніемъ устраивать митинги протеста. Устраивайте собственными силами елки и развлеченія для дѣтей, требуйте возобновленія занятій послѣ праздника въ срокъ, который укажетъ Центральная Дума.

Товарищи, укрѣпляйте свои позиціи въ дѣлѣ народнаго образованія, настаивайте на контролѣ пролетарскихъ организацій надъ школой.

Комиссія по Народному Образованію
при Центральной Городской Думѣ.

From the Commission on Public Education of the Central City Duma.

Comrade workingmen and workingwomen!

A few days before the holidays, a strike has been declared by the teachers of the public schools. The teachers are siding with the burgeoisie against the Workers' and Peasants' Government.

Comrades, organize Parents' Committees and pass resolutions against the strike of the teachers. Propose to the District Soviets of Workers' and Soldiers' Deputies, the Trade Unions, the Factory-Shop and Party Committees, to organize protest meetings. Arrange with your own resources Christmas trees and entertainments for the children, and demand the opening of the schools, after the holidays at the date which will be set by the Central Duma.

Comrades, strengthen your position in public education, insist on the control of the proletarian organizations over the schools.

Commission on Public Education
of the Central City Duma.

THE COMMISSION ON PUBLIC EDUCATION. The Bolsheviks had the majority in the newly elected Petrograd Duma. They sought to arouse public sentiment in protest against the teachers' strike.

Россійская Соціалъ-Демократическая Рабочая Партія.

ПРАВДА

Цѣна 25 коп.

ЦЕНТРАЛЬНЫЙ ОРГАНЪ Р. С.-Д. Р. П.

№ 33 (260). Суббота. ЕЖЕДНЕВНАЯ ГАЗЕТА. 23 (10) февраля 1918 г.

Нѣмецкіе генералы организовали ударные батальоны и врасплохъ, безъ предупрежденія, напали на нашу армію, мирно приступившую къ демобилизаціи.

Но уже сопротивленіе организуется. Оно растетъ и будетъ рости съ каждымъ днемъ. Всѣ наши силы отдадимъ на отпоръ германскимъ бѣлогвардейцамъ!

Ибо они идутъ, чтобы вернуть помѣщикамъ отобранныя крестьянами земли. Они идутъ, чтобъ возстановить хозяйскія права и хозяйскій произволъ на фабрикахъ и заводахъ. Они идутъ, чтобъ вернуть бывшимъ помѣщикамъ и хозяевамъ Романовымъ — тронъ, земли и милліарды.

Рабочіе, крестьяне, солдаты! На защиту совѣтской республики! Всѣ, не медля, въ ряды Красной арміи соціализма!

Россійская Коммунистическая Партія (большевиковъ).

ПРАВДА

Цѣна 30 коп.

ЦЕНТРАЛЬНЫЙ ОРГАНЪ КОММУНИСТИЧЕСКОЙ ПАРТІИ (большевиковъ).

№ 45 (271) Суббота. ЕЖЕДНЕВНАЯ ГАЗЕТА. 9 марта (24 февраля) 1918 г.

Русскіе контръ-революціонеры, съ княземъ Львовымъ во главѣ, создали на Дальнемъ Востокѣ новое правительство.

Предатели вступили въ союзъ съ японскими имперіалистами, чтобы закабалить страну.

Помѣщики и капиталисты изъ-за возстановленія своей власти надъ рабочими и крестьянами продаютъ Японіи Дальній Востокъ.

Къ оружію, рабочіе и крестьяне! Вставайте всѣ, какъ одинъ человѣкъ, на борьбу за великую революцію!

Всѣ на защиту соціалистическаго отечества!
===== КЪ ОРУЖІЮ! =====

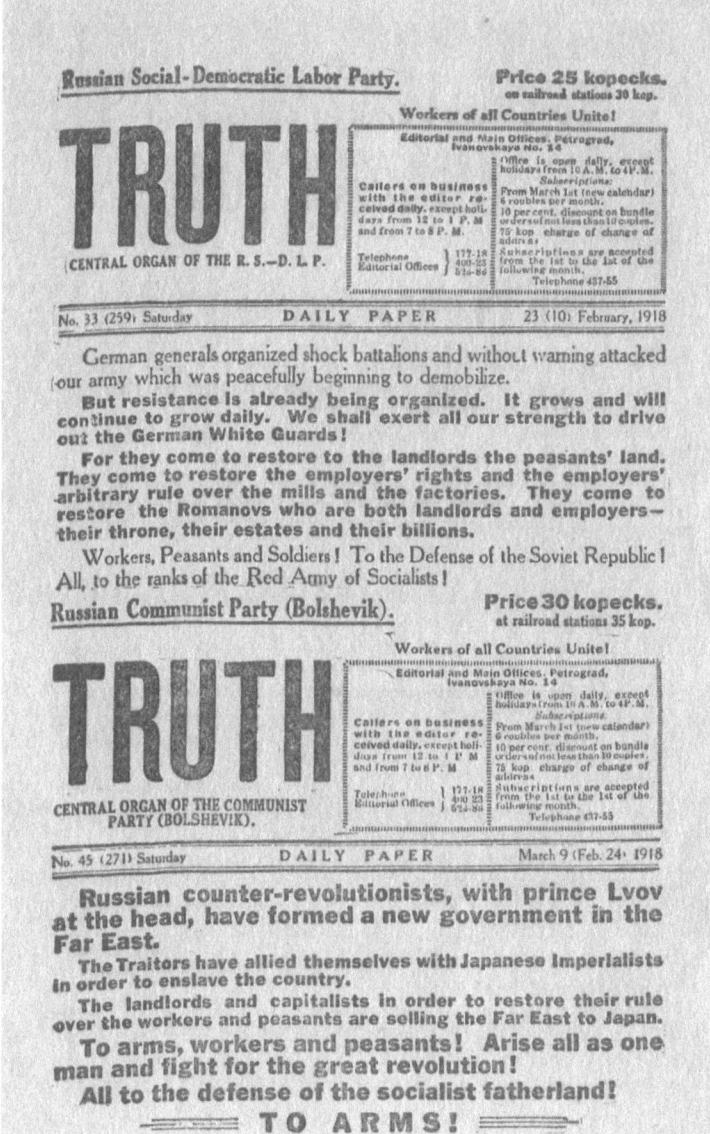

Pravda (**Truth**). Two half-pages of the official Bolshevik newspaper, calling the people to arms against the Germans and Japanese. In issue No. 33, February 23, the price is 25 kopecks. In issue No. 45, two weeks later, the price is 30 kopecks. The two issues show likewise the change of name in the Party. Note also the double number in the date line, "23 (10) February." By Soviet decree the old Julian calendar—13 days behind the rest of the world—was replaced by the Gregorian calendar.

ОТ САМАРСКОЙ ФЕДЕРАЦИИ АНАРХИСТОВ

ПО ПОВОДУ „ДЕКРЕТА".

Враг безсилен. Враг падает ниже и ниже. И в своем падении кощунствует. И в своем падении клевещет. И пускается на самыя отвратительныя провокационныя меры.

Враг угнетенных — он жаждет господства, и страшнее всех для него анархисты, поднявшие высоко знамя свободы.

И враг распространяет злостную клевету, что свобода эта простирается до насилия женщин. От нашего имени распространяет он своими грязными руками «Декрет о социализации женщин».

Какая грубая, нелепая провокация!

Веками, всюду и повсюду анархисты борются со всякими декретами и законами всяких властей, — так могут ли они сами выпускать декреты?

Враги всякого насилия, — могут ли анархисты требовать или даже допускать принудительнаго отчуждения женщин?

Сколько же найдется таких буридановых ослов, что поверят этой провокации, что впрягут себя в стан этих гадюк шипящих?

Нет и нет! Стремясь натравить на нас безсознательныя массы, враг не разсчитал и обнажил только свою грязную душеньку.

Увы! — он еще не узнал всей остроты нашего оружия — так узнает!

Смерть провокаторам! Безпощадная смерть! На месте — без колебания — всеми средствами и всяким оружием!

И всякий, кто — тайно или явно — будет поддерживать эту клевету, прикидываясь одураченным ягненком, — будет объявлен соучастником этой темной банды, будет объявлен провокатором. И постигнет их участь одна...

И всякий, кто — с нами или не с нами — но честно живет и борется, будет помогать нам в расправе, будет сам мстить этим ядовитым гадам подымающейся реакции.

Для расправы огня хватит у нас!

И все средства будут хороши!

Самарская Федерація Анархистов.

FROM THE SAMARA FEDERATION OF ANARCHISTS

IN VIEW OF THE "DECREE"

The enemy is impotent. The enemy is sinking ever lower and lower. And in his fall he blasphemes. In his fall he slings mud at us. He stoops to the most hideous provocatory measures.

The enemy of the oppressed—he thirsts for domination. He fears the Anarchists who have raised high the banner of freedom.

The enemy is spreading malicious calumny, insinuating that our freedom includes violence and rape. In our name he is spreading with his own soiled hands the "Decree about the Nationalization of Women."

What crude, absurd provocation!

For ages, everywhere, the Anarchists have fought against all kinds of decrees and laws no matter by what authorities these were set up. How then can they themselves issue decrees?

Enemies of all violence, how can the Anarchists demand or even allow force in the treatment of women?

How many such asses will be found who will be ready to believe the provocateurs and who will appear in the camp of these serpents?

No, never! In his attempt to set against us the ignorant masses, the enemy did not calculate correctly and only exposed his own filthy soul.

Alas! he does not yet know the power of our weapon—but he will know it!

Death to the provocateurs! No mercy for them! On the spot—without hesitation—by all means, with any weapon!

And everyone, who—secretly or openly—supports this calumny, by pretending that he is an innocent lamb who has been duped by someone, will be considered an accomplice of this black band, as a provocateur. And they will meet the same fate.

Everyone—whether he be with us or not—but who lives honestly and struggles for his living, will help us dispense justice, and will himself mete out vengeance to these venomous reptiles of reaction.

We have enough fire for this purpose!

And all means will be fair!

Samara Federation of Anarchists.

FROM THE SAMARA FEDERATION OF ANARCHISTS. In order to blacken the Anarchists, it was said that they had declared for the Nationalization of Women. Infuriated at this slander, they put out this hot repudiation. The so-called "Decree for the Nationalization of Women," of course, had no existence anywhere in Russia. Even the most extreme groups never considered the idea. It was a monstrous canard invented by the enemies of the revolution.

Bread!

For the defenders of the peasants' land taken from the landlord.

Bread!

To win the fight against the threatening danger of German slavery and bourgeois' serfdom it is necessary to supply IMMEDIATELY all northern Russia with bread.

Bread!

To the fighters for the power of the peasant, worker and soldier.

To the peasants of all the bread-producing districts and provinces

BROTHER PEASANTS!

Dear brothers! From the depths of our souls we, fighting revolutionists, appeal to you. ANSWER THE CALL! The last hour of the decisive battle strikes. This is the question at stake.

LAND TO THE TOILERS WITHOUT COMPENSATION, THE FACTORIES, SHOPS AND BANKS.

Send us bread, that we may not be broken by hunger and that we may be able to hold up our bayonets against the cut-throats of the world.

THE SOCIALISTS FATHERLAND IS IN DANGER!

Bread! Bread! Bread!

Bring your bread to the empty elevators and granaries, to the shipping-points on railways and the wharves of navigable rivers.

Our railroads have broken down on account of unprecedented disorders. Cowards, marauders and speculators having put on soldiers' uniforms are doing violence at the railway stations and are thus hindering the regular movement of trains. True and class-conscious soldiers, peasants and workers of the Revolution! We appeal to you to aid those guarding our railways, and to stop the hooligans from further violence. All these destroyers of the railways are helping our bitter enemy—the German bourgeoise, and are therefore—without the law.

Bread! Bread! Bread!

INDEX

abolition of capital punishment 92
Abramov 142
Abramovich, Raphael Rein 62, 62n5
Alexandrov 28
Allied capitalists enter Russia through Vladivostok 135
Allies crush the Soviet 149–50
All-Russian Congress of Soviets (First): Williams attends xvii
American Bar Association Journal: praises Williams's book xxii
American reaction to revolution 160–61
American Red Cross 22n2
"American Works": produces American cars 139–40
Antonov 138
Antonov-Ovseyenko, Vladimir A. 79, 79n4; leadership of 86–93; prevents execution of monarchists 86–94

Babushka. *See* Breshko-Breshkovskaya, Ekaterina K.
Bakunin, Mikhail 29
balalaika 31n1
Ball, John 143
Barkley, Alben xxiii
Beatty, Bessie (Elizabeth) xvii, xix, xxii, 7, 22n2; witnessed taking of Winter Palace 65
Berkman, Aaron 7
Biletsky, Leonid 92, 92n6
Black Hundreds 5, 5n1, 23, 23n5
Bolshevik Party 17n8
Bolshevik: opposed by peasants, anarchists, Germans 104; policies of 113–14; produce circular for British soldiers 181–82; strength of 110–13; underestimated 17n8
Bolsheviks trained in America 18–19
Bolshevism, peasants wary of 36–37

bourgeois: call for reprisals 151–54; sabotage of 96–99; strike 20
Breshko-Breshkovskaya, Ekaterina K. 20n16
Brest-Litovsk, Treaty of xx
Bronstein, Lev D. *See* Trotsky, Leon
Bryant, Louise xvii, xxii: witnessed taking of Winter Palace 65, 65n2
Budenny, Semyon M. 168, 169n3
Bukely, Rudolph 175
Burtsev, Valdimir L. 93, 93n9

Candide 135n2
Cheka 98
Cherm: prison described 128–32; prisoners described 129–32
Chernov, Victor M. 26, 26n7, 104
Chicherin, Georgy V. 124, 124n1
Chkheidze, Nikolai 14n4, 15; asks Williams to address Congress 14
Church, wealth of 34
"Committee of Salvation" 95, 99–100
Committee on Public Information (USA) 103
Communist Party 166
Constituent Assembly 106–08
Cossacks 5, 5n1, 28, 78
Counter-Revolution: begins 78–80; Soviet fights back 149–51
Cycle Corps 58, 59n4
Czecho-Slovaks 149–50

Dan, Fyodor I. 61, 61n1
Dead Souls 41
Debs, Eugene V. xv
Declaration of the Rights of Working and Exploited Peoples 107, 185–87
Decree for the Nationalization of Women 167
Dell, Floyd xxii–xxiii
Denikin, Anton I. 110n7, 182
Dictatorship of the Proletariat 114
diplomacy now led by workingmen 143–44

Dukhonin, Nikolai N. 91
Duncan, James 17
Duranty, Walter 187
Dybenko, Pavel 46, 46n1
education 113
eight-hour law 113
El Dorado 135
émigrés: find refuge in Vladivostok 135–36; unmoved by Cherm 132; view of the revolution 121–23
Engineers' Castle 82, 82n6
Extraordinary Commission (Cheka) 99

Far East Soviet 134
Field of Mars 15, 15n5
First All-Russian Congress of Soviets 24; Williams attends xvii
flyers (posters) 66–67, 76–77, 97–98; 102–03, 115–16
foreign agents in Williams's detachment 114
French Quay 82, 82n5

Gogol, Nikolai 41, 41n1
Goldstein, Moisei M. *See* Volodarsky, V.
Gompers, Samuel 103, 103n7
Goodsell, Fred 163
Gorky, Maxim 39, 39n6, 72, 183–84
Gumberg, Alex 22, 22n2, 65; travels with Williams 42–43

Hartford Theological Seminary xv
honeymoon of the Revolution 7

In the Claws of the German Eagle: Williams published xvi
Industrial Workers of the World (IWW) xxii

Jerome 150
Jordan 138
Journey into the Revolution: Petrograd, 1917–1918, Williams family publishes xxiv
Jukov, President. *See* Zhukov, Georgy
July Days xviii

Kaledin, Aleksei M. 75, 75n1, 186
Kamenev, Lev B. 109, 109n2, 180
Kerensky, Alexander: fights back against rebellion 58–59; flees from Reds 78; Williams meets xvii; Williams wants to hear 13, 13n2
Khrushchev, Nikita xxiv
Kimball, Mrs. Jessie Y. 7
Kolchak, Alexander 182
Kollontai, Alexandra M. 28, 28n10, 46n1, 99
Kornilov, Lavr G. 45, 45n5, 46, 49, 55, 136
Krasnoschekov, Alexander 18, 18n9, 139, 144
Krasnov, Peter N. 93, 93n8
Krylenko, Nikolai V. 63, 63n6
Kuntz, Charles 111–12, 111n8; joins foreign detachment 114; joins Williams in going home 117; leaves Petrograd with Williams 121; works with Petrovich 125–26

Lawrence Textile Strike xvi
Left Socialist Revolutionists 106, 106n11
Lenin, Vladimir xvii, 18, 18n10, 28; comes out of hiding 58; mission to withdraw Russia from World War I xx; on revolution 170; praises workers 109; underestimated 17n8; wants Williams to form foreign detachment 114; worries about revolution 110; writes letter of passage for Williams 124
Lenin: The Man and His Work: Williams publishes xxii
Liebknecht, Karl 173, 173n1
Lifschiz, Jerome 143
Lunacharsky, Anatoly xix, 109, 109n3

"Magna Carta of the Russian Revolution" 107
Man on Horseback, The 41–44
Marietta College xv
Martov, Julius 62, 62n4
Marx-Engels Institute 27n9
Maverick Congregational Church xv, xvi
Melnikov, Konstantin 138, 138n5, 153–54, 171
Mensheviks 15
Military Port 140–41
Milyukov, Pavel 5n3, 6–7
Milyutin, Nikolai 109, 109n2
Murovsky, Captain 142

nationalization of banks 100
Nationalization of Women, Decree for the 167, 196–97

Neibut, Arnold 19, 19n14, 171
Nekrasov, Nikolai A. 35, 35n4
new order 114
Nicholas II 5n2, 13
Night Asylum, The 39
Nikeferov, Pyotr 138, 138n6
Nikolayev, General 107–08
Nizhnii-Novgorod" established 15; Williams visits home there 15–6
Nogin, Victor P. 109, 109n2
Nolde, Boris E. 56, 56n2

Overman Committee xxii

Palace of Motherhood 113
Panina, Countess Sofia V. 99, 99n4
Peasant and Worker 143
peasants wary of Bolshevism 36–37
People's University 143
Peresvet 7, 7n7
Peshkov, Aleksei Maksimovich. *See* Gorky, Maxim
Peter the Great 19
Peters, Yakov Kh. 110, 110n4
Petrograd 13
Petrovich, Andrei 124–27
placards and posters 189–99
pogroms 100, 100n6
Pokrovsky, Mikhail N. 110, 110n5
Popov 142
Potemkin, Grigory 23n
Pravda 20, 194–95
Preminsky 138, 150
Present Government of Russia, The xii
prisons 128–32
Provisional Government 6n5
Pugachev, Emelian 5n1

Quay with Sphinxes 82n5

Radomsylsky, Ovsei-Gershon. *See* Zinoviev, Grigory
Ransome, Arthur xxii, 168
Rasputin, Grigory 5, 5n2
Razin, Stenka 5n1
rebellion breaks out 55–59
Red Banner 143
Red Funeral 154–55
Red Heart of Russia, The 48n4

Redding, Jo 133
Reds oppose Counter-Revolution 78–83
Reed, John xvii, xxii, 22n2, 81; publishes *Ten Days that Shook the World* xxii; travels with Williams 43, 43n4; with Williams makes illustrated sheet 105; with Williams visits Petrograd Prefect of Police 112; witnessed taking of Winter Palace 65
Reinstein, Boris 43, 43n4
revolution 80–81, 171–72
revolutionaries abolish capital punishment 92
Riazanov, David B. 27, 27n9
Robbins, Raymond xiii, xxii, 104, 104n9, 167
Rodzianko, Mikhail V. 55, 55n1
Romanov dynasty destroyed 6
Root Mission, xvii, xciii–xix, 17, 17n8, 22
Root, Elihu 17
Rozenfeld, Lev B. *See* Kamenev, Lev B.
Russian navy 47–50
rubashkas 21
Russian navy taken over by sailors 46–48
Russian village, Williams describes 30–41
Russians, The: The Land, The People, and Why They Fight xiii
Rykov, Aleksei I. 109, 109n2

Saakian, Sargis (Sako) 26, 26n8
Sadovnikov 126–27
sailors 47–50
Samara Federation of Anarchists 196–97
Sartov 15–16
Second All-Russian Congress of Soviets 60
Semyonov, Grigory M. 142–43, 142n1,
Sevretsev 144
Shatsky, Stanislav 95, 95n1
Shiffrin, N. 173
Sinclair, Upton xxi
Singer sewing machine 35
Socialist Revolutionary Party 15
Soldier, The 20
Soviet (Council) of Workmen Deputies 6
Soviet resistance 163
Soviets: proclaimed by Russian government 63; restrained looters 71–72
Soviets of Soldiers Deputies 6
Spargo, John 110n6
Sputnik xxiv
Squersky 163
Squier, Lucita xxiii

St. Michael's Castle 82n6
Stalin, Joseph 18n10
steppes of Russia 121–27
Sukhanov, Constantin 136, 150, 158–59, 167, 171
Sukhanov, Nikolai xix
Sukhomlinov, Vladimir A. 92, 92n7

Tauride Palace 23, 23n3, 24, 25
teachers' strike 192–93
Ten Days that Shook the World xxii
Tereshechenko, Mikhail I. 71, 92
Thacher, Thomas D. 162, 162n1
Third Congress of Soviets 185
Through the Russian Revolution xv, xxii
To All Workers of Petrograd 190–91
"To the People" movement 61n3
Train of Death 175–77
Trans-Siberian Express 121–27
Treaty of Brest-Litovsk xx
Trotsky, Leon 26, 27: refuses to sign First Treaty of Brest-Litovsk 114; rejects intelligentsia 62; thinks revolution too lenient in beginning 93
Truman, Harry xxiii
Tunganogi 144, 171
Tyutchev, Fyodor 65, 65n1

Ulianov, Vladimir. *See* Lenin, Valdimir
Union of Miners 140
Utkin, Pyotr Vasilyevich 138, 138n4, 172

Valjean, Jean 130, 130n2, 132
Vladivostok 135
Vladivostok Soviet: becomes refuge for émigrés 135–36; educates the people 143–44; influence of 139–45; organizes an army 141–43; organizes industry 139–41
Volodarsky, V. 19, 19n13, 171
Voltaire 135n2
von Hoffman, General 114
Voskov, Samuel 19, 19n12

wealth of the church 34
Wells, H. G. 166
White Guards 79, 79n2
White Nights 13

Williams, Albert Rhys: background of xv–xxiv; confiscation of papers xxi; delayed in China xxi; goes home 117; granted visa by Chinese 164; leaves Petrograd with Kuntz 121; marries Lucita Squier xxiii; motivation of xvi; prisoner of Counter-Revolution 163; publishes book on Lenin xxii; publishes *The Bolsheviks and the Soviets* xxii; receives letter from Lenin to pass through lines xxi; refused a passport by Japanese 164; revisits Russia xxiv; saved by Squersky 163; serves as a war correspondent xvi, xvii; speaks to workers in Petrograd 89; survey of the life of xv–xxiv; takes Siberian Express 121–27; travels with Gumberg 42–43; tries to volunteer for Red Army xx; visit to and description of Russian village 29-40
Williams, Rhys (son) xxiii
Wilson, Woodrow 17, 160
Winter Palace 65–73
Women's Battalions of Death 42, 42n3
Woskov. *See* Voskov, Samuel
Wrangel, Pyotr N. 168, 169, 169n4

Yanishev, Mikhail Petrovich xix, 19, 171, 179; burial of 180; tells about America in Russian village 29–40
Yarchuk, Efim 23, 23n4
Yudenich, Nikolai 168, 168n2, 169
Yunkers 46, 46n2, 68, 79

zemstvo 34, 34n3, 41
Zenith Battery 58, 59n4
Zhukov, Georgy 99n5
Zinoviev, Grigory 28, 10
Zoya 153

Figure 1. One of the 10,000 city and village Soviets in which, as a peasant said, "we are teaching ourselves how to rule ourselves." This is the Petrograd Soviet to which 20,000 workers have been elected in four years.

Figure 2. The masses hearing Lenin express their demands. "Under the pitiless pelting of facts I have been driven to the conclusion that if Lenin and 18 other Bolshevik (leaders) had perished, events in Russia would have taken much the same course. The robbed and oppressed masses —a hundred millions of men and women—moved toward the goal of their long unfulfilled desires like a flow of molten lava that no human force can dam or turn aside."—PROFESSOR E. A. ROSS

Figure 3. Bolshevik poster in Russian and Arabic Characters for the Peoples of the East: "Proletarians of all Countries, Unite!"

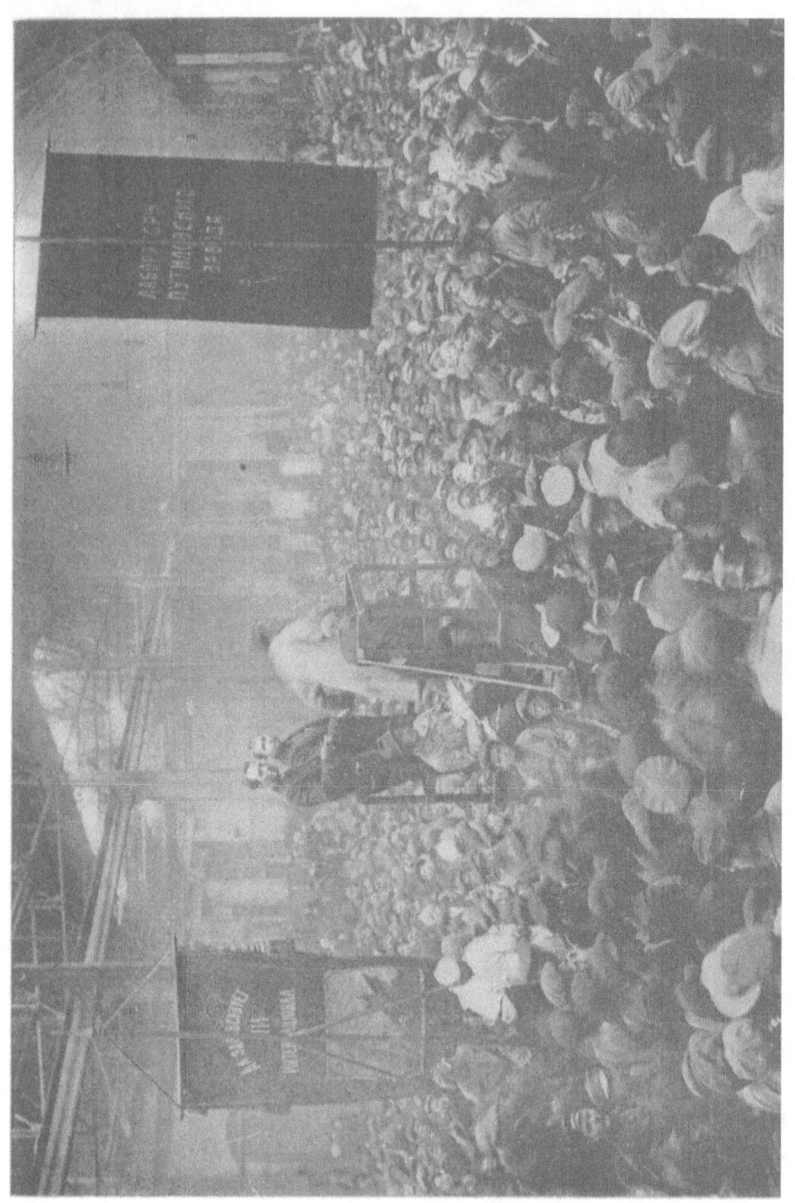

Figure 4. One of the great Cathedrals of the Communist Faith—the Putilov Factory in Petrograd. Banners and speakers proclaim the International unity of all races and peoples.

Figure 5. Petrograd Demonstrates—The river of red flowing by the Admiralty. To the left is the Street of Grand Noblemen, now called the Street of Village Poverty to remind men forever whence came the splendrous buildings.

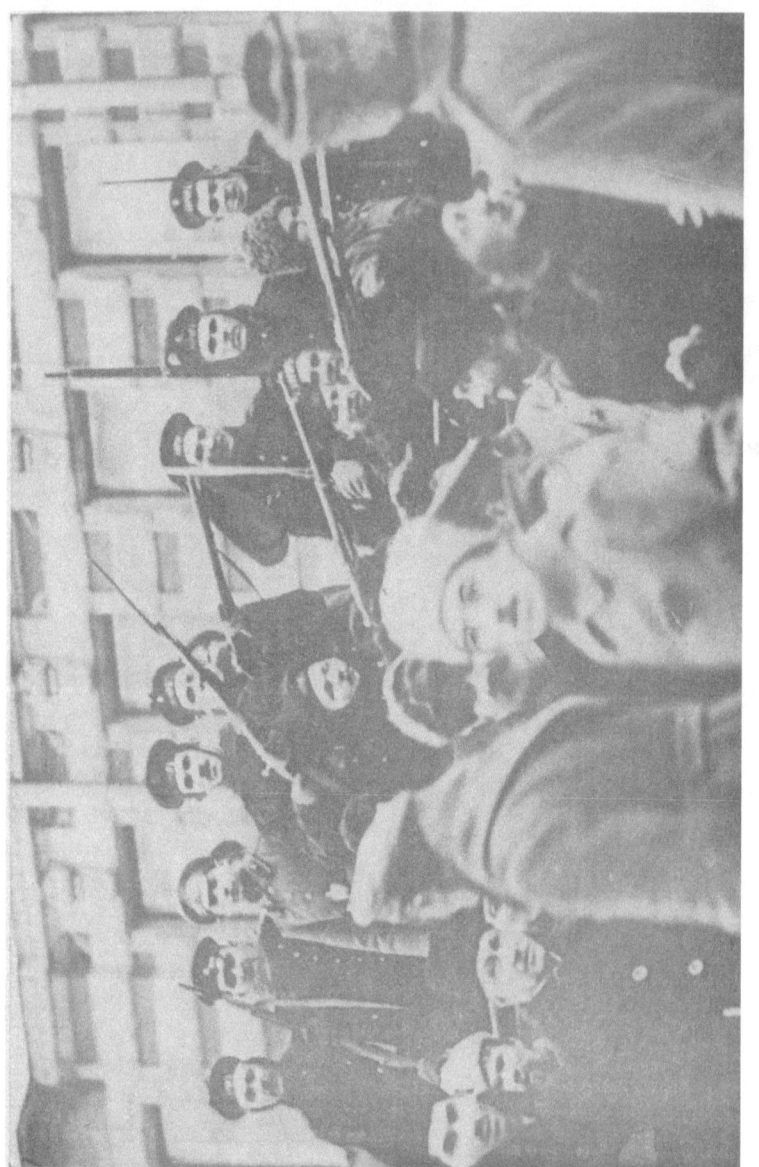

Figure 6. The storm petrels of the Revolution—the sailors—first to raise the red flag in the fleet, always first to hurry to the rescue of the Soviets.

Figure 7. Escaping the bullets in the July Uprising by lying flat on the pavement. This picture is a hardy perennial. Any disturbance in Russia is liable to bring it forth again as the authentic photograph of the event..

Figure 8. The paradoxes of Russia—the peasants, shrewd and superstitious, cruel and kind, communistic and individualistic, baffling to Tolstoy, irritating to Gorky. What will they make of the new Russia?

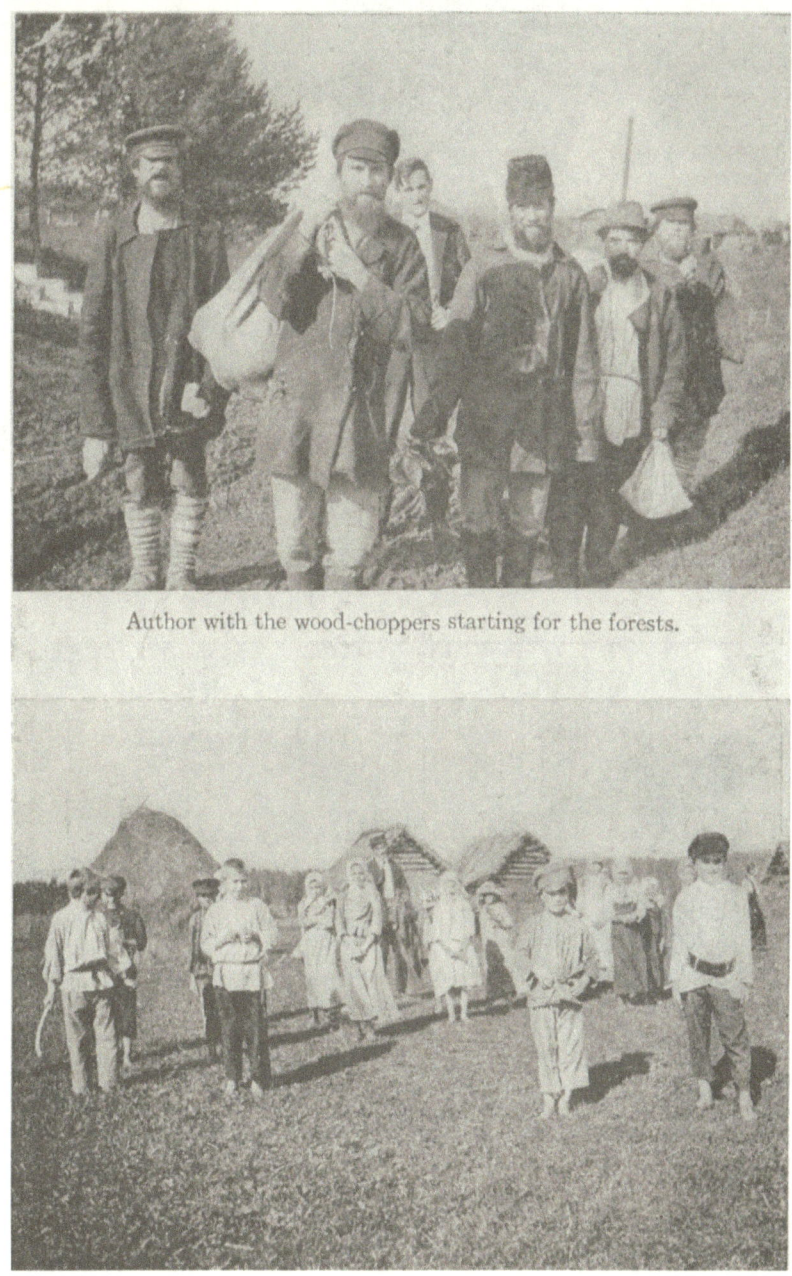

Figure 9. Author with the wood-choppers starting for the forests (above). Across the fields with the children gleaning the oats and rye (below).

*Some father has driven
His daughter, disheveled,
Into the street,
Without cause or mercy.*

*The snow cuts her face,
The wind's breath is icy,
But the heart of the father
Is colder than these.*

*Is the father to blame
For mistreating his daughter?
He was taught by the priest
That woman is sin.*

*Now the Soviet teaches
A new vision of women,
As comrades of men,
Old woes are forgotten.*

Figure 10. The lot of Russian peasant women under the old regime was not all so happy as depicted in chapter 3. Their social position was distinctly inferior to men and they were often treated as drudges and menials. When the Soviet

*Two old women lament
Old days of sorrow,
When prayers went unheard
And the grave was relief.*

*But no more does the stick
Fall upon women's shoulders.
Free and equal they march,
Comrades of men!*

*"Dry your tears, Women!
A new day is here,
When old superstitions
Bring no ignorant fear.*

*Shake off slavish bonds,
Discover your wings,
Fly from ancient darkness
To the light of new days."*

later came into power it sought to make women conscious of their new rights and privileges. To this end the Soviet Government issued posters like this one: FORWARD TO THE LIGHT.

Figure 11. Obliterating the Past. Colossal statue of Czar Alexander III being dismantled after the Soviet came into power. Note the workman at extreme top fixing rope on the crown. *(See next page.)*

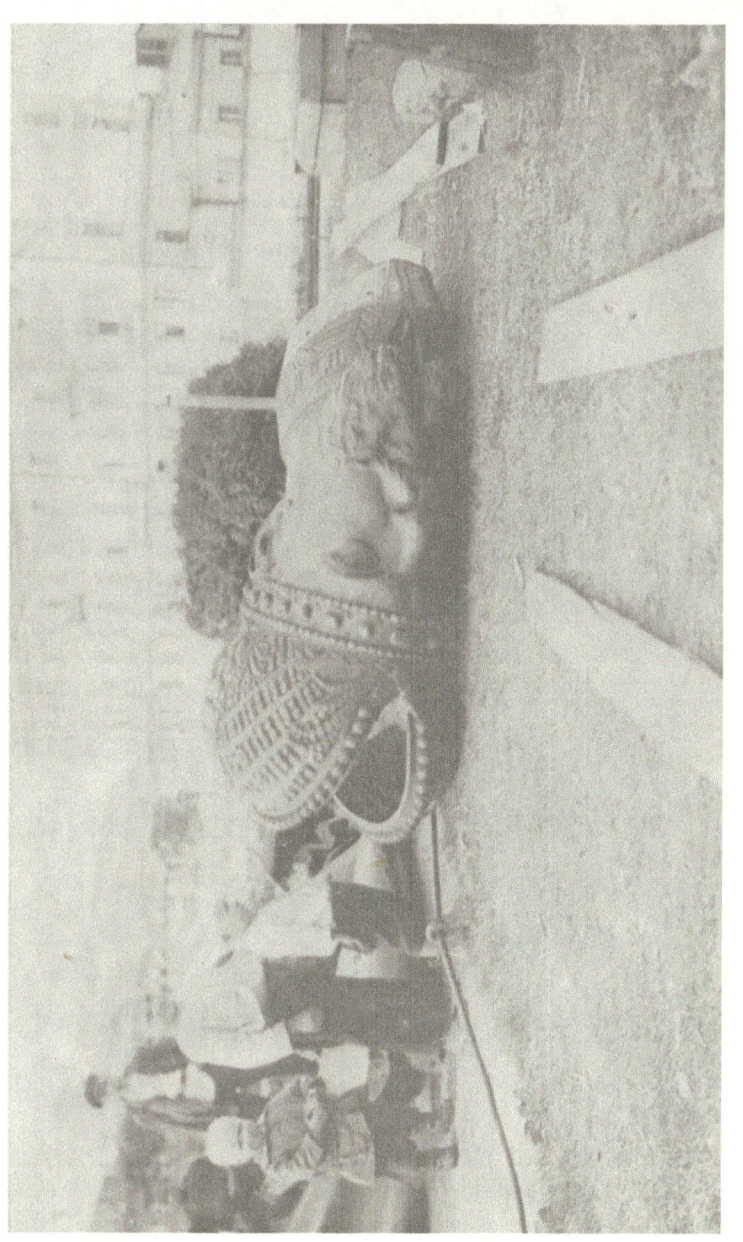

Figure 12. "How are the mighty fallen!" Children gazing into the bronze head from the dismantled statue of Czar Alexander III.

Figure 13. "The Illiterate Is A Blind Man: Everywhere Pitfalls and Misfortunes Await Him."—Soviet Poster to Encourage Education.

Figure 14. The Red Peasant, Soldier, and Workingman (on the left) to the Cossack (center): Cossack, with whom are you? With us or with them?—(The landlords, generals and capitalists.)

Figure 15. One of the crack Bolshevik regiments marching to Smolny under banners emblazoned with *All Power to the Soviets, Long Live the Revolution.*

Figure 16. On the night of November 7 we saw the Winter Palace (left) stormed by the Red Guards. Here they are massed before the base of the Alexander column (right).

Figure 17. Bolsheviks with one of the armored cars that quelled the White uprising. The cars were christened Proletariat, International, The Red Commune, Lenin, etc.

Figure 18. Fighting from doors and windows in the War of the Reds and Whites. Despite the rat-tat-tat of the machine-guns, the theaters and market-places were crowded.

Figure 19. Antonov, Commander of the Red Guards, who held back the revolutionary mob until it came to its senses.

Figure 20. A course of instruction in history and economics for those seeking admission into the Communist Party.

Figure 21. After joining the Communist Party, every member must take regular military exercises. Also all—

Figure 22. ... Communists are expected to do emergency work without pay—called "Saturdayings."

Figure 23. "In order to have more, it is necessary to produce more. In order to produce more, it is necessary to know more."

Figure 24. Under the Czar, this Royal Palace was for a few nobles and their lackeys; now under the Soviet, it shelters hundreds of crippled and orphaned children. The former name, Czar's Village (Tsarskoye Selo), is changed to Children's Village (Detskoye Selo). *(See next page.)*

Figure 25. Play and exercise in the former Palace Park, now the Children's Colony.

Figure 26. Girls at work learning how a Bolshevik cow gives milk.

Figure 27. Boys modeling in clay. Heads are shaved to guard against the typhus louse.

Figure 28. The Moscow Children's Theater. Child-actors and audience enjoying Barrie's *Peter Pan*.

Figure 29. "Chaos is necessary to the birth of a new star," said Nietzsche. Out of Russian chaos rose the powerful Red Army—its emblem the five pointed star, its commander Trotsky.

Figure 30. The Reception Committee which held up our train expecting to take off the Czar, recovering from their disappointment.

Figure 31. A Siberian mother standing by the dead body of her Bolshevik son, killed fighting against the Restoration of the Czar.

Ivan was idling, reading no books, taking to no occupation. Life was a bore to him: the days dragged on endlessly; he didn't know what to do with himself! But then he met his friend Paul to whom he complained that life was a bore. Paul said: "If you like, I shall introduce you to a friend of mine. Then life will become a joy and you will be a new man: a whole day will pass with the swiftness of a single minute." "Introduce me to him," said Ivan. "Good! come to see me on Sunday."

On Sunday Ivan went to see Paul. "Here is my friend," said Paul, "a book. It will acquaint you with everything; it will tell you what people are living on the earth, as well as what people lived here millions of years ago; you will learn what is taking place on the surface of the earth, as well as under the surface and in the sky. Your friend the book will teach you how you may live fully and be helpful to others. You will never be bored again. It will change you so that you will no longer know yourself. It will give you a hundred eyes, the strength of a giant, the wisdom of a sage! And you will never find a friend better able to advise you in the critical times of your life."

Figure 32. A True Friend!—Soviet Propaganda Poster for Education

Figure 33. White troops moving forward in Siberia. In the attempt to strangle the Soviets a steel ring of bayonets, of versts long, was thrown around Russia.

Figure 34. One of the terrible Red Guards. I spent several days with this band of 700 peasants fighting against the Whites "For Land and Freedom."

Figure 35. Intervention in Russia begins—the Allied armies crush the Vladivostok Soviet. The Stars and Stripes, the French Tricolor, the Union Jack and the Rising Sun flag of Japan flying from the Czech Building.

Figure 36. The Red Funeral—the protest of the unarmed masses against Intervention. Coffins of the longshoremen slain in defense of the Soviet carried through the streets on the way to the American consulate.

Figure 37. "The Red Army Has Crushed the White Guard Parasites—Yudenich, Denikin, Kolchak.—Comrades! Fight Now against Infection. Annihilate the Typhus-bearing Louse!"—Soviet Health Poster.

Figure 38. A soldier of the Red Army captured by the Whites. He confesses he is a Communist and is bound to a stake to be shot.

Figure 39. Some of the Bolshevik prisoners on the *Train of Death*, 2,000 of whom were shot, starved, or frozen to death.

Figure 40. The President of the Soviet Republic is Kalinin—not Lenin. Kalinin is here seated in front of a village hut conferring with the peasants.
Dr. Wm. A. Wovschin Collection.

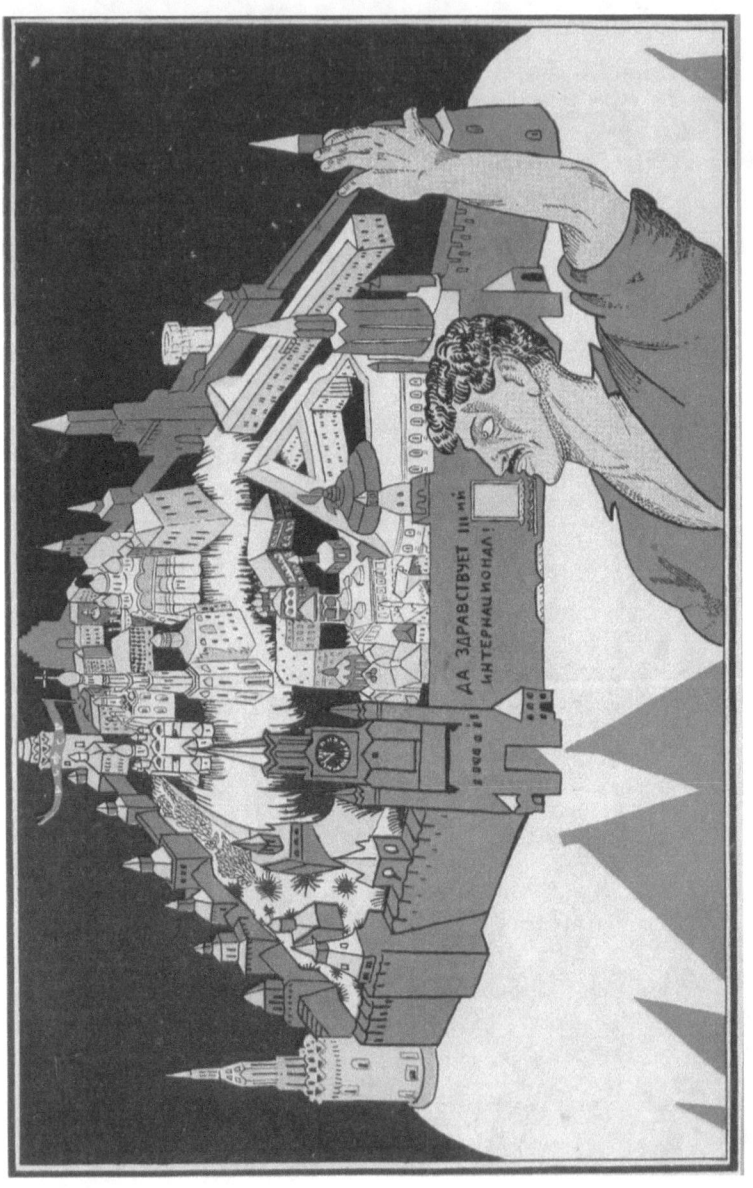

Figure 41. Poster reproduction of the famous Kremlin. The Russians say: "Above Moscow is the Kremlin, and above the Kremlin are only the stars." Inscribed on the walls is the slogan, "Long Live the Third International."

www.ingramcontent.com/pod-product-compliance
Lightning Source LLC
Chambersburg PA
CBHW032020230426
43671CB00005B/147